D0148476

The Ideals of Global Sport

PENNSYLVANIA STUDIES IN HUMAN RIGHTS

Bert B. Lockwood, Series Editor

A complete list of books in the series
is available from the publisher.

The Ideals of Global Sport

From Peace to Human Rights

Edited by

Barbara J. Keys

PENN

UNIVERSITY OF PENNSYLVANIA PRESS

PHILADELPHIA

Published by
University of Pennsylvania Press
Philadelphia, Pennsylvania 19104-4112
www.upenn.edu/pennpress

Printed in the United States of America on acid-free paper
10 9 8 7 6 5 4 3 2 1

A Cataloging-in-Publication record is available from the Library of Congress

ISBN 978-0-8122-5150-0

CONTENTS

INTRODUCTION

The Ideals of International Sport

Barbara J. Keys

"Sport has the power to change the world," South African president Nelson Mandela told the Sporting Club in Monte Carlo in 2000. "It has the power to inspire, it has the power to unite people in a way that little else does. It speaks to youth in a language they understand. . . . Sport can create hope, where once there was only despair. It is more powerful than governments in breaking down racial barriers. It laughs in the face of all types of discrimination."[1]

Sentiments such as these have been uttered by politicians, diplomats, intellectuals, journalists, athletes, and fans, in various guises and with varying emphases, since the origins of international sporting competition in the second half of the nineteenth century. Today we are saturated with messages about the benefits of international sporting competitions. They promote peace. They teach fair play and mutual understanding. They combat racial, ethnic, gender, religious, and national discrimination. In more recent years, the list has expanded at a dizzying rate: international sports bodies now claim to fight poverty, protect the environment, and promote human rights. Critics often appropriate these claims as they push for reality to better match the rhetoric. The voices of doubters—those who dispute the claims outright—are few in number and nearly inaudible amid the cacophony of celebration.

The claims are plentiful and pervasive, but the evidence to back them is sparse and weak. When moral claims are made, it is rarely in the spirit of advancing an argument for which convincing examples need to be provided in the face of skepticism. More often, moral claims are made in the spirit of incantation, like a liturgy based on faith, not facts.

Take the longest-serving and most deeply rooted of these claims: that international sporting events generate transnational bonds of friendship and mutual understanding that make the world more peaceful. During the Cold War, this notion was contested on the grounds that international sport increases the risk of conflict by exacerbating national rivalries. George Orwell famously condemned international sport as "war without the shooting."[2] Such sentiments faded after the end of the Cold War, and the mantra of peace is now virtually unchallenged.

If the proposition that international sport fosters peace were credible, we would expect to see social scientists flocking to test and measure this effect. There would be a sport counterpart to the vast scholarship scrutinizing the "democratic peace theory," which holds that democracies rarely go to war with each other.[3] But there is no field of study devoted to "the theory of international sport and peace." The leading journal of peace and conflict studies, the *Journal of Peace Research*, has never in its history published an article about the peaceful effects of international sport competition.[4]

Sport scholars who claim that the link between sport and peace is real often do little more than cite gestures that have no clear consequences, such as North and South Korean athletes marching together under the same flag during the opening ceremony at the 2000, 2004, and 2018 Olympic Games despite the two nations being technically in a state of war.[5] The International Olympic Truce Centre (IOTC), with funding from the International Olympic Committee (IOC), has existed for nearly two decades but begins from the assumption that sport and peace are linked and then offers weakly correlative examples instead of probing cause and effect. The IOTC produces propaganda such as a hundred-page booklet on the truce's role in "the toolkit for peace," which claims that "The universal nature of [the IOTC's] message creates the potential for the Truce to act as a global 'integrator,' balancing the multiple dependencies and complexities within the world, while understanding the primacy of sport as a conduit for peace." The Olympic Games, this booklet asserts, are a reminder "of just how easy it can be to overcome difference when there is shared commitment and all-round goodwill."[6] The IOTC's motto is "If we can have peace for 16 days, then maybe, just maybe, we can have it forever."[7] Critic John Hoberman calls these sorts of incantations simply delusional.[8]

To understand these claims—why so many people make them and why so many people believe them—it is not enough merely to test them as true or false.[9] The claims are important far beyond the question of their veracity: they constitute a system of meaning and a way of imagining the international. As a set of beliefs, they shape behavior and practice. Moral claims about sport occupy an important but largely overlooked place in a constellation of international idealisms that have gripped the global imagination in the last century and a half. The moral benefits that we expect of international sport are embedded in a wider constellation of internationalist aspirations, from a long tradition of peace movements and organizations seeking to foster international understanding to more recent causes such as protecting the environment and promoting human rights.[10]

"Before our common tie of humanity, differences in manners and customs among races mean next to nothing. . . . We have learned the noble spirit which should prevail in the future by our friendship with all the nationalities of the world."[11] This sort of sentiment has often been offered about international sports events such as the Olympic Games. In this case, however, the remark describes the Harvard International Seminar, a summer school in the 1950s and 1960s for early-career intellectuals, politicians, journalists, and artists run by Henry Kissinger, who was then a rising political scientist. Like the organizers of countless similar endeavors, Kissinger justified his venture on the grounds that bringing together people of different nationalities would produce "mutual understanding," an aspiration that became commonplace after World War II.

This new mantra was taken up by an extraordinary range and number of groups. They devised programs based on the assumption that intolerance led to enmity and that enmity led to war, whereas tolerance, respect for diversity, and mutual understanding created conditions for a more peaceful world. Thus, for example, the constitution of the United Nations Educational, Scientific, and Cultural Organization (UNESCO), formed in 1945, declared that "Since wars begin in the minds of men, it is in the minds of men that the defenses of peace must be constructed. . . . Ignorance of each other's ways and lives has been a common cause, throughout the history of mankind, of that suspicion and mistrust between the peoples of the world through which their differences have all too often broken into war." Mutual understanding was not intended to erase difference but rather to promote the capacity to empathize with the perspectives of others. This cultural broadening was supposed to make peace more likely, though the pathway from understanding to peace was rarely specified.[12]

The Harvard International Seminar was an eight-week program that brought together about forty participants from around the world. They lived together in Harvard's dormitories. They ate meals, attended cocktail parties, toured museums, and watched baseball games together. They took the same classes, listening to lectures by outside experts and seminar students as well as discussing and debating the major problems of the day. The program fostered deep learning and rigorous engagement with international issues. Participants enthused about how well they understood the perspectives of other nationalities after the program.

How can more ephemeral sports events dedicated to physical contests achieve the same kinds of results as intensive educational programs such as the Harvard International Seminar? Athletes interact socially at international sports events, most famously in the Olympic Village, but the raison d'être of these events is competition, which can foster animosity as readily as amity. It is true that elite athletes are often very internationally minded: they have coaches from around the world, travel frequently, and adopt training advances based on research from many countries. But does competing together lead athletes to have greater understanding of other cultures, greater empathy, or greater depth of knowledge about other nations' problems and perceptions? There is remarkably little research to show that it does.[13] Yet our convictions are entrenched. A search of media databases for "sport" and "mutual understanding" from 2008 to 2014 pulls up nearly 1,000 hits in English-language media outlets in over fifty countries.[14]

The claims made for sport are not limited to how it shapes the minds of athletes. Major events such as the Olympic Games draw billions of indirect participants who absorb messages while comfortably ensconced on sofas in front of TV screens or computers. Spectators are also supposed to gain in international understanding by watching athletes of different countries competing amicably under equal conditions. It is not entirely far-fetched to suggest that by watching, enjoying, and celebrating the successes of athletes from many countries, even if rejoicing above all in the medals won by their own national representatives, spectators may achieve a deeper appreciation of a common humanity.[15] But again, no rigorous studies have tried to assess such effects.[16]

Sporting competitions are of course also tied to elitism, corruption, doping, extravagant commercialism, and intense rivalries and hatreds. The tenacity with which proponents praise the moral values of international competition may be related to the desire to direct attention away from or conceal the less savory aspects of mega-events—features that might make the large audiences for these events less enthusiastic about them.[17] No other events draw the level of global attention that the Olympic Games and the men's soccer World Cup attract. In 2012, an estimated 70 percent of the world's population participated in some way in the Olympic Games; figures for the 2010 men's soccer World Cup show close to half the world's population watching at least some of the coverage.[18] Corporations pay millions of dollars to associate themselves with images of excellence, fair play, and high achievement. It is telling, then, that the moral claims made around international sporting events have grown in ambition in tandem with their scale and the revenues they generate.

The moral ambitions associated with international sport have deep roots, thanks to the grandiose visions of Pierre de Coubertin, the French aristocrat who founded the modern Olympic Games in 1894.[19] Coubertin aspired to be a social reformer, and his notions about the benefits of sport were linked to notions about education, the importance of art, the harmonizing of physical and intellectual development, and the value of competition and achievement. He saw sport as a tool to increase national military preparedness but also as a way to promote peaceful internationalism and mutual understanding—though, as critics have pointed out, despite universalist pretensions, his Olympic Games systematically discriminated against women and the working classes.[20] Although many scholars of the Olympic Games refer to a coherent philosophical tradition they call "Olympism," its principles are abstract and diffuse.[21] There is no foundational text, no "Olympic bible." Coubertin's writings are scattered, his ideas were expressed unsystematically, and his influence on broader intellectual thought has been extremely limited.

The organization he founded, the IOC, has attempted to delineate its moral aims with ever greater precision over the last century. Its first charter, in 1908, contained only one reference to "lofty ideals" but no details about what those were.[22] The 2016 charter calls "Olympism" "a philosophy of life" based on "respect for universal fundamental ethical principles." In addition to claiming that the practice of sport is a human right, it describes the Olympic "spirit" as one of "mutual understanding with a spirit of friendship, solidarity and fair play," without discrimination of any kind. The charter states that the goal of Olympism is "to place sport at the service of the harmonious development of humankind, with a view to promoting a peaceful society concerned with the preservation of human dignity."[23] Grand goals, indeed.

Both the IOC and the Fédération Internationale de Football Association (FIFA), the international soccer federation that runs the soccer World Cup, have had recent leaders who believed themselves worthy of the Nobel Peace Prize.[24] Founded just a decade after the IOC, FIFA also embraced internationalist ideals, though to a much lesser extent. Jules Rimet, who headed FIFA from 1921 to 1954 and started the men's World Cup, was, like Coubertin, a sportsman who saw sport as philanthropy—a means of building good character that could bring moral progress to individuals and friendliness to international affairs.[25] In recent decades, soccer and other competitions have worked much harder to associate themselves with peace initiatives and anti-racism efforts, with an eye toward countering corruption scandals and the taint of mammoth commercialism.[26]

We find talk of peace and mutual understanding among enthusiasts of every sport played at an international level, from archery to weightlifting. A typical example is the legendary Pakistani cricketer Imran Khan, who suggested that cricket played "a healing role" when India and Pakistan, two regional powers that have been locked in conflict, were trying to defuse tensions. Writing about a Pakistani cricket team's tour of India in 1999, Pakistan Cricket Board chairman Shaharyar Khan titled his book *Cricket: A Bridge of Peace*. Khan concluded that "after a lifetime in diplomacy, attempting, mostly unsuccessfully, to overcome tension, hostility and conflict," Indians' warm reactions to the Pakistani team convinced him that "cricket's vast untapped energy could be harnessed for understanding and tolerance."[27]

Further evidence of the entrenchment of the sport-peace link is the phenomenon known as sport for development and peace (SDP), which might be likened to a twenty-first-century version of the nineteenth century's muscular Christianity. Kicked off in the heady atmosphere of the 1990s when the Cold War ended and a new world order beckoned, SDP is an umbrella term covering a wide variety of groups and programs that use sport as a tool for development or postconflict reconciliation. SDP programs work toward many different aims, such as improving maternal health, preventing the spread of HIV/AIDS, and encouraging democracy. Many of these programs involve sport for sport's sake: promoting sport because it is supposed to improve health and community cohesion. Hundreds or possibly thousands of organizations around the world have SDP programs that channel billions of dollars in private and government funds to aid efforts. Although SDP is about local sport rather than elite international sport, its moral overtones are entirely consonant with those made by international sport's most vigorous boosters. This alignment explains SDP's enthusiastic embrace by the United Nations (UN), sports organizations including the IOC and FIFA, and corporations eager to showcase corporate social responsibility.[28]

As with other claims made about international sport, very little evidence exists to show that SDP programs are efficacious, despite their rapid spread. One recent review of SDP in Africa concluded that "there is currently no available evidence that supports or refutes the assumption that sport can positively influence development outcomes."[29] Few programs are evidence-based, and few include the kind of monitoring and evaluation that would demonstrate positive effects.[30] The vast majority of the academic research on SDP has been carried out in the developed countries where the researchers reside, and what has been done is often unreliable because donors who fund research are looking for affirmation of positive effects rather than criticism.[31] The traditional development sector, which views meeting basic needs as more urgent than providing leisure activities, has been skeptical of SDP. Recent research suggests that participation in sport yields benefits only in conjunction with programs directly tied to health, education, or employment.[32]

Paradoxically, pervasive rhetoric about peace coexists with its inverse: plentiful talk of war. International sporting competitions are laced with war and military metaphors and are described as battles in which teams might be "destroyed" and honor might be lost or gained. Athletes are called warriors. Coaching rooms are referred to as war rooms. Sport journalism is rife with metaphors of violence. Reciprocally, politicians and military leaders often use sport analogies to sanitize war.[33] The peace/war paradox is similar to the relationship between nationalism and internationalism in sport: international sporting competitions express both, and the potency of sport as a medium for nationalism fuels its power as an internationalist force.[34] The rhetorical power of peace promotion in international sport is intertwined with its kinship to war. Because it showcased physical prowess at a time when military power depended on the health and fitness of human bodies, sport was intertwined with militarism from the earliest days of international sports competitions. The promise of peaceful outcomes sublimate and distract from sport's ties to war. It might even be said that the close relationship of international sport and war makes claims of peace necessary to legitimize sport as entertainment.

If evidence is so lacking, why do so many people around the world continue to believe in international sport's capacity to achieve moral outcomes? This volume explores these questions first by analyzing the most enduring claims made by proponents of international sport and then by focusing on the newest brand of idealism: human rights. The volume aims to examine the functions that these idealistic claims have served, the kinds of politics they have abetted, and why, when, and to whom they have been believable. The chapters make the case that sport mega-events do not merely offer a representation of global order; they also create, reinforce, and propagate normative views about that global order, helping to constitute the moral rules and expectations that guide and inspire it.

The chapters span a range of disciplinary approaches, including history, political science, and anthropology, by scholars from different parts of the world—from the United States and the United Kingdom to Australia, Brazil, Canada, South Korea, and Russia, using sources in Chinese, Korean, Thai, Portuguese, and Russian in addition to English. Some authors specialize in fields other than the study of sport and have brought their expertise to this issue for the first time. Others have spent years studying the social and political dimensions of international sport.

This volume aims to invigorate new conversations in the fields of sport studies, the history of human rights, and the history of internationalism. An enormous body of work covers the political dimensions of the Olympic Games and the soccer World Cup. The main lines of inquiry were delineated by Barrie Houlihan in his 1994 *Sport and International Politics* and have remained little changed since then. Scholars analyze international sport as a vehicle for national prestige and legitimacy, economic interests, and cultural exchange. Increasingly, scholars outside of sport studies have shown an interest in these topics.[35] But as yet there are few studies that locate international sport's idealisms in the context of internationalism more broadly. This volume builds on a growing interest within sport studies in breaking out of the traditional framework of topics and approaches in international politics by situating sport in the realm of ideas and taking it seriously as a vehicle for idealistic internationalism.[36] In doing so, the contributors aim to demonstrate the relevance of sport as an internationalist idiom to the study of internationalism more broadly. This volume also treats the history of human rights in a context that, despite the high global visibility of sport, human rights scholars have entirely neglected.

Part I surveys the most enduring idealistic claims associated with international sport: that sport promotes mutual understanding and friendship, peace, antidiscrimination, and democratic mind-sets and practices. Each author tackles the task not with sweeping generalizations but instead through close analysis of a case study, asking how a particular claim has operated in a particular context. Simon Creak, in looking at the entrenched notion that sports competitions lead to friendship and mutual understanding, surveys the roots of this idea in Coubertin's thought and then tests the idea as it has played out in the Southeast Asian (SEA) Games, a regional version of the Olympic Games that relies heavily on friendship-building for legitimation. Creak, who combined anthropological and historical methods by attending SEA Games, interviewing officials, athletes, and spectators, and researching their history in the archives, finds little evidence that the Games have led to increased regional cooperation, mutual understanding, and friendship in a region beset by rivalries but argues that participants in the SEA Games do experience positive interpersonal bonds. Despite the widespread tendency to anthropomorphize international relations by imbuing them with notions derived from interpersonal relationships such as friendship, there is little evidence that interpersonal bonds formed at sports events translate into international political bonds.

Cross-national sports contacts are not only alleged to promote friendship and mutual understanding, of course, but are also supposed to lead to a more peaceful world. The assumed connection between sport and peace is most strongly exemplified by the close relationship that the IOC has developed with the UN since the 1990s. The UN's core mission is to secure peace, and the UN has embraced the Olympic Games as a means of working toward this goal. But as Roland Burke explains, the convergence between the UN and the Olympics is surprisingly recent. Aside from a UNESCO initiative to take over the staging of the Olympic Games in the 1970s, the two bodies saw little interest in cooperation in the decades after World War II. It was only in the 1990s that the UN looked to associate itself with the IOC in the hope that Olympic virtues would bolster its own credibility. Since then, UN spokespeople have repeatedly invoked versions of the mantra that "Olympic values are UN values." For its part, the IOC, plagued by rising costs and the taint of corruption, saw an alignment with the UN as a way to burnish its own image. The most salient marker of this new rapprochement was the Olympic Truce, introduced in 1993 and reinscribed annually since then. The truce, a reinvention of a tradition from ancient Greece, urges countries at war to call a truce during the Olympic Games. This one small step toward peace is then supposed to lead to more steps. Burke regards the political marriage between the IOC and the UN as "transparently delusional," but the institutional resources invested in the effort point to the enduring potency of this delusion.

Asked to give hard evidence of the beneficial effects of international sports competitions, proponents of global sport most often cite antiracism. Discrimination on the basis of race, politics, and religion has been formally prohibited by the Olympic Charter since 1949. This new provision arose from the global tide that linked racism to the origins of World War II. In that sense, the Olympic Charter's antidiscrimination clause was sibling to the UN's Universal Declaration of Human Rights (UDHR), even if sport was never mentioned during the long months of debate in the declaration's drafting. But like the UDHR itself, the IOC's new provision was mostly hortatory.

Few cases of racism in sport were more clear-cut and egregious than the one presented by apartheid South Africa, because apartheid affected every area of life and injected racial discrimination into every aspect of South Africa's international sporting contacts. Yet as Robert Skinner explains in his chapter on antiracism, the IOC avoided confrontation as long as it could. Only the threat of a major boycott of the 1968 Olympic Games—a boycott supported by the Soviet Union—led the IOC to exclude South Africa, and only continued pressure extended that exclusion. Despite the reluctance with which the ban was pursued, it provided the IOC with considerable moral authority, giving it unearned credence as one of the leaders in the struggle against apartheid.

Exclusion from the Olympics was only one part of the story of antiracism and sport mega-events. The Commonwealth and several international sporting bodies succeeded in cutting most contact with South African sport by the late 1970s. As Skinner explains, sport became a political resource for the many groups fighting against South African apartheid, and the egalitarian claims deeply embedded in sporting discourse became an important tool for those pressing for reform. Sport has sometimes been a site for making or reinforcing racist claims, but the long and highly public battle against apartheid in sport deepened the association between sport and antiracism. When apartheid ended, commentators claimed with some justification that "sport had triumphed over racism."[37] In Skinner's view, this triumph was achieved not because of any inherent morality in sport but instead because of changes in global norms that shaped sport during the process of decolonization.

Sports enthusiasts, at least in democratic countries, have long claimed that international sport is inherently democratic. The rules of sport make it egalitarian: everyone can participate, all participants are subject to the same rules, and winners and losers are determined by merit. American sportswriter John Tunis expressed a common view when he wrote in 1941 that Americans considered democracy and sport "identical" and saw sport as an ideal incubator of democratic behavior.[38] The organizers of the Asia Games during the Cold War made similar claims. Philippine vice president and secretary of foreign affairs Carlos Garcia said in 1954, for example, that the Asia Games were linked to the "permanence of democratic institutions all over the world."[39]

Joon Seok Hong examines how well claims of democracy promotion hold up in the oft-celebrated case of the 1988 Seoul Olympic Games. These Games coincided with the South Korean transition from dictatorship to democracy, and many observers have cited the intense international media scrutiny brought by the Olympics as the deciding factor in pushing the regime toward peaceful reform rather than repression. When Beijing hosted the Games in 2008, some observers predicted that the same forces might achieve similar results in China. As Hong argues, however, South Korea's democratization had been set in motion long before the Games and was propelled by factors that had little to do with the hosting of the sporting event. In addition, as Hong notes, the IOC has always explicitly disavowed interest in democratization and even sees benefits to having the Games hosted in dictatorships that can easily guarantee public support.

In recent decades, the organizers of sport mega-events have been pressured to adopt more and more causes. Beginning in the 1990s, activists forced organizers of sport mega-events to address environmental degradation. Organizers now consider reducing the amount of waste generated, using renewable energy sources, creating carbon offset schemes, promoting public transportation, reducing water pollution, and much more. At the Olympic Games, "legacy" has become a buzzword.[40] With the costs of staging the Games reaching tens of billions of dollars, much of it used to construct elaborate venues that soon crumble from disuse, sports organizers have begun to take more proactive measures to ensure that hosts include long-term social and cultural planning that provides benefits beyond the short span of the events themselves.

A central contention of this volume, however, is that the next major frontier for idealistic internationalism in sport is human rights. In Part II, contributors assess the potent relationship that has developed between global human rights discourse and sport mega-events. Since the end of the Cold War, human rights has become the world's moral lingua franca, and the 1990s saw the first major campaign to make a sport mega-event compatible with human rights. In ways that are strikingly similar to the pattern established during the apartheid years, the IOC resisted the "intrusion" of human rights, but as those pressures grew and were increasingly taken up by governments as well as nongovernmental organizations (NGOs), the IOC has had to adapt. It has now embraced the language of human rights in host city contracts. FIFA and other major sports organizations have also come to accept the basic premise that human rights considerations must be a factor in the staging of international competitions. The debate is no longer over whether human rights are relevant and instead revolves around which human rights, for whom, and how.

Explaining why the two largest human rights organizations, Amnesty International and Human Rights Watch, came to abandon their early indifference toward sport mega-events, my chapter argues that the end of the Cold War gave human rights groups an incentive to widen their list of targets to include events such as the Olympics. When Beijing bid for the 2000 Olympic Games in 1993, Human Rights Watch was the first to see the Olympic Games as an opportunity to bring human rights discussions to new audiences. That bid failed for reasons that have since been attributed to human rights concerns in the aftermath of the 1989 Tiananmen Square massacre. The effects of Human Rights Watch's sustained anti-Beijing campaign are impossible to tie directly to the IOC's final vote, but it is likely that this small NGO can claim significant responsibility for thwarting the ambitions of the world's most populous country. Beijing's second bid—this time successful in winning the 2008 Olympics—brought Amnesty International squarely into the Olympic human rights debate. Many other groups also decided that human rights language was a useful tool in pressing for reform. The chapter suggests that both human rights behemoths should be studied as would any other organization, taking into account organizational dynamics and self-interest instead of assuming altruistic motives. Although the IOC and FIFA have haltingly and reluctantly become more receptive to human rights arguments, serious questions remain about how much they can and are prepared to do to force changes on national governments.

Dmitry Dubrovskiy takes us to the beginning of the current debate over whether the human rights of citizens in host countries should matter to sports events. He examines human rights controversies at the two "Russian" Olympic Games: the Soviet Union's 1980 Moscow Olympics and the Vladimir Putin regime's 2014 Sochi Winter Olympic Games. The 1980 Moscow Games, Dubrovskiy notes, established a familiar pattern. Some observers claimed that holding a major international event such as the Olympic Games in an authoritarian state could be a spur to reform. They argued for using the event to press for openness and dialogue. Others countered that the staging of a major event would provide a rationale for increasing repression. They were convinced that awarding a major event to repressive regimes that did not "deserve" them made the international community complicit in giving those regimes legitimacy and prestige. Dubrovskiy's rich research in Russian-language sources lends support to the latter view for both of these events. The biggest differences he finds between 1980 and 2014 are that the use of boycott threats have receded and that 2014 saw a measure of success: a transnational LGBT rights movement mounted a highly visible campaign that led the IOC to strengthen its antidiscrimination provision.

Jules Boykoff reminds us that human rights violations occur as a direct result of every sport mega-event, not just those hosted by dictatorships.

Concerns framed in the language of human rights have been prominent at recent Olympic Games in Atlanta (1996), Salt Lake City (2002), Athens (2004), Vancouver (2010), and London (2012). Forced evictions to clear sites for new construction are a recurrent point of contention no matter where sports events are held, with claims about property rights and due process turning the issue into a contest over rights. Host cities in democratic countries often place security concerns ahead of protections for free speech and the right of assembly, for example, by passing special laws to curtail basic civil liberties. Debates over social and economic issues crop up frequently, notably in recurrent debates over whether economic benefits such as increased tourism can possibly compensate for the mind-boggling sums spent on staging mega-events. But as Boykoff notes, these issues get less traction as human rights issues than do civil liberties, reflecting a strong Western tendency to prioritize civil and political rights over social and economic rights.

No sporting event has generated more controversy than the 2008 Beijing Olympic Games, which became a flashpoint for human rights concerns. Eschewing the standard terms of the debate, Susan Brownell argues that no one has yet developed the tools to measure the human rights impacts of sport mega-events on hosting countries and that the term "human rights" is probably both too complex and too opaque a rubric to be an assessment tool in any meaningful sense. She chooses instead to map the realm of discourse. In her account, Chinese efforts first to bid for the Olympics in the 1990s and then to host them in the 2000s brought Chinese policy makers and opinion leaders to "engage with the concept of human rights" and adopt elements of international human rights discourse. Brownell's conclusions align with the arguments of advocates for sporting dialogue who contend that hosting mega-events is a force for openness, although she reaches her conclusion through a different logic and with more tentative conclusions. Engagement with hosting the Olympic Games brought human rights concepts into popular discourse in China, she claims, changing "the nature of the conversation between the governed and those who govern," with effects as yet unknown. According to Brownell, we cannot yet measure the effects that the 2008 Games had on human rights, but we can see consequences "in the realm of vocabulary, discourse, and the exchange of ideas."

Taking the story up through 2016, João Roriz and Renata Nagamine examine Brazil's experience hosting two mega-events, first the 2014 FIFA men's World Cup and then the 2016 Summer Olympic Games. Both events took place in the wake of large-scale social protests in 2013 and 2014 over long-standing economic and social problems; the 2016 Games came on the heels of major political and economic crises. Through a careful analysis of Brazilian media coverage, FIFA and IOC statements, reports issued by intergovernmental bodies, official statements by the Brazilian government, and the activities of local and international human rights groups, the authors show that by the time the events took place, all sides talked about protecting and promoting human rights, but official and unofficial actors imbued that talk with very different meanings. FIFA organizers spoke about protecting disability rights and working against sexual exploitation and racism. Local groups focused their protests on combating police violence, mitigating problems related to housing and evictions, and protecting free speech. The crucial distinction was that the rights issues touted by organizers conferred value on the sports events—say, endowing them with the capacity to combat racism—whereas pressure groups organized around rights issues that brought into sharp relief the negative repercussions of the events: increased repression from police, housing problems, and restrictions on civil liberties.

As Roriz and Nagamine rightly conclude, human rights constitutes an appealing language to all sides today. It seems to be invested with universal appeal and even the capacity to transcend politics. Human rights appear to have a grounded specificity because they are spelled out in international legal instruments. They seem therefore to offer more solid ground for measuring the moral benefits of international sporting events than the highly amorphous ideals of friendship and peace, whose broader effects on international politics, if they exist, can only be tenuously linked in causal relationships to sporting events. Yet as the chapters in this volume show, human rights is a malleable concept that can be put to highly varied and even contradictory uses. Its increasing use as the language around which sport mega-events are judged will shift the content and flavor of debates but will not provide the grounds for greater certainty about how such events shape the world.

Notes

1. Nelson Mandela, *Notes to the Future: Words of Wisdom* (New York: Atria, 2012), 113.

2. For a vigorous critique, see John Hoberman, "The Myth of Sport as a Peace-Promoting Force," *SAIS Review* 31, no. 1 (Winter–Spring 2011): 17–29.

3. For an excellent recent analysis of progress and problems in this field, see Christopher Hobson, "Democratic Peace: Progress and Crisis," *Perspectives on Politics* 15, no. 3 (September 2017): 697–710.

4. Based on a keyword search of the journal contents for "sport" and "peace" and for "Olympic*" and "peace." For an interesting account of the difficulties of explaining an observable decline in wars as well as wars for conquest, see the controversial study of the 1928 Kellogg-Briand Pact to outlaw war by Oona A. Hathaway and Scott J. Shapiro, *The Internationalists: How a Radical Plan to Outlaw War Remade the World* (New York: Simon and Schuster, 2017), and the critique by realist Stephen M. Walt, "There's Still No Reason to Think the Kellogg-Briand Pact Accomplished Anything," *Foreign Policy*, September 29, 2017, foreignpolicy.com/2017/09 /29/theres-still-no-reason-to-think-the-kellogg-briand-pact-accomplished-anything/.

5. See Ramon Spaaij, "Olympic Rings of Peace? The Olympic Movement, Peacemaking and Intercultural Understanding," in *The Olympic Movement and the Sport of Peacemaking*, ed. Ramón Spaaij and Cindy Burleson (London: Routledge, 2013), 6.

6. Rachel Briggs, Helen McCarthy, and Alexis Zorbas, *16 Days: The Role of the Olympic Truce in the Toolkit for Peace* (Athens: International Olympic Truce Centre, 2004), 19.

7. See the official blog of the International Olympic Truce Centre at olympictruce.wordpress .com/olympic-truce-history/global-revival/.

8. Hoberman, "Myth of Sport," 27.

9. Sport is sometimes likened to religion, and it is worth pondering the parallels between the study of Christianity and the study of sport. As legal scholar Paul Kahn writes,

> Until the turn of the twentieth century, the study of Christianity was not an intellectual discipline. It was, instead, a part of religious practice. Its aim was the progressive realization of a Christian order in the world—reform within the Christian community, and conversion abroad. Only when the theological project became capable of suspending belief in the object of its study could a real discipline of religious study emerge. The discipline had to give up questions about the truth of Christian beliefs, as well as questions about the correct beliefs of the true Christian. It had to take up, instead, the question of the shape or character that Christian beliefs give to the subject's experience.

Paul W. Kahn, *The Cultural Study of Law: Reconstructing Legal Scholarship* (Chicago: University of Chicago Press, 1999), 2.

10. More than twenty years ago, the provocative sport scholar John Hoberman called for comparative studies of the Olympic Games as a species of internationalism, similar to the Boy Scouts and the Esperanto movement. Though often cited, his article has inspired relatively little research, perhaps because sport scholars have little expertise beyond sport and because scholars outside of sport studies still rarely take up sport. John Hoberman, "Toward a Theory of Olympic Internationalism," *Journal of Sport History* 22, no. 1 (1995): 1–37. For a view of sport and human rights covering the rights of athletes and issues such as privacy and child labor in the manufacture of sporting goods but leaving out the broader rights concerns that have preoccupied groups such as Human Rights Watch, see Richard Giulianotti and David McArdle, eds., *Sport, Civil Liberties and Human Rights* (London: Routledge, 2006).

11. Extracts from Letters from Participants, Yahuhiro Nakasone, Member of the House of Representatives of the Japanese Diet, n.d. [c. 1952–1968], Part II, Series I, Box 131, Folder 15, Henry A. Kissinger Papers, Yale University, New Haven, CT.

12. Barbara Keys, "Die Spinne im Netz: Ideenpolitik im Kalten Krieg [The Diplomacy of Ideas in the Cold War]," *Zeitschrift für Ideengeschichte* 11, no. 4 (Winter 2017): 19–29.

13. As leading sport scholar Bruce Kidd wrote recently, the IOC "rarely examines . . . actual [educational and psychological] results . . . among high performance athletes, let alone among the diverse populations of the world." Bruce Kidd, "Cautions, Questions and Opportunities in Sport for Development and Peace," *Third World Quarterly* 32, no. 3 (2011): 606. However, see Jim Parry's argument that sport has intrinsic values such as fair play that can lend themselves to interpersonal understanding and respect: Jim Parry, "The Power of Sport in Peacemaking and Peacekeeping," in *The Olympic Movement and the Sport of Peacemaking*, ed. Ramón Spaaij and Cindy Burleson (London: Routledge, 2013), 15–28.

14. Based on a search of Factiva.

15. I made this argument in Barbara J. Keys, *Globalizing Sport: National Rivalry and International Community in the 1930s* (Cambridge, MA: Harvard University Press, 2006).

16. For recent scholarship on the values of international sport, see Graeme Hayes and John Karamichas, *Olympic Games, Mega-Events and Civil Societies* (London: Palgrave Macmillan, 2011), which looks in part at sport's value systems but takes a sociological approach focused on the present, and Dikaia Chatziefstathiou and Ian Henry, who in *Discourses of Olympism: From the Sorbonne 1894 to London 2012* (Basingstoke, UK: Palgrave Macmillan, 2012), adopt critical discourse analysis to understand Olympic knowledge.

17. In a similar way, corporate philanthropy can be used to deflect attention from, say, tax avoidance. For a sport-related example, see Sean Dinces, "'Nothing But Net Profit': Property Taxes, Public Dollars, and Corporate Philanthropy at Chicago's United Center," *Radical History Review* 125 (May 2016): 13–34.

18. International Olympic Committee, "London 2012 Olympic Games Broadcast Report," 2012, www.olympic.org/documents/ioc-marketing-and-broadcasting; "FIFA 2010 World Cup South Africa Television Audience Report," FIFA, 2010, www.fifa.com/mm/document/affederation /tv/01/47/32/73/2010fifaworldcupsouthafricatvaudiencereport.pdf.

19. The best study of Coubertin is by John MacAloon, *This Great Symbol: Pierre de Coubertin and the Origins of the Modern Olympic Games* (Chicago: University of Chicago Press, 1984).

20. Kevin Wamsley, "The Global Sport Monopoly: A Synopsis of 20th Century Olympic Politics," *International Journal* 57, no. 3 (2002): 395–410.

21. The best analyses of "Olympism" are by the philosopher Jim Parry. See, e.g., Parry, "The Power of Sport"; Susan Brownell and Jim Parry, *Olympic Values and Ethics in Contemporary Society* (Ghent: Ghent University, 2012), www.scribd.com/document/214700588/2012 -Brownell-Parry-Olympic-Values-and-Ethics-in-Contemporary-Society-240712.

22. Comité International Olympique, *Annuaire* (Lausanne: International Olympic Committee, 1908).

23. *Olympic Charter* (Lausanne: International Olympic Committee, 2016), 11. The charter took effect on August 2, 2016.

24. On FIFA's Sepp Blatter, see David Conn, "Sepp Blatter After the Fall: 'Why the Hell Should I Bear All the Blame,'" *Guardian*, June 19, 2017, www.theguardian.com/football/2017 /jun/19/sepp-blatter-fifa-president-corruption-; on the IOC's Juan Antonio Samaranch, see, e.g., Stephen Wenn, Robert Barney, and Scott Martyn, *Tarnished Rings: The International Olympic Committee and the Salt Lake City Bid Scandal* (Syracuse, NY: Syracuse University Press, 2011), 21.

25. Alan Tomlinson, *FIFA: The Men, the Myths and the Money* (London: Routledge, 2014), 54.

26. On such efforts in FIFA, see, e.g., Jon Garland and Michael Rowe, *Racism and Anti-Racism in Football* (London: Palgrave, 2001); on the Handshake for Peace that began in 2014, see

"Fact Sheet," FIFA, resources.fifa.com/mm/document/afsocial/fairplay/02/24/23/42/factsheet _en_neutral.pdf. See also Christiane Eisenberg, "From Political Ignorance to Global Responsibility: The Role of the World Soccer Association (FIFA) in International Sport During the Twentieth Century," *Journal of Sport History* 32, no. 3 (Fall 2005): 379–393.

27. Kausik Bandyopadhyay, "Feel Good, Goodwill and India's Friendship Tour of Pakistan, 2004: Cricket, Politics and Diplomacy in Twenty-First-Century India," in *The Politics of Sport in South Asia*, ed. Subhas Ranjan Chakraborty et al., 54–70 (New York: Routledge, 2009).

28. For an introduction, see Simon Darnell, *Sport for Development and Peace: A Critical Sociology* (London: Bloomsbury, 2012).

29. Laurenz Langer, "Sport for Development—A Systematic Map of Evidence from Africa," *South African Review of Sociology* 46, no. 1 (2015): 66.

30. Bruce Kidd, "Cautions, Questions and Opportunities in Sport for Development and Peace," *Third World Quarterly* 32, no. 3 (2011): 604.

31. Cora Burnett, "Assessing the Sociology of Sport: On Sport for Development and Peace," *International Review for the Sociology of Sport* 50, nos. 4–5 (2015): 387.

32. Kidd, "Cautions, Questions and Opportunities," 606.

33. See, e.g., J. A. Mangan, ed., *Militarism, Sport, Europe: War Without Weapons* (London: Frank Cass, 2003).

34. See Keys, *Globalizing Sport*.

35. For one notable example, see the work of Andrei S. Markovits; for a survey, see Barbara Keys, "International Relations," in *Routledge Companion to Sport History*, ed. S. W. Pope and John Nauright, 248–267 (New York: Routledge, 2010).

36. One study of the ethics of "Olympism" assumes it to be a "discourse" that exists for a few people involved in the Games, not a broad set of ideas that are contested by many actors. See Chatzeifstathiou and Henry, *Discourses of Olympism*. Jean Harvey et al. in *Sport and Social Movements: From the Local to the Global* (London: Bloomsbury, 2013) examine how five social movements have used sports events to advance their causes by challenging "the political and economic order of sport." See also Jules Boykoff, *Activism and the Olympics: Dissent at the Games in London and Vancouver* (New Brunswick, NJ: Rutgers University Press, 2014); Barbara Keys, "The Early Cold War Olympics: Political, Economic, and Human Rights Dimensions, 1952–1960," in *The Palgrave Handbook of Olympic Studies*, ed. Helen Jefferson Lenskyj and Stephen Wagg, 72–87 (New York: Palgrave Macmillan, 2012).

37. See chapter 2 in this volume.

38. John R. Tunis, *Democracy and Sport* (New York: A. S. Barnes., 1941), 1, 8–10, 5, 39.

39. Quoted in Stefan Hubner, *Pan-Asian Sports and the Emergence of Modern Asia, 1913–1974* (Singapore: NUS Press, 2016), 133.

40. See John J. MacAloon, "'Legacy' as Managerial/Magical Discourse in Contemporary Olympic Affairs," *International Journal of the History of Sport* 25, no. 14 (2001): 2060–2071.

PART I

The Core Ideals

CHAPTER 1

Friendship and Mutual Understanding

Sport and Regional Relations
in Southeast Asia

Simon Creak

Of the growing list of moral claims attached to international sport, perhaps none is more widely repeated than the suggestion that such contests promote friendship and mutual understanding. Associated especially strongly with the Olympic Games, this claim can be traced to Pierre de Coubertin's justification for establishing the modern Games in the late nineteenth century. "Wars break out because nations misunderstand each other," Coubertin famously argued. "We shall not have peace until the prejudices which now separate the different races shall have been outlived. To attain this end, what better means than to bring the youth of all countries periodically together for amicable trials of muscular strength and agility?"[1]

After a century that saw 100 million war-related deaths, it hardly seems worth debating whether the rise of international sports competitions has diminished international conflict.[2] As Barbara J. Keys argues in the introduction to this volume, the linking of sport, friendship, and mutual understanding is part of a liturgy—which includes fair play, sportsmanship, a level playing field, mutual respect, and so on—based on circular reasoning and little resort to evidence. As with all liturgical texts, we learn more from trying to understand the social and cultural conditions that explain the persistence and resonance of such ideas than by trying to determine their "truth."

This chapter examines these themes not through the Olympics themselves but instead through the example of the Southeast Asian (SEA) Games, a biennial sport mega-event founded in 1959. By any conventional measure, the countries of Southeast Asia—Brunei, Cambodia, Indonesia, Laos, Malaysia, Myanmar (Burma), the Philippines, Singapore, Timor Leste, Thailand, and Vietnam—lie on the periphery of world sport. At the 2016 Rio Olympics the eleven countries garnered a total of five gold medals, which was unprecedented; four years earlier in London they won none at all, and in all prior Olympiads (1896–2008) they collected a total of thirteen.[3] Unlike their Northeast Asian neighbors, moreover, no country in Southeast Asia has ever bid for the Olympics, let alone hosted them.

Paradoxically, this peripheral status makes Southeast Asia an ideal example of the global reach and pervasiveness of Olympic idealism. Despite the region's limited on-field success, Southeast Asia has embraced Olympic ideals through hosting and participating in its own sport mega-events. The Asian Games and the short-lived but politically significant Games of the New Emerging Forces (GANEFO) are also examples of the spread and adaptation of Olympic idealism in this region that have drawn significant scholarly interest, but the SEA Games provide an ideal lens for examining the rhetorical and political uses of notions of friendship in international sport.[4]

Since the event's founding, organizers have consistently promoted the SEA Games as a means of enhancing friendship, mutual understanding, and cooperation in Southeast Asia. Despite much evidence both on and off the field that the Games have not fostered intraregional "friendship," the claims endure because they serve important functions at a variety of levels. At a diplomatic level, they resonate with the pursuit of regional cooperation in Southeast Asia, a persistent if sometimes elusive goal since decolonization and the creation of a region of nation-states. Despite changing visions of regionalism since then, the model of Olympic internationalism has been sufficiently malleable to adapt as required.

This political dimension is reinforced at an interpersonal level, where the marriage of sport, friendship, and mutual understanding forms a key discursive foundation of the SEA Games. In this latter sense, athletes, spectators, and officials are socialized into the rhetoric of friendship and mutual understanding, which becomes a lens for interpreting their own experiences of forming intercultural connections. It is this coexistence of different meanings of the relationship involving sport, friendship, and mutual understanding— as political metaphor, intercultural discourse, and interpersonal experience—that accounts for the durability and adaptability of idealistic claims of promoting friendship and understanding through sport.

Sport, Friendship, and Mutual Understanding

In Asia, the links between friendship, international sport, and politics have been overt. Indonesia's GANEFO of 1963 was framed as an alternative to the "imperialistic" Olympic Games and was ostensibly devoted to recovering Coubertin's true "Olympic ideals," including the promotion of sport "so as to cement friendly relations."[5] In a region with many socialist states, social-ist rhetoric about "friendship" and "socialist brotherhood" was especially prominent, including in the realm of sport. From the 1950s to the late 1980s, the People's Republic of China (PRC) advanced the ideal of "friendship first, competition second." Although "friendship sport" was ultimately incompat-ible with notions of athletic excellence and thus "seriously flawed," in the assessment of one scholar, it proved to be an "ingenious and effective" tool of diplomacy.[6]

Sport scholars have considered the notion of friendship, usually cover-ing it as part of the wider category of Olympism, but few studies interro-gate the term "friendship" itself and its application to the context of sport. Despite obvious differences between categories of friendship—friendship among individual athletes and friendship among countries—the term itself is left untheorized. Rather, whichever kind of friendship is being evoked, the term (like other key features of Olympism) is examined as a moral category, a positive value that is "good" because it transcends narrow sectional inter-ests, while the range of meanings contained in references to "friendship" are overlooked.

As political philosophers are quick to point out, friendship has distinct if clearly related social and political dimensions. At a social level, friendship involves dyadic or reciprocal relations between individuals or small groups such as families who share a direct and interpersonal relationship char-acterized by closeness and a degree of intimacy. We all know this kind of friendship; it is the intuitive sense of the term applying to the private and personal domain. The notion of friendship between political groups, such as nation-states, is more contested. For some realist scholars, the very pos-sibility of political friendship is dubious. According to political philosopher Graeme Smith, however, the "privatization" of friendship is a recent historical development and is evidence of modernity's trend toward individualization. In ancient times, he argues, political friendship was "a central and pressing concern."[7] The recent surge of interest in the topic among political philos-ophers suggests that political friendship might provide a useful conceptual tool for understanding modern politics, both domestic and international.[8] Drawing on this subfield, this chapter argues that the first step in understanding notions of friendship in sport is to disarticulate their social and political connotations and consider their political dimensions as part of a broader phenomenon in international relations.

Coubertin's notion of Olympic internationalism emerged from his belief that education could promote mutual understanding and thus peace between nations. This understanding of peace and intercultural relations was not only "fundamentally rationalistic," as his biographer John MacAloon writes, but also idealistic. It was equally true of Coubertin's suggestion that athletic contests could provide a means of fostering such education. Behind Coubertin's theory, MacAloon argues, lay a form of "popular education, or to be more precise, 'popular ethnography.'" The 1896 Athens Olympics "drew athletes, officials, and spectators alike" into making contact with their counterparts from other countries and thus "into condensing, expressing, and exchanging images and judgments on exotic national characters, social institutions, and styles of life."[9] It was through this immersive, ethnographic experience of mixing with people from other cultural backgrounds—and the interpersonal friendships that would result—that mutual understanding would develop and peace would prevail.

Coubertin's idealistic vision of Olympic internationalism did not go unquestioned. The French nationalist Charles Maurras, who in 1899 would help to found the right-wing l'Action française, viewed the Olympic idea as a vulgar form of antinational cosmopolitanism, as "nothing but a confused mixing of nationalities reduced [to nothing] or destroyed." Yet Maurras's view changed dramatically as he watched the Athens Games and observed "the maintenance of the different [national] spirits": "No, countries aren't yet socially dissolved. War isn't dead yet. In former times, peoples interacted through ambassadors. These were intermediaries, buffers, which the new order of things tends to suppress. The races, released from the earth's gravity, served by [modern technologies of] steam and electricity, are going to interact without proxies, to insult one another mouth to mouth, and to turn one another's stomachs." The Olympics, he declared, had "become the happy battlefield between races and languages."[10]

Maurras's critique forced Coubertin to clarify his theory of internationalism, including its relationship with patriotism, nationalism, and cosmopolitanism. Whereas Maurras believed that internationalism could guarantee nationalism and patriotism (which he viewed as the same thing), Coubertin saw internationalism as "a bulwark against ignorance, chauvinism, and war," the dark underbelly of nationalist sentiment.[11] In this respect, Coubertin drew a distinction between patriotism, the healthy love of one's own nation, and chauvinistic nationalism. In his aptly titled article "Does Cosmopolitan Life Lead to International Friendliness?" he carefully distinguished "true internationalism" from cosmopolitanism. As the latter was based on a material life—European aristocrats swanning around the world thanks to new technologies, in ignorance of the foreign cultures they merely consumed—it would never result in "friendliness." By contrast, proper internationalism emerged from intellectual engagement or "study": "this is the true secret of international friendship; ignorance maintains prejudices; study alone expels them. In order to understand a country, it is not enough to see it live; its present state must be compared with its recent past." He even said it was "regrettable that one should visit a country before he has made such a study."[12]

In Coubertin's justification for the Olympic Games, internationalism was the product of mutual education between patriots of different countries. "Properly speaking," he wrote, "cosmopolitanism suits those people who have no country, while internationalism should be the state of mind of those who love their country above all, who seek to draw to it the friendship of foreigners by professing for the countries of those foreigners an intelligent and enlightened sympathy."[13] According to MacAloon, Coubertin's category of cosmopolitanism effectively absorbed Maurras's idea of internationalism (summarized by MacAloon as "cross-national contacts that assert differences and divide men from one another").[14] Coubertin's true internationalism took into account the social and cultural differences among nations, but, MacAloon concludes, "far from dividing and repelling men from one another, national differences were to be celebrated as different ways of being human; their recognition was the first step toward peace, friendliness and what the baron would later call *le respect mutuel*."[15]

Coubertin's article, though it did not discuss the Olympic Games, encapsulated the ingenious doubleness that would make the Olympics synonymous with both nationalism and internationalism. In this view, Olympic athletes represented their nations but were also "internationalists almost by definition." Athletes, together with officials and even spectators, were "drawn into rich contact with the cultures of their foreign opponents and comrades."[16] Three decades later, with the Olympics established as a feature of international public culture, Coubertin reviewed the logic once more: "To ask the peoples of the world to love one another is merely a form of childishness.

To ask them to respect one another is not in the least utopian, but in order to respect one another it is first necessary to know one another."[17] From this knowledge would emerge friendship and mutual understanding, and through these ingredients would emerge a diminished prospect of war.

The idealism and amateurism of Coubertin's ethnology was evident in his theory of internationalism. But as MacAloon also points out, the Olympic Games and the social sciences were infantile creations of the same era, products of the same political transformations of the late nineteenth century. In this respect, it is hardly surprising that Coubertin's theory of internationalism lacked sophistication; more striking is what happened afterward. While the academic discipline of anthropology would deal with questions of culture with an ever-increasing degree of theoretical sophistication, Coubertin's principle linking sport, friendship, and intercultural relations took on an ossified form that, unlike other elements of Olympism (such as amateurism and the participation of women), has remained remarkably resistant to critical analysis ever since.

Despite its prominence in the writings of Coubertin, the word "friendship" did not appear in the Olympic Rules—later the Olympic Charter—until the 1950s. Before then, the official statutes included only vague reference to the two main duties of the IOC: making the Olympic Games "more and more perfect, worthy of its glorious past and conforming to the high ideals" of those who revived the Games (especially Coubertin, mentioned by name from 1949), and taking "all proper measures to conduct modern athletics in the right way."[18] From 1956, the latter of these obligations was expanded to include explicit reference to amateurism, and it was in this context that the word "friendship" found its way into the official rules. According to the new phrasing, the IOC would be responsible for "guiding, and leading amateur sport along the right lines, thereby promoting and strengthening friendship between the sportsmen of all countries."[19] Although a detailed genealogy of the Olympic Charter is beyond the scope of this chapter, it is noteworthy that explicit reference to friendship first appeared during the postwar era: "The Age of Transnational Evangelism," in John Hoberman's felicitous phrasing.[20] Nevertheless, the term referred to the relationship among individual athletes, as Coubertin himself had originally conceived.

Over the following decades, the emphasis on friendship and understanding continued to intensify. In the 1970s, the Olympic Rules were restructured so that "the aims of the Olympic Movement" (previously referred to as the IOC) were highlighted in paragraph 3, the third of the "Fundamental Principles."[21]

A few years after this modification, the themes of sport, friendship, mutual understanding, and peace took on their most elaborate expression, which was also most faithful to the writings of Coubertin. In 1978 the rules stated that "The aims of the Olympic movement are . . . to educate young people through sport in a spirit of better understanding between each other and of friendship, thereby helping to build a better and more peaceful world."[22]

Although the wording and focus of the IOC's official aims have continued to change, friendship and mutual understanding remain key discursive themes. In the current Olympic Charter (2017), the fourth "fundamental principle of Olympism" posits that "The practice of sport is a human right. Every individual must have the possibility of practising sport, without discrimination of any kind and in the Olympic spirit, which requires mutual understanding with a spirit of friendship, solidarity and fair play."[23] Coubertin's rationalist logic of promoting peace through friendship, and friendship through sport, also lives on. According to the IOC's "Promote Olympism in Society" web page, "The goal of the Olympic Movement is to contribute to building a peaceful and better world by educating youth through sport practiced without discrimination of any kind and in the Olympic spirit, which requires mutual understanding with a spirit of friendship, solidarity and fair play."[24]

More than a century after Coubertin first asserted the relationship between sport, friendship, and mutual understanding, the theory underpinning this claim remains undeveloped, though not for lack of effort. A 2007 article in the IOC's *Olympic Review* titled "The Olympic Values" offers four pages of exegesis on "core values" of Olympism: excellence, friendship, and respect. Its author Steven Maass explains that friendship "encourages us to consider sport as a tool for mutual understanding among individuals and people from all over the world. The Olympic Games inspire humanity to overcome political, economic, gender, racial or religious differences and forge friendships in spite of those differences."[25] In the form of intellectual hagiography, the author traces the history of this value through the personage of Coubertin, "the man behind the values," and the inspiration he took from the ancient Olympic Truce:

The Olympic Movement is, at its heart, about people. The value of friendship is steeped in the tradition of the ancient Olympic Truce and refers, broadly, to building a peaceful world through sport. The athletes express this value by forming life-long bonds with their team mates, as well as their opponents. Today, the Olympic Movement expresses this value by reaching citizens of more than 200 countries and territories and applying a fundamental humanistic approach to all its actions.[26]

In spite of these efforts, the reader is left with little more than general platitudes. As philosopher Jim Parry has observed, "Friendship, Excellence, Respect is a slogan that might be adopted by almost any organization." Although Parry is sympathetic to Olympism and its social potential, he criticizes the slogan as "a weak and uninformative formulation."[27]

Conscious of cynicism toward such slogans, Maass concedes that "critics may argue that sport has had minimal effect in creating this sort of utopian existence." Yet in a striking example of how Olympic ideas can be remolded, he simply reverses the causal direction so that "the modern Olympic Games, in conjunction with the broader Olympic Movement, have relied on these [core] values to create one of the greatest social phenomena of our times."[28] In this curious logic, it is no longer the Olympics that instill values of excellence, friendship, and respect; rather, these values created the Olympics. Maass thus reinforces the liturgical quality of the claim that sport promotes friendship and mutual understanding. Turning to Asia and Southeast Asia, we can see another way in which the liturgical features of friendship have been reinforced: by conflating social friendship with political friendship in the quest for regional cooperation in the postwar era.

The Asian Games

After the South East Asia Peninsular (SEAP) Games, as the SEA Games were originally known, were established in 1959, the IOC recognized them as being among several "regional games" under IOC patronage. The most influential inspiration for the SEAP Games was the Asian Games, first held in newly independent India in 1951. Partly modeled on the prewar Far Eastern Championship Games and West Asiatic Games, the Asian Games embodied the anticolonial and Pan-Asian values of the Asian Relations Conference, convened by Indian prime minister Jawaharlal Nehru in 1947 and attended by many other Asian leaders. It was during the conference in New Delhi that Guru Dutt Sondhi, Indian IOC member and founder of the West Asiatic Games, gained support for the idea of an Asian Games as a means of promoting the Asian Relations Conference's goal of enhanced regional relations.

Nehru agreed, and four years later 478 athletes from eleven countries came together in New Delhi to compete in the first Asian Games.[29]

The official aims of the Asian Games were twofold: to improve physical fitness, especially among youths, and to promote international friendship and cooperation.[30] Although the second of these aims clearly invoked the idealistic internationalism of the Olympics, there was a slight shift in emphasis. Whereas Coubertin believed that peace would result from friendship between individual athletes, officials, and spectators and the mutual understanding of foreign cultures that would develop, Nehru and Sondhi placed greatest emphasis on friendship among nations. In February 1951 two weeks before the inaugural Asian Games commenced, Nehru asserted that the Asian Games would "bring together the youth of many countries and thus help, to some extent, in promoting international friendship and cooperation. In these days, when dark clouds of conflict [in Korea] hover over us, we must seize every opportunity to promote this understanding and cooperation between nations."[31] In 1966, Sondhi—by then a senior vice president and "doyen member of the IOC"—put a similar emphasis on the nation, stating that Coubertin's "chief aim" had been the use of sport to develop "sportsmanship and goodwill and understanding between the nations of the world."[32]

Though perhaps unintentional, the enhanced emphasis on the nation was a logical product of the postcolonial context. According to Nehru, the Games sought to recover a historical spirit of good relations in Asia, which had been interrupted under colonial rule when "the countries of Asia . . . lost contact with each other."[33] In the contemporary context, a new international calamity—the Korean War—threatened to engulf the nations of Asia, highlighting the need for regional friendship. In sum, Nehru viewed the Asian Games as a means of promoting friendship among the new and emerging nations in a continent torn apart by colonialism and ongoing conflict between global powers. Ironically, despite highlighting this nationalist perspective in his own remarks, Sondhi would critique this interpretation of Asian Games friendship as aberrant.[34]

By the second and third Asian Games in the Philippines (1954) and Japan (1958)—both steadfast allies of the United States—a Cold War-inspired, anticommunist regionalism had superseded the anticolonial regionalism of the first Games. As in the Olympics of the 1950s, the starkest indicator of this shift was the inclusion of the U.S.-allied Republic of China (ROC), which in turn guaranteed the exclusion between 1954 and 1970 of the PRC.[35] But this was also part of a broader pattern. In Manila eight countries participated in the Asian Games for the first time, all of which—including the ROC, the Republic of Korea, and the Republic of Vietnam—were "free world" allies of the United States or colonies of U.S. allies.[36] With the sidelining of the communist bloc, Asian Games discourses of friendship and understanding became limited to "free world" nations. As Stefan Huebner writes, "the image of Asia . . . communicated was that of a community of countries either pro-American or neutral in the Cold War."[37] This pattern would be reproduced in the SEAP Games, which excluded the Democratic Republic of Vietnam.

Friendship in the SEAP Games

The SEAP Games were founded by military-ruled Thailand, a key U.S.-backed anticommunist bulwark in Southeast Asia. While in Tokyo for the 1958 Asian Games, Thai sporting officials met with Southeast Asian counterparts and agreed to establish a "little Asian Games" among six countries located in mainland Southeast Asia: Burma, Cambodia, Laos, Malaya, South Vietnam, and Thailand. The city-state Singapore was added as an afterthought the following year, when it also gained full internal self-government.[38] Forming the SEAP Games Federation (SEAPGF) to oversee the games, officials decided to hold the event every second year, between the Olympic Games and the Asian Games, and awarded the inaugural SEAP Games of 1959 to Bangkok in recognition of Thailand's foundational role. With the single exception of 1963, the biennial schedule has been maintained ever since. The SEAP Games became the SEA Games in 1977, two years after communist revolutions led to the withdrawal of Vietnam, Cambodia, and Laos, when the archipelagic countries of Indonesia, the Philippines, and Brunei joined and the word "Peninsular" was dropped. The Indochinese countries remained members of the SEA Games Federation (SEAGF), rejoining the games between 1983 and 1995, and in 2003 newly independent Timor Leste brought the number of participating nations to eleven.[39]

As in the Asian Games, which provided the main model, the official objectives of the SEAP Games were twofold. The first goal—to improve the performance of peninsular athletes at the Asian and Olympic Games—was motivated by Thai concerns that Southeast Asia lagged behind other Asian nations in sporting standards. "Our teams are not strong. . . . Our standards are low," stated Olympic Council of Thailand (OCT) deputy president Luang Sukhum Naipradith, who is celebrated as the official founder of the SEAP/SEA

Games. According to an article introducing the official report of the 1959 games, probably penned by Sukhum himself, "Such a contest, if held at just the right time, well before the Asian and Olympic Games, will indeed enable the athletes to improve their skills, thus preparing them for better performance in the two older international meets."[40]

It was the second objective that organizers believed to be the most critical. According to the same report, "The most important fact remains that the contest among these nations of the region will no doubt foster good understanding, goodwill and cooperation."[41] This view was based on Thailand's recent experience of conducting bilateral sporting contests with its newly independent neighbors, which had "become instrumental in rendering closer the already existing bonds of friendship among the competing nations."[42] According to Lieutenant General Praphat Charusatien, president of the OCT, the SEAP Games would "better the already existing bonds of friendship among various member nations of the Games."[43]

For many organizers and government officials, friendship meant friendship between nations. In seeking cabinet support for the proposed SEAP Games, Praphat—who was also deputy prime minister and minister of the interior in the Thai junta—argued that the SEAP Games would "cement friendship between the six neighboring countries . . . situated in the Golden Peninsula [mainland Southeast Asia], thus increasing closeness and intimacy." Sport, he stressed, without further explanation, was "one of the best means of cementing friendship."[44] Sukhum likewise asserted that the event would promote "good understanding, goodwill and cooperation" in the peninsular region, because "the various countries in the Peninsula [share] among them a great affinity in practically all respects, such as the way of life and climate as well as physical appearance."[45] The SEAPGF's official symbols reinforced these themes, with an official flag featuring a rosette of six yellow gold rings—referring to the six original SEAPGF members—against a light blue background. These rings were "intertwined," according to the official statutes of the SEAPGF, "to denote friendship, brotherly love and unity of purpose."[46]

Inevitably, given the regional ructions of the Cold War, it was not long before political realities challenged the idealism of the newly founded SEAP Games. Less than two weeks before the opening ceremony, Cambodia withdrew from the SEAP Games due to fears over the safety of its athletes and officials. The immediate cause for concern was anti-Cambodian protests in Bangkok, sparked by Cambodia's decision to refer a high-profile border dispute to the International Court of Justice. But the dispute was also an indication of the Cold War animosity between the two countries' leaders: Field Marshal Sarit Thanarat, the charming and ruthless dictator of Thailand who was heavily backed by the United States, and Prince Norodom Sihanouk, the neutralist prime minister of Cambodia who condemned Thai and U.S. interference while courting aid from China (as well as the United States). In 1963 Cambodia cancelled the third SEAP Games, which it was scheduled to host, when it backed Indonesia's GANEFO. Cambodia then withdrew in 1967, when again scheduled to host, and also in 1969.[47] In 1966 when Cambodia held a major multisport event in Phnom Penh, it was the second or "Asian" GANEFO, an event that drew Cambodia into a very different circle of friends consisting of Second World and Third World nations.

Although Cambodia rejoined the SEAP Games under the pro-U.S. regime of Lon Nol (1970–1975), further challenges emerged. In 1975 communist revolutions in South Vietnam, Cambodia, and Laos led to their withdrawal from the SEAP Games. The Coalition Government of Democratic Kampuchea (CGDK), which enjoyed international recognition over the Vietnam-installed People's Republic of Kampuchea, rejoined the renamed SEA Games between 1983 and 1987, but the CGDK's participation kept Vietnam and its ally Laos out of the SEA Games until 1989. Although the main impediment to Vietnam's earlier return was the presence of the Khmer Rouge-backed CGDK team, Vietnam's nonparticipation highlighted the deep political divisions that existed between it and the Association of Southeast Asian Nations (ASEAN).[48] Hardly a priority in these years, regional sports "friendship" was an obvious casualty of these developments.

It was not just regional politics but also the sports events themselves that undermined regional bonhomie. From the mid-1980s, host countries began to load the program with sports they expected to win, including a growing list of "local" or traditional (i.e., non-Olympic and non-Asian Games) sports. Despite modifications to SEA Games rules allowing host nations to include up to eight such sports, critics condemned the practice as being unfair, unsportsmanlike, and even corrupt. Although this practice was reciprocal in the sense that all host nations did it and in turn reaped the benefits of inflated medal tallies, claims of regional friendship in the SEA Games were increasingly ridiculed as empty clichés. In more recent years with the SEA Games program expanding to include up to forty-three different sports (in 2007), many more than the Olympics, this trend has led some observers to wonder about the purpose and future of the SEA Games.[49]

Anthropomorphizing International Relations

Despite these challenges, SEA Games' discourses linking sport, friendship, and mutual understanding have remained ubiquitous over the past sixty years. This resilience can be attributed to the event's qualities as a spectacle, which generates the suspension of disbelief, and the vagueness of "friendship" as a normative value, which encourages the confusion—or conflation—of its social and political registers. Whereas social friendship invokes the intimacy, authenticity, and universal experience of friendship as a private and personal relationship, political friendship connotes the scale and significance of international relations and the latter's implications for regional order. The slippage between these two categories of friendship, which in some ways are incommensurate, helps to account for the resilience of friendship as a SEAP/SEA Games value. We can think of this slippage as the anthropomorphizing of international relations.

As we have seen, SEAP Games founders tended to invoke a political meaning of friendship among multiple nations. As in the Asian Games, this emphasis could be explained by the postcolonial context, including the emergence of a new regional order of nation-states. Between 1945 and 1957, decolonization re-created Southeast Asia as a region of nation-states. While Thailand had avoided colonization, its neighbors, including the other five original members of the SEAPGF, had obtained independence between 1947 and 1957, and Singapore achieved internal self-government in 1959. With external affairs policies no longer determined primarily by imperial powers, the countries of Southeast Asia sought for the first time to engage with one another on the basis of Westphalian sovereign equality, now expressed in the norms of the United Nations. As the new nations of Southeast Asia pursued good neighborly relations, promoting regional friendship took on an urgency that was both practical and symbolic. Sport was a significant—but hardly the only—means through which such "friendship" was pursued.

In most countries in the region, sport was overseen by senior politicians, military officers, and civil servants—an indication of the national importance and prestige attached to the field. Some of these leaders captured the political significance of the SEAP Games as a means of reinforcing the new regional order of nation-states. In December 1959 at a farewell ceremony in Kuala Lumpur for Malaya's athletes, Deputy Prime Minister Tun Abdul Razak, president of the Olympic Council of Malaya, declared that

Today, as a result of the rebirth of liberty in Asia, Asians are free to choose their own ways and it is particularly fitting that the [SEAP] Games should first take place in Siam which is the oldest free nation in this region. I am confident that as the years go by the S.E.A.P. Games will help bring this small family of nations even closer together, and so promote the spirit of goodwill, peace and harmony which we always cherish in this part of the world.[50]

Praphat, the Thai interior minister and OCT president, invoked similar ideals in describing the SEAP Games. Only through "brotherly relations" such as those fostered by the SEAP Games, he proposed, "could peace and independence in this area be maintained according to the ideals of the United Nations."[51]

The idea of promoting regional relations—and friendship—through sport reflected and reinforced other areas of regional cooperation in the early Cold War period. In the case of Thailand, where the junta was no less anticommunist than its U.S. patrons, regional cooperation was pursued primarily as a means of containing Vietnamese and Chinese communism. The best known of these ventures was the Southeast Asia Treaty Organization (SEATO), founded in 1954 and headquartered in Bangkok, although the capacity of SEATO to promote regional relations was limited by its small membership from the region (only Thailand and the Philippines) and the impression of U.S. domination.[52] Nevertheless, there were other less well-known regional ventures with greater local input. Between 1954 and 1957, Thailand proposed or supported at least three other regional organizations—made up of various combinations of Malaya, South Vietnam (both free world allies of Bangkok), Laos, Cambodia, and Burma (all officially neutralist)—that reinforced the country's pursuit of anticommunist regionalism in mainland Southeast Asia.[53]

Like the SEAP Games, these initiatives focused on cultural cooperation rather than political ties, even though their anticommunist basis explicitly betrayed political motivations. None of these proposals came to fruition, but they provided further evidence of a belief in cultural cooperation as a means of promoting anticommunist friendship. In all cases, this anticommunism was exemplified by the absence of the Democratic Republic of Vietnam, despite its belonging geographically to the peninsular region.

Another parallel between SEAP Games friendship and the broader political context was evident in U.S. involvement. Although Sukhum is remembered as the founder of the SEAP Games, the OCT was advised by an American, David Dichter, a junior officer in the Bangkok branch of the U.S. Information Service who was the honorary coach of the Thai Athletics team. Dichter's involvement was unplanned but was consistent with American strategies for influencing Thai society in line with U.S. strategic interests. In a long cable to the U.S. State Department in Washington, Dichter's superior stressed the policy benefits of the SEAP Games for promoting regional cooperation and "mutual understanding among peninsular Southeast Asians." "Uniting the states of the region through international sports should give them greater strength to resist Communist subversion," he added, since they would look to one another as a means of improving their athletic standards rather than to "propaganda-loaded all expense-paid tours offered by Red China."[54]

In this way the SEAP Games highlighted the emergence of rival Cold War friendship circles in the region, pitting free world friends against socialist and/or nonaligned friends. This was clearest in Cambodia's decision to side with Sukarno's GANEFO in 1963, the only time since 1959 that the SEAP or SEA Games have not been held, and in Sihanouk's Asian GANEFO three years later, which represented a rival to the fifth Asian Games, held two weeks later in neighboring Thailand. Whereas the Asian GANEFO attracted mostly socialist countries, with a few nonaligned contingents also attending, the latter welcomed primarily free world teams.[55] Underlining the polarized nature of regional sport at this time as the Vietnam War tore the region in two, Thailand's neighbor Laos, then engulfed in a civil war, was represented by rival teams at the two competitions: the socialist Lao Patriotic Front in Phnom Penh and the official national team of the Royal Lao Government in Bangkok.[56]

In subsequent decades, SEA Games discourses of regional friendship—and later "family"—evolved in response to developments in regional politics. The first of these was the formation in 1967 of ASEAN, originally comprising Indonesia, Malaysia, Singapore, the Philippines, and Thailand. Although the archipelagic states of Indonesia and the Philippines were considered significant powers in Asian sports, they were not members of the SEAPGF. Within two years, Singapore and then Malaysia were calling for the SEAP Games to be expanded or, if necessary, supplemented by an ASEAN or Southeast Asian Games including these two countries.[57] Inclusion, they argued, would boost standards and spread the burden of hosting the games, a serious issue given that due to war, Cambodia, Laos, and South Vietnam were unable to host. Although the Thais originally blocked the proposal, they relented after the three Indochinese countries withdrew in 1975. Two years later Indonesia and the Philippines were admitted along with the British protectorate of Brunei, and the SEAP Games were renamed the SEA Games (minus "Peninsular"). Southeast Asia's primary regional sports event now included all five members of ASEAN along with Burma and Brunei.

ASEAN's detractors frequently criticize it for being a mere "talk shop." But as historian Anthony Milner notes, talk "can be productive in identity terms," and one thing ASEAN has long talked about is friendship.[58] As the membership of the renamed SEA Games was expanded to include all five ASEAN nations, SEAP/SEA Games discourses of friendship increasingly invoked the political parallel of ASEAN. In 1975 as Malaysia and Singapore pushed for expansion, the *Straits Times* (Singapore) suggested that "Another good reason why they [Indonesia and the Philippines] should [join] is that they are members of Asean, a body dedicated to precisely the same objectives as Seap"—that is, regional friendship and cooperation.[59] Two years later as this "new chapter" was being written, Philippines Olympics chief Colonel Nereo Andalong declared that "Sport is the major area of co-operation. We are fully committed to the cause of ASEAN co-operation, and there can be no better way of achieving it than through sport." Such effusiveness affirmed *Straits Times* columnist Percy Seneviratne's belief in Coubertin's vision of realizing "international respect and goodwill" through sport. While Senevirante regretted that "the Olympic Games have veered away from the original objectives" of transcending politics, "the South-east Asian Games have a special warmth that is a triumph for idealism in sport."[60]

A decade later on the eve of his country's second time as host to the Games, President Suharto of Indonesia employed similar language, reminding his athletes "of the importance of friendship and harmony among Asean members," the "fundamental spirit" behind the SEA Games.[61] The same year another observer, writing in the context of ASEAN's twenty-first anniversary celebrations, argued that regional sporting ties exceeded even the ties of ASEAN, since they "go back some four decades."[62]

ASEAN friendship was also a key theme when Laos and Vietnam returned to the SEA Games in the late 1980s. When Laos returned with a "token" team in 1989, it was to bring "friendship and solidarity to Asean countries," according to the head of the Lao delegation.[63] In Laos, significantly, this rhetoric (especially "solidarity," a powerful word in the socialist lexicon) still borrowed most directly from that of existing sporting ties with "fraternal socialist countries." Since 1980 this designation had referred to Vietnam and Cambodia, with which it met regularly in triangular "friendship competitions" and the socialist bloc in general, particularly in the context of the Moscow Olympics.[64] Now with the warming of regional relations and the imminent fall of the Berlin Wall, membership of this "extended socialist family," as it was also called, was being superseded by new notions of sporting friendship with non-communist neighbors in the region.

The association between SEA Games and ASEAN friendship was reinforced by the One Southeast Asia vision of the 1990s, when after the international settlement on Cambodia, existing members decided to expand ASEAN to Vietnam (1995), Laos and Myanmar (1997), and Cambodia (1999). In 1997, a reluctant Indonesia agreed to host the SEA Games only "in order to keep the celebration of the ASEAN Family Games going."[65] The same year, the official SEA Games anthem included the verse

Although our cultures are not the same we are one big family . . .
We ASEAN together at SEA Games arena to compete is the game . . .
And the honor of our nations will remain . . .
And we attain unity, pride and honour, that's our aim.[66]

Official SEA Games mottoes introduced in 1997 celebrated themes of unity and friendship in the age of One Southeast Asia. In Indonesia that year the motto was "Spirit, Unity and Honour."[67] More recent versions have included "One Heritage, One Southeast Asia" (Philippines, 2005), "Spirit, Friendship, Celebration" (Thailand, 2007), "Generosity, Amity, Healthy Lifestyle" (Laos, 2009), "United and Rising" (Indonesia, 2011), and "Clean, Green and Friendship" (Myanmar, 2013). At the opening ceremony in Naypyitaw in 2013, the Myanmar sports minister explained that "The SEA Games Federation has been hosting SEA Games with the aim of fostering friendship. . . . Myanmar is hosting the SEA Games under the motto of 'Green, Clean & Friendship' with the aim of fostering and enhancing friendship among ASEAN countries by sports."[68]

Because Myanmar had not hosted the Games since 1969, the emphasis of the 2013 Games was on celebrating the country's symbolic reentry to the region, particularly after its political reforms of 2007–2011.[69] The following year to cap off this symbolic reemergence, the country chaired ASEAN for the first time. This theme of regional emergence has been common in the past two decades, with Brunei (1999), Vietnam (2003), and Laos (2009) hosting the SEA Games for the first time and Cambodia scheduled to do so in 2023.

Friendship as a Social Relation

Despite the increasing emphasis on geopolitical aspects of regional friendship, SEA Games officials and observers have also celebrated the promotion of friendship at a more intimate level of social and interpersonal relationships. This aspect of friendship typically emerges from people's direct or ethnographic experience of the games as spectators, officials, and athletes.

As MacAloon notes in his study of Olympic spectacle, the rituals of the opening ceremonies effect "social transitions or spiritual transformations" through the modeling of shared humanity or "humankind-ness," the "transcendental ground" of the rituals.[70] In the SEAP/SEA Games, which largely replicated this principle at a regional level, these rituals and the spectacle of the ceremonies helped spectators (including the press) overlook evidence of regional conflict. According to *Siam Nikorn* (Bangkok), in the inaugural games of 1959 the opening ceremony was "spectacular" and unforgettable, "the most impressive and grandiose image" created by the "biggest opening to a sports competition Thailand has ever seen." Revealingly, the writer conflated the spectacle of symbolic unity among individual athletes with that of unity among participating nations. Most impressively, the march of athletes represented "a strong and stable movement . . . driving us to think of close relationships among the six nations. . . . This [the SEAP Games] has become a symbol of love, sportsmanship, [and] friendship of neighboring countries in the Golden Peninsula region." Despite Cambodia's withdrawal at the last minute, "this beautiful and impressive image" would be re-created in future games in "every country in the Golden Peninsula, including Cambodia."[71] More than half a century later, the spectacle of the opening ceremony still commonly results in the pattern of pre-Games controversies being forgotten.[72]

In the mold of Coubertin's original vision, other observers draw more explicit and instrumentalist links among interpersonal friendship, mutual understanding, interstate relations, and peace. In the aftermath of the roundly praised inaugural Games in 1959, the Bangkok newspaper *Siam Rath* explained that "Travelling to compete in sport represents a good opportunity for athletes to socialize and become familiar with each other, and to get along well. When the people have mutual understanding, increasingly friendly relations between countries will follow."[73] Visiting officials echoed this theme. The Burmese team manager, for example, remarked that the SEAP Games would cement friendship and promote "better understanding of people in each country."[74] Others noted isolated disagreements over refereeing and other issues, but these were minor. One report even suggested that small controversies such as these could help "build up meaningful friendship" similar to arguments between a husband and wife.[75]

As in the Olympics, the SEA Games Village is often thought to exemplify the value of friendship. In 1973, Singapore's organizers suggested that the location of the village in suburban Toa Payoh, a new housing estate, would promote friendly relations: "The idea is to make the contestants feel at ease, live in a friendly atmosphere, and to get to know each other—and Singaporeans—well. As a result, stated Games chief E. W. Barker, 'There is no doubt that the seventh Seap Games will draw the various participating nations closely together and catalyse the spirit of co-operation.'"[76] The same logic applied in reverse. Four years later in Kuala Lumpur, a Singaporean columnist bemoaned the lack of communal eating facilities at an otherwise model SEA Games Village at the University of Malaya, since the contingents "would not get much of a chance to mix with each other." This "negated" the central point, he asserted, "of bringing together about 2000 sportsmen in one arena for the intangible promotion—and fusion—of their cultures."[77]

Talk of the social aspects of friendship has often been most pronounced among officials and athletes—those people with the most intimate experience of the SEA Games. As noted earlier, Games founder Sukhum stressed the goal of "good understanding, goodwill and cooperation," and David Dichter, the American coach and adviser, brought to Thailand a similar faith in the capacity of sport to forge interpersonal relations, which he drew from his experiences as a high school and college athlete. A quarter century later, Thai Olympic chief and IOC member Marshal Dhawee Chullasarp reaffirmed this view. While gold medals were important, friendship was more so: "I believe sports is the best ammunition in the world to keep peace. . . . You see, medals are only symbols. But friendship means harmony between two groups of people."[78] This sentiment was doubly significant for the former defense minister, according to his interviewer, because a "border battle [presumably with anti-CGDK Vietnamese forces] has fired his military belly." (The irony of a senior military commander preaching peace through sport was seemingly lost on the reporter.)

The themes of friendship (and secondarily, family) arise often in discussions with officials and athletes. In recent years, particularly during the twenty-eighth SEA Games in Singapore in 2015, I have conducted twenty interviews with SEAGF members, including several whose involvement in the SEA Games stretches over many decades. These officials (mostly but not solely men) refer to two kinds of friendship. First, almost without exception, they mention the twin objectives of the SEA Games, including regional friendship and cooperation. Here, friendship is part of the institutional rhetoric of the SEAGF, in which members are well versed. Unless asked, officials elaborate little on what friendship means in this context; it is simply an abstract statement about the positive associations of the SEA Games and international sport.

In contrast, officials tend to be far more specific and animated about the friendships they share with each other through membership of the SEAGF, which they refer to warmly and unanimously as the "SEA Games family." These friendships, often forged over several decades, commonly build on officials' earlier experiences as athletes, which they consider inseparable from their careers as sports administrators. Officials are frank about the tensions that exist in the SEAGF, particularly over sports selection. Nevertheless, they believe that the warmth and longevity of their personal friendships allow the SEAGF to navigate these difficulties. At the same time, they generally pay little attention to higher-level political issues arising from the Games, which sometimes dominate media coverage. While aware that the SEA Games take place in a political context and rely on government funding to run the Games, the people at the heart of the SEA Games family see politics as largely irrelevant to their own primary task, which is to ensure the successful running of the Games every two years. Due to the small size, biennial frequency, and cooperative approach to running the SEA Games, officials draw a clear distinction between the family feel of the SEAGF and the more formal and remote style of cooperation in the Asian and Olympic Games.

In a similar way, SEA Games athletes embrace the social notion of friendship with their counterparts from other countries. Though the SEA Games dominate the regional sporting calendar every second year, Southeast Asian athletes cross paths in a range of other events on a regular basis. These experiences can begin from a young age. One interviewee, a twenty-six-year-old male marathon runner from Singapore, recalled forming friendships in the ASEAN schools championships, which have lasted over a decade. Through such connections athletes can get to know their competitors reasonably well, although language limitations mean that they are most likely to befriend competitors with a similar language background.[79] Even more than for SEAGF officials, these ideas of friendship are immune to the political disputes that can mar media coverage of the Games. Seemingly oblivious to the noise going on outside, this group of people are among the truest converts to the idea of friendship in sport, although there appears to be considerable variation from sport to sport.

These examples are not intended to suggest that Coubertin had it right or that the SEA Games—as one journalist argued—have succeeded in realizing the baron's vision where the Olympics have failed. The views of athletes, officials, and spectators attest to a shared conviction in official discourses of friendship, but a shared discourse does not imply that regional sports competitions have produced mutual understanding or peace. What the examples demonstrate is the widespread persistence, despite ample evidence to the contrary, of moral discourses linking sport to friendship. On one level, this connection is aided by the simple repetition and rhetorical familiarity of this moral claim and by the way in which the spectacle itself generates a suspension of disbelief. Despite the great weight of evidence to the contrary, journalists, officials, athletes, and other observers continue to learn and then repeat an international and highly institutionalized language that rapidly becomes familiar to them.

The persistence of friendship discourses in sport also owes much to the vagueness with which the claim has been defined. The confusion of social and political aspects of friendship has conflated two very different forms of relationship, both of which have inherent appeal to different groups. The political connotations of friendship suggest that the SEA Games play a role in creating a regional order of nation-states, which has evolved from the Thai-led anticommunist regionalism in mainland Southeast Asia of the 1950s to the regionalism of the ASEAN-5 in the late 1970s and the vision of One Southeast Asia since the 1990s. Although officials liked to maintain the fiction that sport is removed from politics, sport and politics have shown themselves to be two sides of the same regionalizing coin.

Parallel to these developments, the social and interpersonal connotations of friendship—*real* friendship, we might say—suggest that the SEA Games do promote interpersonal or social relations. This aspect of friendship remains crucial to the moral claims of the SEA Games, for it evokes the impression of genuine warmth and intimacy and reinforces the belief that sport transcends politics. This can be very helpful when noisy and predictable nationalist controversies undermine the claim that the SEA Games promote friendship among the countries of the region. Curiously, the existence of these two quite different kinds of friendship does not seem to have occurred to SEA Games observers. Observers frequently slip unselfconsciously between social notions of friendship (between individuals) and political notions of friendship (between countries). This slippage gives the rhetoric of friendship a certain malleability and adaptability, because friendship really does mean different things to different people. In a complex and conflict-ridden world, it is perhaps the hiddenness—in plain sight—of friendship's double meaning that best explains the persistence and power of the moral claim that sport serves friendship and mutual understanding.

Notes

1. Pierre de Coubertin, "The Olympic Games of 1896," *Century Magazine* 53 (1896): 53, cited in John MacAloon, *This Great Symbol: Pierre de Coubertin and the Origins of the Modern Olympic Games* (New York: Routledge, 2013), 262.

2. On the debate over whether violence, including death from war, is declining, see Steven Pinker, *The Better Angels of Our Nature: Why Violence Is Declining* (New York: Penguin, 2012); cf. Pasquale Cirillo and Nassim Nicholas Taleb, "The Decline of Violent Conflicts: What Do the Data Really Say?," November 27, 2016, NYU Tandon Research Paper No. 2876315, ssrn.com /abstract=2876315.

3. These thirteen gold medals were split by the region's two powerhouses, Thailand with seven and Indonesia with six.

4. For the Asian Games, see Stefan Huebner, *Pan-Asian Sports and the Emergence of Modern Asia, 1913–1974* (Singapore: NUS Press, 2016); Fan Hong, *Sport, Nationalism and Orientalism: The Asian Games* (London: Routledge, 2013). For GANEFO, see Russell Field, "Splitting the World of International Sport: The 1963 Games of the New Emerging Forces and the Politics of Challenging the Global Sport Order," in *Sport, Protest and Globalisation*, ed. Jon Dart and Stephen Wagg, 77–99 (London: Palgrave Macmillan, 2016); Ewa Pauker, "Ganefo I: Sports and Politics in Djakarta," *Asian Survey* 5, no. 4 (1965): 171–185.

5. Quoted in Richard Espy, *The Politics of the Olympic Games* (Berkeley: University of California Press, 1979), 81.

6. Guanhua Wang, "'Friendship First': China's Sports Diplomacy During the Cold War," *Journal of American-East Asian Relations* 12, no. 3 (2003): 133–153. On socialist Laos, see also Simon Creak, *Embodied Nation: Sport, Masculinity, and the Making of Modern Laos* (Honolulu: University of Hawai'i Press, 2015), 201–207, 209–216.

7. Graham M. Smith, "Friendship and the World of States," *International Politics* 48, no. 1 (2011): 15.

8. See recent special issues of *Critical Review of International Social and Political Philosophy* (2007) and *International Politics* (2011).

9. MacAloon, *This Great Symbol*, 262.

10. Quoted in ibid., 262–263.

11. MacAloon, *This Great Symbol*, 263.

12. Quoted in ibid., 265.

13. Quoted in ibid., 265–266.

14. Ibid., 266.

15. Ibid., 266.

16. Ibid., 266.

17. Quoted in ibid., 268.

18. This wording is taken from International Olympic Committee, *Olympic Rules* (Lausanne: Heliographia, S.A., 1946), 6. Prior to 1933, the IOC statutes were published only in French, but the quoted objectives were the same. See, for example, Comité International Olympique, *Statuts du Comité International Olympique* (Lausanne: Comité International Olympique, 1924), 3–4.

19. International Olympic Committee, *The Olympic Games: Fundamental Principles, Rules and Regulations, General Information* (Lausanne: International Olympic Committee, 1956), 11.

20. John Hoberman, "Toward a Theory of Olympic Internationalism," *Journal of Sport History* 22, no. 1 (1995): 28.

21. International Olympic Committee, *Olympic Rules and Regulations: Rules Approved in Munich 1972* (Lausanne: International Olympic Committee, 1973).

22. International Olympic Committee, *Olympic Charter: Provisional Edition* (Lausanne: International Olympic Committee, 1978), 4.

23. International Olympic Committee, *Olympic Charter: In Force from 15 September 2017* (Lausanne: International Olympic Committee, 2017), 11.

24. International Olympic Committee, "Promote Olympism in Society," 2018, www.olympic.org/the-ioc/promote-olympism. In addition, the second fundamental principle of Olympism "is to place sport at the service of the harmonious development of humankind, with a view to promoting a peaceful society concerned with the preservation of human dignity."

25. Steven Maass, "The Olympic Values," *Olympic Review*, no. 63 (2007): 30.

26. Ibid., 32.

27. Jim Parry, "Physical Education as Olympic Education," in *Olympic Values and Ethics in Contemporary Society*, by Susan Brownell and Jim Parry (Ghent: Ghent University Press, 2012), 31.

28. Maass, "The Olympic Values."

29. "Report of the First Asian Games Held at New Delhi, March 4 to 11, 1951 (Under the Patronage of the I.O.C.)," *Bulletin du Comité International Olympique*, no. 27 (June 1951): 43. See also Huebner, *Pan-Asian Sports*, 102–111.

30. "The Asian Games: A Short History," *Bulletin du Comité International Olympique*, no. 96 (November 1966): 39. See also Huebner, *Pan-Asian Sports*, 111–114.

31. Cited in Huebner, *Pan-Asian Sports*, 112.

32. G. D. Sondhi, "A Policy for Asian Games," *Bulletin du Comité International Olympique*, no. 25 (January 1951): 45.

33. Cited in Huebner, *Pan-Asian Sports*, 113. Nehru's history ignored many precolonial conflicts.

34. Sondhi, "A Policy for Asian Games," 45–46.

35. At New Delhi in 1951, India welcomed observers from the PRC while shunning the ROC team. See Huebner, *Pan-Asian Sports*, 110. For the "China issue" at the Olympics, see Susan Brownell, "'Sport and Politics Don't Mix': China's Relationship with the IOC during the Cold War," in *East Plays West: Sport and the Cold War*, ed. Stephen Wagg and David Andrews, 253–271 (London: Routledge, 2007).

36. Huebner, *Pan Asian Sports*, 129.

37. Ibid., 145.

38. Other countries from the region, such as Indonesia and the Philippines, also expressed interest in joining but would be forced to wait almost two decades for admission.

39. Simon Creak, "Eternal Friends and Erstwhile Enemies: The Regional Sporting Community of the Southeast Asian Games," *TRaNS: Trans-Regional and -National Studies of Southeast Asia* 5, no. 1 (2017): 150–151.

40. *Official Report of the Organizing Committee of the First South East Asia Peninsular Games, Bangkok, Thailand, December 1959* (Bangkok: Siva Phorn Limited Partnership, 1961), 1; see also "Thai 'Little Asian Games' Idea Told," *Bangkok Post*, May 26, 1959, 6. Thai people are usually referred to by their first names (here Sukhum). "Luang" is a title bestowed by the king, which thus betrays Sukhum's high status and close connections to the king. Formerly a royal aide, Sukhum was head of the Civil Service Commission in 1959.

41. *Official Report*, 2. See also "Thai 'Little Asian Games' Idea Told," *Bangkok Post*, May 26, 1959, 6; for an example of how this narrative has been institutionalized, see SEA Games Federation, *SEAP and SEA Games History: 50th Anniversary of SEA Games, 8th December 2009, Vientiane* (n.p., 2009), 15–17. A similar publication or web page is typically reproduced at each SEA Games.

42. *Official Report*, 1.

43. "Thailand Suggests SE Asia Games Here Next December," *Bangkok Post*, May 12, 1958, 6.

44. Praphat Charusatien (OCT) to Secretary of Cabinet, "*Kan-khaengkhan kila rawang prathet khang-khiang*" [Sports Competitions Between Adjoining Countries], March 7, 1959, in Surachit Charuserani, *Pramuan ruang-rao lae khwam-pen-ma khong khaengkhan-kila laem-thong khrang-raek na krungthep phramahanakon wan-thi 12–17 thanwakhom phutta sakkarat 2502* [Compiled Story and History of the 1st South East Asia Peninsular Games in Bangkok, December 12–17, B.E. 2502 (1959)] (Bangkok: Government Lottery Office Publishing, 1959), 12–13, National Archives of Thailand (NAT) M/3/905 2754 M.1. The key word in the Thai phrase translated here as "friendship," *samphan maitri* (relations [of] friendship), is *maitri*, a Pali-Sanskrit derivation meaning "amicability, friendship, goodwill, (to be on) good terms" (see www.thai-language.com/id/144327).

45. *Official Report*, 2.

46. Ibid., 17.

47. Creak, "Eternal Friends and Erstwhile Enemies," 157.

48. "Vietnam Wants to Take Part," *Straits Times*, July 26, 1979; "Vietnam out of SEA Games," *Straits Times*, March 22, 1983.

49. Creak, "Eternal Friends and Erstwhile Enemies," 161.

50. "Malayan Team Leaves for Bangkok," *Straits Times*, December 10, 1959, 12.

51. Praphat Charusathien to U. Alexis Johnson (U.S. ambassador to Thailand), December 24, 1959, UD3267, Box 124 [Old box 20], (1959–1961), 600.3, Record Group 84, National Archives and Records Administration, College Park, MD (hereafter RG 84, NARA).

52. Donald Emmerson, "'Southeast Asia': What's in a Name?," *Journal of Southeast Asian Studies* 15, no. 1 (1984): 10.

53. Creak, "Eternal Friends and Erstwhile Enemies," 152.

54. Despatch 787, American Embassy, Bangkok to Department of State, Washington, "Thai National Athletic Program," May 13, 1958, p. 5, UD3267, Box 111 [Old box 8], 600.3, RG 84, NARA.

55. A small number of countries attended both events, including Japan.

56. Creak, *Embodied Nation*, 160–162.

57. Jo Dorai, "Pesta Sukan May Be First Asean Games," *Straits Times*, December 11, 1968, 24; "A Boost for Sports!," *Straits Times*, December 7, 1969, 10; Bernama, "Asean Games to

Replace Seap?," *Straits Times*, December 3, 1971, 26; Ernest Frida, "Asean Games Win Support," *Straits Times*, December 4, 1971, 26.

58. Anthony Milner, "Regionalism in Asia," *Far East and Australasia 2017* 48 (2016): 45. ASEAN's foundational agreement, the Bangkok Declaration of 1967, referred to the "collective will of the nations of South-East Asia to bind themselves together in friendship and cooperation." See "The Asean Declaration, 8 August 1967," Association of Southeast Asian Nations, asean.org/the-asean-declaration-bangkok-declaration-bangkok-8-august-1967/. Similarly, the more detailed Treaty of Amity and Cooperation (1976), which like many treaties foregrounded friendship in its very title, spoke of the "endeavour to develop and strengthen the traditional, cultural and historical ties of friendship, good neighbourliness and cooperation." See "The Treaty of Amity and Cooperation," Ministry of Foreign Affairs of Japan, www.mofa.go.jp/region /asia-paci/asean/treaty.html.

59. "SEAP: Almost Surely Yes," *Straits Times*, October 12, 1975, 6.

60. Percy Seneviratne, "Opening a New Chapter: Games Assume Sophistication, Status and Stature," *Straits Times*, November 18, 1977, 31.

61. "More Than You Realise," *Straits Times*, November 18, 1977, 12; "Suharto to Athletes: Don't Forget Asean Spirit in Gold Quest," *Straits Times*, August 15, 1989, 14.

62. Lee Wai Wun, "Sport Links Nations of Diverse Cultures," *Straits Times*, January 15, 1989, 27.

63. "Laos Back in Games Fold After 16 Years," *Straits Times*, August 20, 1989, 32.

64. Creak, *Embodied Nation*, 201–205.

65. Organising Committee of the Nineteenth SEA Games, *19th SEA Games 1997: Jakarta, 11–19 October 1997* [Official Report] (Jakarta, 1997), vii.

66. Ibid., 33.

67. Ibid., back cover.

68. The speech was given in the Myanmar language and subtitled in English. The quotation is taken from the subtitles displayed at the stadium.

69. Simon Creak, "National Restoration, Regional Prestige: The Southeast Asian Games in Myanmar, 2013," *Journal of Asian Studies* 73, no. 4 (2014): 853–877.

70. John MacAloon, "Olympic Games and the Theory of Spectacle in Modern Societies," in *Rite, Drama, Festival, Spectacle: Rehearsals Toward a Theory of Cultural Performance*, ed. John MacAloon (Philadelphia: Institute for the Study of Human Issues, 1984), 251.

71. Samon Samonkritsana, "Phap prathap-chai" [An Impressive Image], *Siam Nikorn*, December 15, 1959, 7.

72. Simon Creak, "Sport as Politics and History: The 25th SEA Games in Laos," *Anthropology Today* 27, no. 1 (2011): 14–19; Creak, "National Restoration," 870–872.

73. Editorial, "Sing thi dai chak kila laem-thong" [Things (We) Got from the SEAP Games], *Siam Rath*, December 16, 1959, n.p., NAT K/P7/2502 B.4 Bet-talet kila [Miscellaneous Sports].

74. "Wiatnam phoei het thai phae futboll khong ton" [Vietnamese Reveal Reason For Their Football Defeat of Thailand], *Phim Thai*, December 19, 1959, n.p., NAT K/P 7/2502 Kila tang tang [Various Sports].

75. Samana, "Phap prathap-chai ik-khrang" [An Impressive Image Again], *Siam Nikorn*, December 20, 1959, 3.

76. "Winning Friends Is Just as Important," *Straits Times*, September 1, 1977, 10.

77. "More Than You Realise," *Straits Times*, November 18, 1977, 12.

78. "Friendship First, Success Second," *Straits Times*, May 9, 1983, 39.

79. Mutually intelligible languages include Thai/Lao and Indonesian/Malay (spoken in Indonesia, Malaysia, Brunei, and to a lesser extent Timor Leste and Singapore). In addition, English is spoken widely in Singapore, the Philippines, and Malaysia. Athletes from Myanmar, Vietnam, and Cambodia are more likely to be linguistically isolated, though one would speak some Thai.

CHAPTER 2

Antidiscrimination

Racism and the Case of South Africa

Robert Skinner

A moral ideal of antiracism was one of the defining characteristics of the post-World War II world. Attempts to construct a new international political order, centered on notions of collective self-determination and individual rights, helped to dissolve the assumptions and intellectual frameworks that had underpinned the colonial and racial ideologies that held sway until the global conflict of the 1940s. The new international norms of popular sovereignty and antiracism accelerated in a rapid and dramatic process of decolonization that was largely complete by the mid-1960s. Within this context, international sport became a contested terrain in which new values of antiracism and global solidarities challenged visions of innate social hierarchy that had underpinned colonialism. The rapid expansion of sovereign nation-states transformed worldwide sporting contests into events of global significance in which antiracism featured as a prominent discursive thread.

Within this decolonizing world, the rigid system of apartheid in South Africa seemed to many observers to be the epitome of those political and social norms that had passed with the end of the era of European imperialism. Reflecting on his warning to South African politicians of the "wind of change" sweeping the African continent, British prime minister Harold Macmillan argued in 1960 that apartheid was a "grave error" that contrasted with British policy, based on the belief "that different races can and should live together in partnership."[1] Apartheid's critics argued that the policy had no place in a world shaped by ideals of equality and national self-determination, by decolonization and civil rights. Campaigns to isolate South African sport, expel the country from international bodies, and boycott its involvement in the Olympic Games and other mega-events therefore provide a compelling case study of the struggle to define the global ideal of antiracism in sport.

There is, though, no golden thread of antiracism in the history of international sport; modern competitive sport has in fact had a powerful capacity to embody, rather than challenge, biological theories of race. Sport provided a useful point of reference for late nineteenth- and early twentieth-century scientific racism. In his seminal work on eugenics, *Hereditary Genius*, Francis Galton included "Wrestlers of the North Country" in his parade of talents inherited through good breeding, while anthropologists organized a "Tribal Games" to run alongside the 1904 Olympics in St. Louis to test claims of the "natural" athletic ability of "primitive" peoples.[2] By the 1930s, the symbolic impact of the success of African American sprinter Jesse Owens and the investigations of physical anthropologist W. Montague Cobb had challenged the myth of Nordic athletic supremacy. While genetic interpretations continue to inform popular discussions of sporting prowess, the retreat from scientific racism after World War II helped to encourage the conviction that racial differences were sociologically determined and therefore that inequalities might be overcome with antiracism intervention.[3]

On one level, the ideal of antiracism might be considered an outgrowth of Pierre de Coubertin's philosophy of Olympism, the egalitarian and cosmopolitan vision that inspired his revival of the Games in 1896. But the modern Olympics is an embodiment of internationalism, of the interaction between individuals as representatives of a nation-state, and has found itself caught between a belief in the autonomy of sport and a realist acknowledgment of the influence of national politics. Nevertheless, the Olympic Charter has since 1949 included as part of its first principle explicit opposition to discrimination on the basis of race, religion, or politics.[4] Notwithstanding these expressions of high ideals, the history of antiracism in sport reaffirms the role of international sporting competition as a forum for diplomacy, a potent force in nation building, and a means of gaining access to international institutions.[5] In this context, the particular case study of South Africa cannot be disentangled from histories of decolonization and imperial retreat. While it is possible to characterize the Commonwealth as a field of sporting interaction that provides a disciplinary function on its members, mediating "the terms of admission to the modern developed world" through a "commitment to liberal democracy and market economics," those same mechanisms came to rebound on South Africa as apartheid began to be measured based on the same terms.[6] In short, sport became a political resource in a struggle to define the norms and values of a postcolonial world.

The contest over South Africa is not, then, a straightforward case study in the interactions between the moral ideals of sport and the wider question of antiracism in the late twentieth century. This contest demonstrates that an antiracist ideal in sport was fostered in parallel with and as a consequence of the politicization of sport in an era of decolonization. Much to the regret of the older generation of administrators, political struggles around apartheid and race shattered the assumption that games were a pure and autonomous form of human activity.

Sport and the Cultural Boycott

Over the first half of the twentieth century, discourses of immutable racial difference had fostered the development of a system of segregation in South Africa.[7] Even before 1948, when Afrikaner nationalists came to political power under the vaguely defined banner of "apartheid," South African sport had already taken on a racially segregated character, with white dominance particularly marked in those sports that were most deeply embedded in the culture of empire. In these sports, notably rugby and cricket, white supremacist ideas in South Africa were by no means at odds with segregationist and discriminatory practices found in the organization of sport in Britain, Australia, and New Zealand, but clear differences were already evident by the late 1930s.[8] No South African cricket teams played against India or the West Indies, and white South Africans protested when black players such as the Anglo-Indian Ranji Duleepsinghji were selected to compete against them—although opponents were often willing to comply with segregationist practices, such as New Zealand's omission of Maori players from the rugby team that toured South Africa in 1928.[9] Meanwhile rugby, a sport rooted in the invented traditions of the Victorian public school, had from the 1930s become closely associated with Afrikaner nationalism. The prominence of rugby at leading Afrikaner educational institutions such as the University of Stellenbosch, rugby's apparent symbolic affinity with nationalist ideals, and the importance of Afrikaner players within highly successful Springbok teams have all been adduced as factors in the development of rugby as a sport that played a "unique role in the calculations of the political elite" connected with the Afrikaner National Party.[10] By the second half of the twentieth century, South African sport was therefore marked by the white supremacist practices and nationalist ideals that underpinned the development of political and social segregation and apartheid.

While South African sport had developed along informal lines of segregation over the course of the century, it was not until the 1950s that the South African government sought to codify the meaning of apartheid in sport. In 1956, South African minister of the interior T. E. Dönges issued a statement that defined the contours of apartheid sport through to the early 1970s. Significantly, Dönges articulated a clear principle of total separation within sporting competitions and sports administration. His statement called for all sport to be organized along separate racial lines and for black organizations to seek international recognition only through the auspices of official white counterparts. The statement also stressed the expectation that other countries would abide by "South African custom" in the selection of teams to compete in South Africa.[11] By setting the framework for sports administration and in particular by refusing to recognize nonracial bodies, the state imposed control over sport in ways that had not previously been obtained. In a sense, just as legislation such as the Bantu Education Act (1953) established a framework for state control of a school system in order to impose apartheid, Dönges's statement played a similar role in sport. As with the broader "project," apartheid in sport revealed the underlying confidence in the power of the interventionist state as much as its fundamental racial ideology.[12]

During the 1950s, anti-apartheid campaigners included sport as one facet of their demands for a "cultural boycott" of South Africa. In part this was a response to the increased politicization of sport within South Africa, but sport also provided seemingly fertile ground for international protest. In 1957, the British anticolonial campaign group the Africa Bureau published the "Art and Sport Manifesto" condemning apartheid, while the prominent Anglican anti-apartheid activist Trevor Huddleston argued in his 1956 book *Naught for Your Comfort* that a boycott "might even make the English-speaking South African wake up to the fact that you can't play with a straight bat if you have no opponents."[13] In defining sport as a focus for international anti-apartheid protests, campaigners tended to emphasize the practical advantages rather than supposed moral ideals of sport itself. For Huddleston, the impact of isolation on white South Africans, for whom sport was a key element of collective identity, was more significant than the secular values of sport. In fact, early attempts to mobilize international sport as a vehicle for critical engagement with apartheid were ambiguous.

Huddleston's reference to playing with a "straight bat" hinted at the structures of sporting relations that determined the shape of anti-apartheid protests in the period between 1960 and 1990. Alongside South African involvement in global events such as the Olympic Games (see the following section), the politics of sport and race intersected most clearly in those Olympic sporting events most closely associated with empire and whiteness: cricket and rugby. Cricket was perhaps the exemplary "imperial game," which embodied essential English characteristics and a morality that was entangled with imperialism and white racial identity. Before World War II, renowned black cricketers, such as the Indian Kumar Shri Ranjitsinhji and the West Indian Learie Constantine, had established themselves as stars in the game but not without compromises and challenges subject to contemporary racial prejudices.[14] After World War II, cricket did have the capacity to become a focus for black solidarity and political confidence, exemplified by the appointment of Frank Worrell as the first black captain of a West Indies cricket team in 1960. But even here, moral ambiguities remained. Prior to his appointment, Worrell had sought permission to lead a representative West Indian team on a tour of South Africa with the intention of playing a series of fixtures against "nonwhite" teams. In the face of opposition from Constantine, the African National Congress, and anti-apartheid activists, the planned tour was abandoned. But some supported the tour including the Marxist intellectual C. L. R. James, whose book *Beyond a Boundary* (first published in 1963) remains one of the most compelling accounts of the social and political values and relations intertwined with sport. As James argued, the tour would have seen a "pitiless light . . . thrown on the irrationality and stupidity of apartheid."[15]

Rugby emerged as one of the first major sites of struggle against apartheid in sport. Until the late 1950s, New Zealand rugby authorities had been content to comply with South African principles of segregation, not selecting Maori players for South African tours. While the all-white All Black squad had aroused brief protests in 1949, the Springbok tour of New Zealand in 1956 had almost universal support—including from the New Zealand Communist Party. However, when the New Zealand Rugby Football Union (NZRFU) announced in 1958 that Maori players would again be barred from selection for the 1960 tour of South Africa, public opposition mounted.[16] Originating within churches (and influenced by Huddleston's Christian opposition to apartheid), protest coalesced in the Citizen's All Black Tour

Association (CABTA), which formed by mid-1959 and gathered a petition of over 160,000 signatures against New Zealand compliance with apartheid.[17] The NZRFU largely ignored the protests but claimed that the country had a "reputation for racial tolerance and equality" and that ongoing contacts with South Africa would prompt incremental change in apartheid. The 1960 New Zealand rugby tour showed that sports-focused protest had a genuinely transnational dimension, provoking political debate in those states with historic sporting relations with South Africa as much as providing an opportunity to engage with the issue of apartheid. Rugby, as Thompson argues, was (and remains) central to the international relations of New Zealand. Sporting links were therefore the primary form of exchange between the two countries, and acquiescence with apartheid suggested a very real statement of priorities that challenged New Zealanders to address their own sense of national identity.[18] At the same time, while CABTA was the first large-scale organized protest movement against apartheid in sport anywhere in the world, it was in many ways an inward-looking campaign focused on domestic issues of race within New Zealand. And while CABTA made much of the statement by E. B. Corbett, former minister of Maori affairs, that "sport without morality no longer deserves the name," the issue was one of race relations within New Zealand. As CABTA explained to the South African campaigner Dennis Brutus, the protest was "*not* one against the racial policy of the South African government, but rather against an act of racial discrimination committed by a New Zealand sports organisation."[19] Nevertheless, CABTA revealed the emergence of a politics of antiracism that would present an increasingly powerful challenge within global sport.

Building Isolation: SAN-ROC and the Olympics

The shooting of over sixty supporters of the Pan Africanist Congress in the township of Sharpeville in March 1960 animated anti-apartheid activism around the globe.[20] Global disquiet regarding apartheid reflected and was driven by the crisis that accompanied the intensification of authoritarian measures designed to suppress political opposition in South Africa, just as the process of decolonization in Africa began to accelerate. Decolonization led to the emergence of a vocal Africa Group at the United Nations (UN) that sought to persuade the international community to undertake concrete action against South Africa in the form of economic and trade sanctions.[21]

While fundamental global inequalities set limits on the ability of newly independent African states to shape international diplomacy, the Olympic Games
offered a more promising opportunity to develop international prestige.[22] As
with their counterparts in global political institutions, Third World representatives on sporting bodies sought to enact decolonization on a terrain where
European and imperial agendas had predominated. Within the Olympics,
the effect was to heighten calls for South African exclusion. Initially South
African sports officials sought to deflect responsibility, claiming that efforts
were under way to demonstrate South African alignment with Olympic ideals. This presented some difficulty, given that the first principle of the charter
(antidiscrimination) was in direct contradiction to the official policy set out
by Dönges in 1956. Because of this clear conflict, even though the possibilities
for formal political sanctions receded over the course of the decade, sport
became an increasingly central battleground against apartheid.

During the 1960s, then, the Olympics became a primary focus of anti-
apartheid campaigns led by independent African states. At an International
Olympic Committee (IOC) meeting in March 1960, IOC president Avery
Brundage noted that South Africa had made no discernible progress on the
question of discrimination, but he persuaded the IOC to grant South Africa
until October 1963 to "eliminate racism in sports."[23] While Brundage had
reportedly accepted the inevitability of a confrontation over apartheid in the
late 1950s, the IOC continued to sidestep the issue in part, it has been claimed,
because of an unwillingness to see the departure of "a member of the Olympic
family."[24] Although the 1960 Olympics had seen a glimpse of the potential
for African success when the Ethiopian runner Abebe Bikila became the first
black African gold medal winner in the marathon, Olympic sports continued
to be dominated by Europe and America.[25] As the IOC deadline drew near,
the South Africa Non-Racial Olympic Committee (SAN-ROC) was formed
as a counterpoint to the whites-only official Olympic body in the country.
Despite the imprisonment of its chair, Dennis Brutus, SAN-ROC achieved
a major success in August 1964 when the IOC announced that South Africa
would not be permitted to compete in the Tokyo Olympics.

After Brutus left South Africa for exile in Britain following his release
from prison, SAN-ROC was relaunched in 1966. From London, Brutus combined campaigns against apartheid in sport with wider anti-apartheid efforts,
including a leading role in the World Campaign for the Release of South
African Political Prisoners and the International Defence and Aid Fund, giving him access to a broad international anti-apartheid network.[26] The IOC

meanwhile gave South African officials a lifeline by agreeing to dispatch a committee of investigation to examine the development of nonracial sport in South Africa. In April 1967 before the IOC commission had traveled to South Africa, the new prime minister, B. J. Vorster, announced a number of concessions seemingly designed to address the outstanding issues with the IOC. South Africa would send a single multiracial team to the 1968 Olympics, although members would be selected through segregated boards. Vorster attempted to define the plans as a continuation of existing policy, but for the wider world they were meant to signal a significant innovation in policy.[27] Frank Braun, head of the South African Olympic Committee, was thus able to announce significant progress: one team traveling and living together and competing under one flag with one uniform.

Meanwhile, African states had begun to forge a collective approach to the question of South African participation in the 1968 Olympics. The Supreme Council for Sport in Africa (SCSA), an offshoot of the Organisation of African Unity formed in 1966, announced that its members would reconsider their decision to participate in the Games if South Africa was allowed to compete "without complying fully with the Olympic Charter"; moreover, the SCSA looked beyond the Olympics and for the first time presented the sports boycott as a tactic aimed at apartheid in its widest sense.[28] In the United States, African American civil rights activists and athletes, convinced of the need to engage sports institutions in the wider debate around racism, formed the Olympic Project for Human Rights (OPHR). They saw South Africa's participation in the Olympics as a cause around which the politics of black antiracism might coalesce.[29] When the IOC sought yet again to put off any final decision, its Congolese commission member Jean-Claude Ganga angrily insinuated that Africans were being treated "like costumed apes presented at a fair."[30] Brutus, the globe-trotting anti-apartheid activist, raised the sports boycott at the UN Seminar on Apartheid in the Zambian capital of Lusaka, where he suggested that a coordinated boycott of South Africa would "have repercussions far beyond the field of sport as well as asserting one of the basic values of human relations—fair play and justice."[31] African athletes, he noted, had already withdrawn from international events that included South African competitors.

The IOC commission published its findings in January 1968, concluding that it had discovered sufficient evidence to suggest that South Africa would be able to send a multiracial team to the Olympics. The IOC thus declared that South Africa would be allowed to compete on the basis that it had made progress to conform to the first principle of the Olympic Charter.[32] In response, fourteen African states announced their withdrawal from the 1968 Mexico City Games. In the United States, along with protests from the OPHR, the American Committee on Africa marshaled over sixty U.S. athletes in support of a boycott.[33] Critically, the Soviet Union announced its support for the boycott, fearing that if it did not, it would cede influence in the Third World to China.[34] Faced with the collapse of the Mexico Games, the IOC retreated, announcing that "in view of all the information on the international climate," it had withdrawn its invitation to South Africa.[35]

Vorster responded in typically combative style, arguing that the decision signaled a return to "the jungle," while some in the United States suggested that the ban on South Africa reflected American refusal to stand up to "prejudices of the anarchic countries of black Africa."[36] IOC members certainly reported that its discussions were swayed by "foreboding about the racial problems in the world," including rioting in American cities following the murder of Martin Luther King Jr. and predictions of racial violence in Britain by British Conservative member of Parliament Enoch Powell.[37] The Mexico City Olympics nevertheless passed without a major boycott by either African nations or black athletes connected with the OPHR. The Olympics did, of course, witness one of the most striking and provocative political gestures in modern sport when African American athletes Tommie Smith and John Carlos raised their arms in the Black Power salute as they received their Olympic medals.[38] And yet, while their gesture has become one of the most familiar symbols of black resistance to racism in sport, it was the efficacy of the boycott threat that perhaps stands out more in terms of significance. The focus on apartheid, an exceptional contemporary moral issue, demonstrated the vulnerability of global sporting events as political resources. Moreover, unlike the U.S. protest against Soviet military aggression at the 1980 Olympic Games, the 1968 boycott had the advantage of being rooted in an indisputable question of sporting ideals. But the 1968 Olympic crisis demonstrated the contingent and nascent character of the moral ideal of antiracism in sport. The threatened boycott proved that sport was a viable battleground against apartheid but did not—as the ambivalence of Brundage and the IOC commission showed—uphold a consistent and universal sporting principle.

South African officials sought to sidestep the Olympic ban by organizing the South African Games, following the example of the Games of the New Emerging Forces hosted by Indonesia in 1964 after its ban from the Tokyo Olympics.[39] The South African Games took place in 1969 as two racially separate events, with the main focus being the whites-only competition. As a government-led endeavor, the Games were given ambiguous support by other national bodies. Athletics organizations in a number of countries, notably the United States, France, and Australia, refused to send white teams, although the United States and France did agree to send national teams to participate in other sports along with West Germany, Belgium, New Zealand, and Britain. Again SAN-ROC spearheaded the campaign against the Games, calling on African states to boycott the 1970 Commonwealth Games rather than compete against teams that had participated in South Africa.[40] Ever louder calls were made for South Africa to be expelled from the Olympics, which came to a climax at the May 1970 IOC session in Amsterdam. Despite a melancholy call from Brundage for peace, the committee voted to expel the South African National Olympic Committee after a heated and intemperate speech by its representative, Frank Braun, who spoke of a "vendetta" against the country.[41]

The late 1960s had seen the Olympic Games become a site of struggle around race. Brundage, while not quite a crude racist, had sought to define the question of apartheid in nuanced terms that misunderstood the significance of the issue for African leaders. Or rather, the conflict over apartheid demonstrated the incompatibility of the moral vision of egalitarianism that underpinned Brundage's vision of nonracial sport and the radical claims of those such as SAN-ROC and the SCSA, which believed that the Olympics could not be disentangled from social and economic inequalities and discrimination. In Brundage's view, political actions along the lines of the Smith-Carlos protest were simply an anathema that "had nothing to do with sport."[42] In a way Brundage was correct, as it seems warranted to judge the threatened boycott of the Mexico Olympics as an attempt by newly independent African states to assert their own authority on an international stage. For emerging states, sport was a valuable political resource that could foster national unity, regional solidarity, and a conduit for international influence. Struggles within the Olympic movement arguably provide a cultural parallel to efforts by newly independent states to establish new centers of power at the UN General Assembly.[43] At the same time, the focus on sport was a political expedient that masked ongoing trade relationships between South Africa and the continent.[44] Nevertheless, the often crude attempts by the Vorster government to avoid sporting isolation sat somewhat at odds with its more sophisticated efforts to square "separate development" with postcolonial notions of sovereignty.[45] The expulsion of South Africa from the Olympic Games in 1970 was not so much an indication of the degree to which apartheid had departed from a moral ideal of antiracism as it was a demonstration of the ways that sporting and political antiracist norms became imbricated in a decolonizing world.

"No Normal Sport in an Abnormal Society"

On the threshold of the 1970s, South African sport was in a critical position.[46] While officials struggled to maintain links in the face of an emerging nonracial consensus, international anti-apartheid campaigners increasingly viewed sport as an effective political terrain. Protest thus entered a new phase in the 1970s, when sport became a means to address the system of apartheid as a whole. Prior to the Olympic ban, cricket and rugby had returned to the center of anti-apartheid campaigns in Britain, both within the formal structures of sporting administration and as an opportunity to channel new forms of direct action. In 1968, public interest became focused on the Cape Coloured cricketer Basil D'Oliveira when he was drafted into the England squad for the scheduled tour of South Africa.[47] Vorster refused to accept what he dismissively described as "the team of the Anti-Apartheid Movement," and the tour was cancelled. While sport had again become an issue of high-level diplomacy, the affair was in many ways an "elaborate charade," motivated by the desire to maintain cordial political relations with South Africa as much as historic sporting connections between the two countries.[48]

A new campaign group, the Stop the Seventy Tour Committee (STST), was formed in Britain in 1969, led by the Young Liberal (and future labor minister) Peter Hain with the aim of forcing the cancellation of the forthcoming South African cricket tour of England. At its heart, the STST campaign was grounded on the principle that maintaining sporting contact with South Africa was itself a statement of approval of apartheid. In late 1969, STST campaigners tested direct-action tactics against the Springbok rugby tour of Britain, ensuring that protestors beleaguered the South African team wherever they traveled. The Irish Anti-Apartheid Movement declared that sport could not be disentangled from the wider implications of apartheid: "matches against all-white teams," they insisted, were "regarded, by both black and white, as an agreement with segregation."[49] As the New Statesman put it, South African rugby players had taken on the role of a "roving embassy for apartheid."[50] Decried by establishment critics as "left-wing, workshy, refugee long hairs," the protestors met with an uncompromising response on the part of police, organizers, and supporters of the tour. Rather than deter anti-apartheid campaigners, the confrontations intensified, and by the end of the tour several thousand protestors were in attendance at every Springbok fixture.[51]

As campaigners hoped, the chaotic scenes during the rugby tour had begun to focus attention on the upcoming cricket tour. Prime Minister Harold Wilson, concerned that the tour—and attendant protests—would coincide with a general election campaign, decided that the UK government would not intervene directly but nevertheless would provide "tacit support" for its cancellation. However, by April 1970 Wilson felt obliged to challenge the sport's governing body, the International Cricket Conference, to reconsider its support for the tour, citing the threats to both sporting relations with Commonwealth countries and increased social tensions within Britain.[52] When the issue was debated in Parliament on May 14, opposition to the tour was stated in more obvious terms: Labour member of Parliament and former Olympic athlete Philip Noel-Baker argued that apartheid in South Africa was at odds with "the basic foundation of world co-operation in international sport."[53] While the tour organizers claimed significant public support for the tour, opinion polls suggested that it was of minimal importance for voters during the election campaign. After months of political wrangling, the tour of England was called off in May, and a series of matches against a "World" eleven was organized in its stead. Alongside this and the Olympic ban, 1970 also saw South Africa's suspension from the Davis Cup tennis tournament after the government refused to permit the African American player Arthur Ashe to compete in South Africa. As a consequence, some within South African sport began to talk openly of the need for reform. The South African cricket authorities announced that the national team would in future be selected "on merit," a move that prompted English commentator John Arlott to note that the Stop the Seventy Tour campaign had "in a few months achieved more than the cricket officials have done by fifteen years of polite acquiescence."[54]

Campaigns spread around the Commonwealth in the wake of the success of the STST. In 1971, Australia experienced protests on par with those in the United Kingdom in 1969–1970, which resulted in the cancellation of a proposed South African cricket tour. In the following year, protests in New Zealand intensified as the Labour government led by Norman Kirk turned back on its original pledge of noninterference and called for the postponement of the 1973 Springbok tour of the country.[55] Back in the United Kingdom, Brutus and Hain joined together in the Stop the Apartheid Rugby Tour to protest against the proposed 1974 British Lions tour of South Africa. Although it went ahead, the heavy defeat of the Springboks was viewed in South Africa as a consequence—at least in part—of its selection policy. In Britain, Labour's return to power under Wilson in 1974 was accompanied by a reiteration of the party's opposition to sporting contacts, while in New Zealand the election victory of Robert Muldoon reversed that country's policy yet again, with the government backing the All-Blacks tour of South Africa, which began a matter of weeks after the Soweto Uprising. The continuation of the tour amid mass protest and the brutal government response to the uprising led to widespread condemnation of New Zealand and contributed to the decision by African teams to boycott the 1976 Montreal Olympics.

The 1976 boycott, which focused on a sport that was not part of the Olympics and concerned contacts with a country that had already been expelled from the Olympic Games, failed to gather the degree of support that the Mexico City boycott threat had mobilized eight years before.[56] The Montreal boycott did, however, sharpen the focus of international debate around sporting links with South Africa and, in particular, became increasingly important in Commonwealth diplomacy. As a response, British sports minister Denis Howell initiated discussion of a Commonwealth-level agreement on sport and apartheid, which was brokered by Commonwealth secretary-general Sonny Ramphal at the Gleneagles Hotel in Scotland in July 1977.[57] The Gleneagles Agreement, approved by all members of the Commonwealth, called on governments "to combat the evil of apartheid by withholding any form of support for, and by taking every practical step to discourage contact or competition by their nationals with sporting organisations, teams or sportsmen from South Africa."[58]

By the late 1970s, South African sport had been formally isolated by the Commonwealth as well as a number of international sports bodies. This was in part a consequence of the gathering momentum of campaigns that had originated in the late 1960s that reinvigorated and reframed public engagement with the issue of apartheid in the Commonwealth in particular. By 1980 when the UN Center Against Apartheid started to issue regular reports on individuals who had competed in South Africa, sport had become a routine site for anti-apartheid activism.[59] However, while anti-apartheid had become a recognized feature of international diplomacy by the late 1970s and a kind of consensus had begun to emerge around the cultural boycott, the intensity of opposition to South African sport during the final decade of apartheid would be contingent upon local and historical contexts.

"Constructive Engagement" and "Reform"
in the Context of Sport

During the 1970s, the international isolation of South African sport prompted a series of "reforms" that, in many ways, presaged wider political developments in the following decade. Over the course of the 1980s, however, developments in sport also reflected the contours of international diplomacy, as both the British and U.S. governments took a more accommodating stance toward Pretoria and a new generation of political leaders advocated "constructive engagement" rather than isolation.

In April 1971, Vorster had announced a series of reforms in sports policy defined as "multinationalism," a term that sat squarely within the discourse of high apartheid, centered as it was around a fantasy of "independent" black homelands that were the embodiment of separate development. Vorster's policy allowed black and white South African athletes to compete as individuals at "open international events" and foreign multiracial teams to compete in South Africa against separate black and white teams, as was the case with the British Lions in 1972 and the New Zealand rugby tour of 1976. However, no changes to domestic competition or the internal organization of sport were introduced. In seeking to navigate a path between the norms of international sport and the deeply rooted opposition to any form of racial integration from hard-line nationalists, adjustments to the multinational policy continued throughout the 1970s. In response to the resurgence of protest in South Africa in the mid-1970s, segregation within domestic sport was relaxed as part of wider reformist efforts aimed at the co-option of black communities by the apartheid state. Multinationalism, it has been argued, was the "apogee of apartheid sport"; its quiet retreat into "multiracial sport" in the 1980s signaled an ideological transformation of official sports policy.[60]

For nonracial sport federations, attention shifted from government policy around sports to debates focused on the fundamental principles of apartheid itself. Formed in 1973, the South African Council on Sport (SACOS) crystallized a fundamental division between opponents of apartheid in sports. After an initial period of "strategic unity," SACOS became a focus of contested debate between those firmly committed to a noncollaborationist position and those more open to working alongside "reformist" elements within official sports bodies.[61] For SACOS, noncollaboration became a core principle. It emerged as a response to a particular crisis in domestic sport at a conference organized by Norman Middleton, president of the South African Soccer

Federation, who was frustrated by the decision taken by the Johannesburg City Council to ban the use of municipal football grounds by black teams. SACOS thus started life as the forefront of a boycott campaign against the segregation of sport facilities within South Africa. Under the leadership of Hassan Howa (a key figure in the multiracial South African Cricket Board of Control), SACOS became the center of opposition to "multinationalism," which it regarded as merely a superficial change in policy that left the fundamental structures of racial inequality intact. During the course of the 1970s, SACOS moved increasingly toward the belief that discrimination in sport was based on structural inequality; as Howa put it, apartheid needed to be addressed "from a completely humanitarian angle" rather than a question of sport. In turn, SACOS worked to convince international bodies that sport could only be fully integrated after apartheid had been eradicated. This was therefore the principle that overrode the "cardinal apolitical tenet" of international sport.[62]

By 1984, the contested debates around reform in South Africa were thrown into stark contrast by the sudden resurgence of violent protest and popular resistance. Beginning in the industrial heartland of the Vaal Triangle in mid-1984, a brutal cycle of resistance and repression provided the background for both South Africa's domestic politics and its international relations for the remainder of the decade. At the same time, under Margaret Thatcher in Britain and Ronald Reagan in the United States, South Africa's major trading partners had turned to policies of "constructive engagement" with the P. W. Botha administration in Pretoria. Under Thatcher, the British government became a firm advocate of maintaining links with South Africa, ostensibly in the hope that these would encourage reformers within the apartheid state. As such, indications of a move toward "multiracialism" in South African sport led British sports administrators to consider renewed contacts with South Africa. In fact, some sports officials began to consider moves that even the Thatcher government felt were inopportune. In 1983, a cricket tour proposed by the Marylebone Cricket Club was called off only after personal intervention by the prime minister.[63]

During the early 1980s, the British government thus sent out mixed messages with regard to the international politics of sport. While wary of sanctions in principle, the Thatcher government had urged British athletes to boycott the Moscow Olympics in protest against the Soviet invasion of Afghanistan. The sense that sport was by nature apolitical prevailed among sports officials; however, participation was seen as ultimately a matter of individual conscience. Unofficial "rebel" tours of South Africa continued, while a number of individual cricketers maintained personal contacts with South African cricket. In 1984, the South African athlete Zola Budd found her application for UK citizenship rapidly processed so as to facilitate her participation in the Los Angeles Olympics. Tacit support for South African sport seemed in line with political contacts, notably the state visit by Botha in 1984, and sport emerged as a locus of conflict between anti-apartheid and "anti-anti-apartheid" tendencies.[64] The general sense of British willingness to engage with Pretoria, combined with the ongoing rebel cricket tours and official rugby tours, left the United Kingdom open to censure under the terms of the Gleneagles Agreement and resulted in the boycott of the 1986 Edinburgh Commonwealth Games by over thirty states. In the months preceding the Games, the high-level Commonwealth Eminent Persons Group had visited South Africa and sketched out a basic framework for negotiations between the apartheid state and opposition movements. The Edinburgh Games took on the appearance of a colonial-era "Commonwealth club meeting," which stood in stark contrast to the special Commonwealth summit that concluded, just days after the closing ceremony of the Games, with an agreement for a package of trade and economic sanctions against South Africa.[65]

By the end of the 1980s, South African sports officials, like many business and political leaders, had come to see the need for engagement (at least covertly) between established institutions and those connected with the liberation movement. For movements such as SACOS, these developments presented a political challenge as much as they represented an opportunity. The campaign against racist sport in South Africa was shaped by the politics of the wider struggle against apartheid and must be understood within that context.

In the second half of the 1980s as the confrontation between the state and resistance movements intensified and as violence in South African townships became a matter of everyday life, SACOS moved toward a more integrationist position, arguing that its aim should be to "win over" individuals within government institutions rather than boycott them. By the late 1980s, SACOS members began to openly consider negotiations with official sports bodies.[66] At the same time, just as South African business leaders were beginning to reach out to the leadership of the African National Congress (ANC), sports officials were also seeking to build contacts with exiled liberation movements. In 1988, veteran rugby administrator Danie Cravan entered into negotiations with the ANC over the feasibility of an international rugby tour.

In 1989 a new body, the National Sports Council (NSC), effectively took leadership of nonracial sport from SACOS, working alongside the Mass Democratic Movement to coordinate protest campaigns including those that effectively dogged the 1989–1990 rebel cricket tour led by the former England captain Mike Gatting. The tour, which took place amid the political upheaval fermented by the unbanning of the ANC and the release of Nelson Mandela, ended with the early departure of the mercenaries and the cancellation of a planned second tour. As political negotiations got under way, the NSC came to the forefront of the redevelopment of South African sport. SACOS withdrew from negotiations between established and nonracial sporting bodies, suggesting that any changes would merely be superficial. While Booth has suggested that the NSC leaders were "opportunistic" and inexpert negotiators in contrast to their counterparts in SACOS, the latter were hamstrung by an ideological purity that undermined their ability to work closely with apartheid-era officials. At the same time, the ANC appeared little interested in sport beyond its potential as a way of reassuring white South Africans. Thus, by 1992 most international sports bodies had lifted boycotts, and many had recommenced contacts with South Africa, claiming that "sport had triumphed over racism."[67]

The embrace between President Nelson Mandela and the Springbok captain Francois Pienaar at the 1995 rugby world cup became a cliché of the New South Africa—an image that supposedly demonstrated the power of sport to overcome social division and of South Africa's successful journey from renegade racist state to a fully democratic nation underpinned by values of equality and human rights. In their study of rugby and South African national identities, David Black and John Nauright have shown that sport acts as a force for conservatism and the maintenance of established social divisions as well as a potential driver of social change. South Africa has become, they argue, "firmly enmeshed in the global sports system," subject to the structures of a political economy of sport that both protects the status of sports closely associated with the apartheid era, even as pressure for their reorganization in line with the ideals of a "new" South Africa is maintained.[68] The 1995 Rugby World Cup was a highly significant moment in the construction of a new national identity, but its contradictions were clear: the Springbok jersey worn by Nelson Mandela was intended as a symbol of reconciliation in a new South Africa, but its survival as a marker of sporting success also signaled a political willingness to compromise on the pace of reconstruction.

Sport provided a potent political metaphor for both the apartheid state and global anti-apartheid movements. The progress of the national team—particularly in the imperial games of cricket and rugby—was taken as a potent measure of national character, while the dominance of white athletes might be adduced in support of the fundamental principles of cultural difference that provided the ideological scaffolding of apartheid. Conversely, the apparent contradiction between apartheid and the global norms of equality and universal opportunity that were claimed as the basis of international sport provided anti-apartheid campaigners with a powerful moral argument in support of their attempts to isolate South Africa. Moreover, the obvious inequalities in provision of sports facilities for black and white South Africans provided a stark illustration of the deficiencies of "separate development." But the political conflicts around sport and apartheid were never a straightforward battle for definition of a global ideal.

Anti-apartheid campaigners identified sport as one element of a cultural boycott that had tactical as much as moral value. The focus on sporting contacts sharpened a sense of global complicity in apartheid that gave campaigners in Britain, the United States, and elsewhere a vital impetus when it came to persuading members of the public to act. The boycott and direct action against South African teams were potent elements of the repertoire of the global anti-apartheid movement insofar as they produced transnational spaces of action. The public demonstrations against South African teams in Britain in 1969 and in New Zealand in 1981 provided high-profile opportunities for campaigners to interact with and influence the political system and, by extension, to apply pressure on the apartheid regime itself. The sometimes elaborate games of protest, concession, and reform that surrounded apartheid sport in the 1960s and 1970s were testimony to sport's value as a location of transnational protest. At the same time, of course, the debate around apartheid provided a political opportunity for states to establish, maintain, or extend their international influence, with the role of African states in the movement for South African expulsion from the Olympics being perhaps the most obvious example.

The question of apartheid in sport was firmly set within the framework of the international campaign to isolate South Africa and even then was as much a reflection of local contingencies as it was an embodiment of a global ideal. Indeed, there might be some merit in claiming that there has never been a moral ideal of antiracism in sport as such. Rather, international sport has provided both a resource and a location for struggles over the definition of an antiracist norm in global politics. As the case of South Africa demonstrates, the inflection of antiracism in sport was not a function of inherent moral ideals but rather the gradual adoption of norms that emerged in political and social discourse in the process of decolonization.

Notes

1. "Macmillan: Apartheid a Grave Error," *The Observer*, March 20, 1960.

2. Francis Galton, *Hereditary Genius: An Inquiry into Its Laws and Consequences* (London: Watts, 1892); Mark Dyreson, "American Ideas About Race and Olympic Races from the 1890s to the 1950s: Shattering Myths or Reinforcing Scientific Racism?," *Journal of Sport History* 28, no. 2 (2001): 173–215.

3. Elazar Barkan, *The Retreat of Scientific Racism* (Cambridge: Cambridge University Press, 1993).

4. *Olympic Charter*, 1962 (Lausanne: Comité International Olympique, 1962).

5. Barrie Houlihan, *Sport and International Politics* (London: Harvester Wheatsheaf, 1994), 9–25.

6. Ibid., 146.

7. Douglas Booth, *The Race Game: Sport and Politics in South Africa* (London: Frank Cass, 1998), 12–20.

8. John Nauright, *Sport, Culture, and Identities in South Africa* (London: Leicester University Press, 1997), 24–45.

9. Booth, *The Race Game*, 23.

10. David Black and John Nauright, *Rugby and the South African Nation: Sport, Cultures, Politics, and Power in the Old and New South Africas* (Manchester, UK: Manchester University Press, 1998), 60. See also Albert Grundlingh, "Playing for Power: Rugby, Afrikaner Nationalism and Masculinity in South Africa," in *Making Men: Rugby and Masculine Identity*, ed. John Nauright and Timothy John Lindsay Chandler, 181–204 (London: Frank Cass, 1996); Robert Archer and Antoine Bouillon, *The South African Game: Sport and Racism* (London: Zed, 1982), 56–78.

11. Archer and Bouillon, *The South African Game*, 46.

12. Deborah Posel, "The Apartheid Project, 1948–1970," in *The Cambridge History of South Africa*, ed. Robert Ross, Anne Kelk Mager, and Bill Nasson, 319–368 (Cambridge: Cambridge University Press, 2011).

13. Trevor Huddleston, *Naught for Your Comfort* (London: Collins, 1956), 202.

14. Jack Williams, *Cricket and Race* (Oxford, UK: Berg, 2001).

15. C. L. R. James, *Beyond a Boundary* (London: Yellow Jersey, 2005), 314.

16. Trevor Lawson Richards, *Dancing on Our Bones: New Zealand, South Africa, Rugby and Racism* (Wellington, New Zealand: Bridget Williams Books, 1999).

17. Black and Nauright, *Rugby and the South African Nation*, 82.

18. Richard Thompson, "New Zealand: The Issue of Apartheid and Sport," *Africa Today* 17, no. 6 (1970): 12–13; Richards, *Dancing on Our Bones*.

19. Richards, *Dancing on Our Bones*, 19, 27.

20. Tom Lodge, *Sharpeville: An Apartheid Massacre and Its Consequences* (Oxford: Oxford University Press, 2011). See also Christabel Gurney, "'A Great Cause': The Origins of the Anti-Apartheid Movement, June 1959–March 1960," *Journal of Southern African Studies* 26, no. 1 (2000): 123–144; Rob Skinner, *The Foundations of Anti-Apartheid: Liberal Humanitarianism and*

Transnational Activism in Britain and the United States, c. 1919–64 (Basingstoke, UK: Palgrave Macmillan, 2010).

21. Ryan M. Irwin, *Gordian Knot: Apartheid and the Unmaking of the Liberal World Order* (Oxford: Oxford University Press, 2012).

22. David B. Kanin, *A Political History of the Olympic Games* (Boulder, CO: Westview, 1981).

23. Richard Lapchick, *The Politics of Race and International Sport: The Case of South Africa*, (Westport, CT: Greenwood, 1975).

24. Houlihan, *Sport and International Politics*, 117; Allen Guttmann, *The Games Must Go On: Avery Brundage and the Olympic Movement* (New York: Columbia University Press, 1984), 233.

25. Barbara Keys, "The 1960 Rome Summer Olympics: Birth of a New World?," in *Myths and Milestones in the History of Sport*, ed. Stephen Wagg (London: Palgrave Macmillan, 2011), 295.

26. Denis Herbstein, *White Lies: Canon John Collins and the Secret War Against Apartheid* (Oxford, UK: James Currey, 2004).

27. Booth, *The Race Game*, 96.

28. Lapchick, *The Politics of Race and International Sport*, 92; Booth, *The Race Game*, 97.

29. Amy Bass, *Not the Triumph But the Struggle: The 1968 Olympics and the Making of the Black Athlete* (Minneapolis: University of Minnesota Press, 2002), 140.

30. Quoted in Booth, *The Race Game*, 97.

31. Dennis Brutus, "Lines for Action Against Apartheid," paper presented at the United Nations International Seminar on Apartheid, Kitwe, Zambia, 1967.

32. Lapchick, *The Politics of Race and International Sport*, 110.

33. Bass, *Not the Triumph But the Struggle*, 162.

34. Houlihan, *Sport and International Politics*.

35. Lapchick, *The Politics of Race and International Sport*, 119.

36. Quoted in Bass, *Not the Triumph But the Struggle*, 179.

37. Neil Allen, "Board Surprised at Own Decision," *Times* (London), April 23, 1968.

38. Gary Osmond, "Photographs, Materiality and Sport History: Peter Norman and the 1968 Mexico City Black Power Salute," *Journal of Sport History* 37, no. 1 (2010): 119–137.

39. Houlihan, *Sport and International Politics*, 13.

40. Lapchick, *The Politics of Race and International Sport*, 193.

41. Guttmann, *The Games Must Go On*, 247.

42. Ibid., 245.

43. Ryan M. Irwin, *Gordian Knot: Apartheid and the Unmaking of the Liberal World Order* (Oxford: Oxford University Press, 2012).

44. Houlihan, *Sport and International Politics*, 116.

45. Jamie Miller, *An African Volk: The Apartheid Regime and Its Search for Survival* (Oxford: Oxford University Press, 2016).

46. The slogan was originally used by the South African Council of Sport from the mid-1970s and signaled its hard-line stance in contrast to reformist groups (discussed in the following section).

47. Booth, *The Race Game*, 94–95; Bruce K. Murray, "Politics and Cricket: The D'Oliveira Affair of 1968," *Journal of Southern African Studies* 27, no. 4 (2001): 667–684.

48. Murray, "Politics and Cricket," 683–684; Kevin Jefferys, *Sport and Politics in Modern Britain: The Road to 2012* (Basingstoke, UK: Palgrave Macmillan, 2012), 109.

49. Lapchick, *The Politics of Race and International Sport*, 158.

50. "Apartheid Is Not a Game," *New Statesman*, November 7, 1969, 641–642.

51. Jefferys, *Sport and Politics in Modern Britain.*

52. Lapchick, *The Politics of Race and International Sport*, 174–179.

53. *Hansard*, House of Commons Debates, May 14, 1970, vol. 801, col. 1462.

54. Lapchick, *The Politics of Race and International Sport*, 163.

55. Black and Nauright, *Rugby and the South African Nation*, 84–85.

56. Houlihan, *Sport and International Politics*, 118.

57. Ibid., 140–141; Jefferys, *Sport and Politics in Modern Britain*, 167–268.

58. "The Gleneagles Agreement on Sporting Contacts with South Africa, 1977," The Commonwealth, thecommonwealth.org/sites/default/files/inline/GleneaglesAgreement.pdf.

59. Houlihan, *Sport and International Politics*, 88.

60. Booth, *The Race Game*, 99–109.

61. Ibid., 115–118.

62. Douglas Booth, "The South African Council on Sport and the Political Antinomies of the Sports Boycott," *Journal of Southern African Studies* 23, no. 1 (1997): 56–57.

63. Jefferys, *Sport and Politics in Modern Britain*, 190.

64. Saul Dubow, "New Approaches to High Apartheid and Anti-Apartheid," *South African Historical Journal* 69, no. 2 (April 3, 2017): 304–329.

65. Houlihan, *Sport and International Politics*, 141; Stuart Mole, "Negotiating with Apartheid: The Mission of the Commonwealth Eminent Persons Group 1986," *Round Table* 101, no. 3 (June 1, 2012): 253–260.

66. Booth, "South African Council on Sport," 62.

67. Ibid., 64.

68. Black and Nauright, *Rugby and the South African Nation*, 152–156.

CHAPTER 3

Democracy and Democratization

The Ambiguous Legacy

Joon Seok Hong

Democracy is messy. By design, democracy thrives on division of power, disaggregation of interests, and decentralization of authority. In practice, democracies are not silent; they are noisy and often chaotic. Democratization, or the transition to democracy, can be even more tumultuous as social and political forces rise, decline, splinter, and compete.[1] Whether it is the separation of powers among different branches of government, the system of checks and balances, federalism, judicial review, the rise of civil society, or the assertion of individual rights against state action, democracy in its varied manifestations is inherently driven by a logic of division.

The divisive dynamics of democracy have recently posed challenges to the International Olympic Committee (IOC), as it has encountered increasing hesitancy and failures by countries commonly identified as democracies to host the Olympic Games. For example, in October 2014 Oslo (Norway) withdrew its bid to host the 2022 Winter Games, leaving only Beijing (China) and Almaty (Kazakhstan), both dictatorships, with the former eventually getting the nod.[2] In August 2015, the U.S. Olympic Committee withdrew Boston as its proposed bid city for the 2024 Summer Games after the city failed to get a majority of its residents to support the bid in the face of economic concerns.[3] Later in November 2015, another city looking to host the 2024 Summer Games, Hamburg, withdrew its bid after 51.6 percent of the city's residents voted against it in a popular referendum—just as residents of another German city, Munich, had voted to reject that city's bid for the 2022 Winter Olympics two years earlier.[4] The situation seemed so dire that the IOC took the extra ordinary step in September 2017 of simultaneously announcing that two cities, both from stable democracies, would host successive Summer Games: Paris in 2024 and Los Angeles in 2028. This double selection was unprecedented, departing from the long-established practice of the IOC selecting one city in separate bid processes for each Olympic Games every four years.[5]

The IOC's growing "democracy problem" runs counter to the common perception that the Olympic Games and democracy share conceptual roots and reinforce each other in practice. Victor Cha writes that "based on fair competition, rules, best efforts, and rewards based on merit and performance, sport and sporting competition inherently privilege values that are classically liberal in nature."[6] Many observers have raised concerns about the reluctance of cities from established democracies to host the Olympic Games due to cost concerns and a lack of sustained popular interest as well as about the implications of the related trend of nondemocracies stepping in to fill the void and possibly using the Olympic Games for self-legitimacy at the expense of individual rights or political reform.[7] For example, as Dmitry Dubrovskiy explains in this volume, during the lead-up to the 2014 Winter Games in Sochi, which beat out Pyeongchang (South Korea) and Salzburg (Austria), the Russian government passed an anti-LGBT federal law that caused great controversy, though the uproar did not ultimately jeopardize Sochi's hosting of the Games.[8]

The democracy problem also calls into question the relationship between sport and political change. The 1988 Summer Olympics in Seoul, South Korea, is often lauded as the classic case of how sport in general (and the Olympics in particular) can promote political change and democratization in a host country. Many observers have noted that the 1988 Games contributed to South Korea's transition to democracy, opening up the country to the world's attention. This traditional narrative claims that as images of government crackdown on student protestors were broadcast worldwide, the ruling regime grew increasingly sensitive to foreign pressure from not only the IOC, which was monitoring the local developments closely, but also allies, such as the United States, that were concerned about the implications of continuing political instability.[9] When a nondemocracy hosts the Olympics, parallels are often drawn to the South Korean experience and the promise of democratization. For example, shortly after Beijing won the right (in July 2001) to host the 2008 Summer Olympics, Chalmers Johnson predicted (and hoped) that the Games "might even promote a democratization of China comparable to that which occurred in Korea in 1987" and claimed that the Seoul Olympics "proved [the dictatorship's] undoing," as "the protestors knew that the government dared not use the armed forces [against them] because that would have caused the cancellation of the Olympics."[10]

While increasing attention from abroad may have played a role in South Korean politics in the lead-up to the 1988 Seoul Olympics, this chapter argues that the dominant narrative regarding the transformative powers of the Olympics to bring about democratization overstates the independent effect of the Games to bring about political reform. A closer look at the 1988 Games reveals that the empirical bases for claims are much more complicated. Contrary to the standard view, the 1988 Seoul Olympics (and the more than seven years of preparation involved) amplified multiple unifying forces at work during that period in the international system as well as domestically within South Korea which brought the country together rather than widening the fissures in the South Korean political structure, thereby further encouraging democratization and buttressing the powerful underlying currents of political reform in the country. Foreign media attention may have only tuned into what was happening in South Korea during the period as the Games drew near, but the political changes that the country was witnessing were already decades in the making, with notable moves for political liberalization in April 1960 against President Syngman Rhee and in May 1980 in Gwangju against President Chun Doo-hwan.[11] In short, South Korea democratized not because of the Olympics but in spite of them.

This chapter is organized into three sections. The first explores the connection between the Olympic Games and democracy, critically examining the long-standing position of the IOC to keep politics out of the Games and the implications of such a policy on the constitutive power of Olympics to create political reform. The second section examines the domestic and international unifying forces that constituted the backdrop to the 1988 Seoul Olympics and their implications for the question of whether the Games played a central role in bringing about democratization in South Korea. The final section reflects on the experience of the 1988 Seoul Olympics and its implications, especially in light of South Korea's hosting of its second Olympics in 2018 in Pyeongchang. What emerges is a very ambiguous legacy for the impact of the Olympics on democratization. More generally, despite the inclusion of democratic practices in the pantheon of sport idealisms, for most of the twentieth century democracy promotion has not been considered a goal of international sport.

The Olympics and Democracy

The IOC has not been very influential in promoting democracy, because it has historically chosen not to assume such a role. The word "democracy" is never mentioned in the hundred-odd pages of the Olympic Charter, the governing document of the IOC that codifies its fundamental principles.[12] The document does speak to certain liberal ideals of individual freedom and equality often associated with democracies, calling for the "preservation of human dignity," declaring the practice of sport as a "human right," and prohibiting discrimination "of any kind."[13] Critics have pointed out that the IOC has failed to implement these principles in its governance of the Games, with Human Rights Watch advocating in 2009, in the wake of the 2008 Beijing Olympics, for the establishment of a permanent mechanism to integrate human rights in the Olympic process, including benchmarks on media freedom, labor rights, freedom of expression, and civil liberties.[14]

In early 2017 as part of its Olympic Agenda 2020, the IOC announced that candidate cities would have to commit to certain human rights provisions in the standard host city contracts between the city and the IOC. Specifically, the host city contract would "prohibit any form of discrimination with regard to a country or a person on grounds of race, colour, sex, sexual orientation, language, religion, political or other opinion, national or social origin, property, birth or other status." The host city must also "protect and respect human rights and ensure any violation of human rights is remedied in a manner consistent with international agreements, laws and regulations applicable in the Host Country and in a manner consistent with all internationally recognised human rights standards and principles."[15]

But there is no explicit reference in the Olympic Charter to democracy as the preferred (or even aspirational) governing political ideology or set of political institutions in a bid or host country. The Olympic Charter's silence on democracy may surprise those who subscribe to the normative notion that the Olympic Games are a force for good in the international arena and are specifically an agent of change that works to further the cause of political reform and democratization. For others, its silence on democracy does not come as a surprise, given the IOC's explicit and repeated calls for the autonomy of sport from politics. As Rule 50.1 of the Olympic Charter states, "no kind of demonstration or political, religious or racial propaganda is permitted in any Olympic sites, venues or other areas."[16] The promotion of democracy has never been an explicit policy goal of the IOC, which has repeatedly tried to limit itself to matters directly connected to sport.

Democracy, or any other specified political ideology or system, has never been an articulated IOC criterion for evaluating candidate cities. Instead, a general notion of "public support" for a particular candidate city's bid is taken into account by the IOC when evaluating bids, which typically involves an independent public survey, commissioned by the IOC, of residents from candidate cities and their views on their city's proposed bid to host the Olympics. The IOC also takes into account the level of government support, whether national or local, for a particular candidate city's bid, but there is no assessment on the type of political system involved.

Practically speaking, the focus on public support is indeed important to the IOC, as it is in the interests of the organization to have a successful event in which the local residents are enthusiastic about and likely to participate (and even volunteer to assist) in the Games. However, from the perspective of democratization and as the recent examples mentioned above illustrate, this criterion can be problematic for established democracies that are more likely to be open to a wide range of views from different constituencies regarding the desirability of hosting the Olympics. And in the context of astronomical costs of hosting the Games and concerns about their legacies and post-Games consequences, greater political openness and greater potential opposition will infuse the hosting process with greater uncertainty for democracies.[17]

In its 2015 questionnaire to candidate cities for the 2024 Summer Olympics, the IOC indicated that it was concerned about the potential impact of public referendums on the host selection process, explicitly asking the following questions: "Is there a requirement or intention to carry out a referendum in relation to the staging of the Games in your country/city? Could you be obliged to carry out a referendum by opponents to the Olympic Games project? Is such a referendum already planned and if so provide details?"[18] As Ryan Gauthier notes, countries with a weaker rule of law are less likely to be subject to requirements for a public referendum and have more "streamlined decision-making, which is favourable to international sporting organisations as it requires less need to compromise with opposing forces, and less likely chance of delay in preparing the event."[19]

Similarly, Fédération Internationale de Football Association (FIFA) secretary-general Jerome Valcke publicly admitted in 2013 that "less democracy is sometimes better for organising a World Cup."[20] Valcke was speaking about the preparations for Brazil's 2014 men's World Cup, and he commented that the "main fight we have [is] when we enter a country where the political structure is divided, as it is in Brazil, into three levels—the federal level, the state level and the city level. . . . [There are] different people, different movements, different interests and it's quite difficult to organise a World Cup in such conditions."[21] He contrasted the situation to Russia, which was expected to host the 2018 World Cup, stating that "when you have a very strong head of state who can decide, as maybe Putin can do in 2018[,] . . . that is easier for us organisers."[22]

If there is any "political" criterion that is central to the IOC's selection of host cities, it is political order, not democracy. The Olympic Charter's political agnosticism (and silence on democracy) is similar to the argument of Samuel Huntington, who famously noted that the "most important political distinction among countries concerns not their form of government but their degree of government."[23] Democracy, or any other type of political system, is not inherently synonymous with capacity to govern, because at any one time or place we may find a paralyzed democracy or a dysfunctional autocracy, but the process of undergoing political change is inherently more unstable and fraught with uncertainty. As one study notes, the success of nondemocracies in hosting major sporting events "can, in part, be put down to the absence of democratic processes and the presence of alternative social contracts between rulers (or leaders) and their populations, whereby resources and legitimation are far less of a problem than for nations of the west. . . . It appears that, the strengths of democracy and the associated need for accountability on behalf of political leaders can, in effect, work against those nations competing for the mega-event prize against others."[24] From the IOC's perspective, it is crucial that the host city, the organizing committee, and the national government manage the process in a stable and predictable manner during the seven or more years of preparing to host the Games. As the IOC monitored the developments in South Korea on the eve of the 1988 Seoul Olympics, IOC president Juan Antonio Samaranch is quoted as having said that "If there is no stability, there will be no Games."[25] The messiness that often accompanies democratic process, a virtue at the altar of freedom, can be a major red flag on the steps of the Olympic podium.

The Unifying Forces of the 1988 Seoul Olympics

During the summer of 1987, South Korea experienced its own tumults of democratization as thousands of demonstrators took to the streets to demand political liberalization after decades of authoritarian rule, especially in the wake of President Chun's proclamation in April 1987 to suspend discussions regarding constitutional amendment and other political reforms.[26] As in other countries that have undergone rapid economic development and industrialization, growing political and social cleavages were crucial to South Korea's path to democracy, especially the rise of the country's burgeoning middle class, which increasingly asserted itself against government repression and demanded greater political reforms and protection of individual rights.[27]

South Korea's period of political transition coincided with Seoul's preparations for the 1988 Summer Olympics, which the city was selected to host in 1981. The 1988 Seoul Olympics represented a coming-out party of sorts for the country (as the Tokyo Olympics did for Japan in 1964), as South Korea sought to showcase to the world its rapid economic development and industrialization. It was a project that mobilized the entire populace, transformed the basic infrastructure of the country, and permeated discourse about national pride and identity. Even opposition politicians hesitated to voice strident opposition to the Seoul Games, and some students agreed to confine their protests to campuses as the Games neared. This pivotal moment on the world stage for South Korea was even more meaningful because Seoul had defeated Nagoya (in Japan, which had colonized Korea for over thirty years before the end of World War II in 1945), the other finalist candidate city for the 1988 Summer Olympics, which buttressed widespread nationalist sentiment. South Korea also saw the Games as an opportunity to cement its claim to represent the true Korean nation in its contest of political legitimacy vis-à-vis North Korea. Abroad, the theater of the Cold War and the shadow of two consecutive boycotts during the 1980 Moscow Olympics and 1984 Los Angeles Olympics raised the stakes for the IOC and its then recently elected president, Samaranch, to push for a successful 1988 Seoul Olympics.

The initial idea for Seoul to bid for the Olympics originated during the Park Chung-hee administration in 1979. The Park regime considered the Games an important opportunity to showcase to the world South Korea's successful economic development and modernization. The campaign for the Seoul Olympics was the genesis of a long-standing policy rationale in South Korea: the hosting of a major international event as a key proxy for its national prestige and importance on the world stage. This rationale still holds true decades later, as exemplified by the campaigns to host the 2002 World Cup (the organizing committee for which was led by the same individual, Park Seh-jik, who headed the 1988 Seoul Olympics organizing committee) and more recently with the 2018 Winter Olympics in Pyeongchang, which the city finally succeeded in securing after two initial failed attempts.

In the late 1970s, the humiliation of having had to forgo the 1970 Asian Games in Seoul due to economic difficulties was still fresh on the minds of South Koreans, and such a failure was something that the country did not want to repeat. With growing confidence after the successful hosting of the 42nd World Shooting Championships in Seoul during the fall of 1978, Seoul mayor Chung Sang-chon announced on October 8, 1979, that Seoul would bid for the 1988 Summer Olympic Games. However, just eighteen days later President Park was assassinated, and plans for the bid were temporarily put on hold.[28] When Chun came to office after his 1979 coup, the Olympic project continued, and on December 15, 1980, the IOC announced that four cities were officially designated as candidate cities for the 1988 Summer Olympics: Athens (Greece), Melbourne (Australia), Nagoya (Japan), and Seoul.[29] Melbourne dropped out of the competition in February 1981 followed by Athens, leaving Nagoya and Seoul.[30]

In bidding for the 1988 Games, South Korea was attempting to become the first developing nation and the second Asian country after Japan to host the Olympics. In less than a generation, South Korea rose from the devastation of the Korean War in the early 1950s and transformed from one of the poorest countries in the world into an industrial player in the world economy, with double-digit growth rates in the years leading up to the 1988 Olympics and a per capita gross domestic product of US$1,586 by 1980.[31] From the 1960s when President Park initiated state-led growth initiatives, the government played a central role in industrialization through investments in key industries such as steelmaking and shipbuilding and a focus on exports to larger overseas markets.[32] The government played a pivotal role in the rise of *jaebols* (large business conglomerates), such as Hyundai and Samsung, that continue to dominate the South Korean economy today and received mandates to push into and become national champions in specific industries and markets.[33]

South Korea's rapid economic growth also led to fundamental social changes. For example, by 1980 about 57 percent of the South Korean population resided in urban areas (primarily the Seoul metropolitan area), and by 1985 Seoul had become the ninth most populous city in the world.[34] Urbanization was accompanied by rapidly rising literacy rates in the country. Between 1953 (at the end of the Korean War) and 1963, South Korea's literacy rate increased from about 30 percent to 80 percent; by 1987 during the June protests and on the eve of the Seoul Olympics, the literacy rate stood at about 98 percent.[35]

South Korea's rapid economic development and social transformations had important political implications, as the wealthier and better-educated population created cleavages in the social and political structure of the country. With the infusion of more stakeholders and opinions on policy issues, South Korea was well on its way in the transition to democratization. However, if there was one issue on which all politicians agreed, it was the importance of staging a successful Seoul Olympics, as opposition party leaders Kim Dae-jung and Kim Young-sam both supported the bid. These two Kims could not agree which of them would run on the opposition ticket in the December 1987 presidential elections, ultimately splitting the opposition vote and effectively handing the incumbent party candidate (and head of the Seoul Olympic Organizing Committee) Roh Tae-woo the presidency and sapping the popular momentum for political reform that had brought down Chun.

Even the ardent student demonstrators who had occupied streets and campuses throughout the country found it difficult to project their voices in the midst of unified support for the Seoul Olympics. They found less support than they did even a year earlier in 1987 when the middle class joined in the protests against Chun. While the Roh government attempted to silence dissent in the lead-up to the Games by setting up designated "peace parks," many South Koreans expressed misgivings about the impact of such protests on the 1988 Games. In August 1988, the *New York Times* reported that "many Korean are expressing concern that student protests could embarrass the nation," noting that a planned protest by Yonsei University students, who were calling for North Korea to cohost the event, failed to attract the support of the general public.[36] As one student protest leader admitted, "We are very worried because of the cold reaction from the people."[37]

When South Korea won the bid, Chung Soo-chang, president of the Korean Chamber of Commerce and Industry, commented that "the Olympic games will give us the momentum to stage another economic takeoff and to gain international recognition of Korea's diplomatic and political position."[38] The goal of continued economic growth and the potential for the 1988 Games to contribute to it was a message that had great appeal to the South Korean populace. Many had witnessed and benefited from the ever-enlarging economic pie. As IOC vice president Richard Pound accurately noted, for South Korea, "nothing could stand in the way" of successful hosting of the 1986 Asian Games and the 1988 Seoul Olympics. These were entrée to international recognition, acceptance, and membership in the family of nations. This was a feeling shared by all South Koreans.[39]

The theme of the XXIV Olympiad was "Harmony and Progress." The head of Seoul's organizing committee, Park Seh-jik, stated in his opening address that "Our world has overcome numerous obstacles to finally come together here from East and West, North and South under the sky of Seoul. We have leaped over ideological and political barriers to share in a celebration of 'harmony and progress,' which we earnestly hope will endure long after these Games are over."[40] The theme was appropriate, since there was top-down mobilization of the entire country as well as bottom-up popular support and belief in the value of the Games to showcase and help continue South Korea's rapid economic growth.

Another unifying factor in the lead-up to the 1988 Games was the contest between Seoul and Nagoya, the two remaining candidate cities. Anti-Japanese sentiments in South Korea from the period of Japanese colonial rule (1910–1935) were still fresh, and many South Koreans badly wanted to beat Japan. Japan had previously hosted the Summer Olympics in 1964 in Tokyo and the 1972 Winter Olympics in Sapporo, the former of which was Japan's own coming-out party after its role and defeat in World War II.[41] Ironically, in many respects the South Korean bid for the 1988 Games was modeled on the trajectory of the 1964 Tokyo Games, not unlike the economic policies and developmental model for rapid industrialization that the Park government benchmarked for South Korea's economic rise.[42]

As Pound observed, the Japanese may have been overconfident about Nagoya's chances with the 1988 Games, given the country's past experience in hosting the Games and concerns about South Korean politics and South Korea's tense relationship with North Korea: "It was unimaginable to them that they might not be successful in a head-on competition with Korea."[43] Pound recounts an attempt by the Japanese to embarrass the South Korean bid by planting a question with a Soviet IOC member regarding South Korea's loans from Japan in order to cast doubt on the financial soundness of Seoul's bid. Seoul brought in economic expert Yoo Chang-soon, South Korea's former deputy prime minister in charge of economic planning and prime minister, to respond that the loan was for economic development purposes and was not out of the ordinary.[44] The question backfired on Japan when it was exposed as having been planted.[45]

While Japan was overconfident with its chances, it may also have been hampered by local resistance to Nagoya's bid. When the city was preparing its bid, many citizens' groups in Japan protested, arguing that the 1988 Games would be a waste of public expenditures and might have a negative ecological impact.[46] In fact, hundreds of activists from Japan traveled to Baden-Baden, Germany, the site of the IOC meeting to announce the winner of the 1988 Games.[47] While these protests may not have single-handedly been fatal to Nagoya's bid, they raised questions about local public support for the city's bid and planted doubts about popular consensus in the Japanese city. Christian Tagsold has called these Nagoya-related protests "probably the first popular anti-Olympic movement in Asia."[48]

South Korea, on the other hand, was much more unified in its bid for the 1988 Games, and there was no widespread opposition to the bid itself even if some South Koreans thought that their chances against Japan were slim. South Korea surprised many observers when IOC president Samaranch declared Seoul the winner in a convincing manner, with a vote of 52 to 27, over Nagoya.[49] When South Korea won the bid, one Japanese observer noted that "the South Koreans have been trying to catch up to Japan ever since the 1960's and now they believe they have reached their goal."[50] Another commented that "In their eyes . . . beating the Japanese at anything automatically means raising their international prestige," noting that Nagoya's bid was mainly a regional effort, "but in Korea, it was taken up as a national campaign."[51]

A third unifying factor in Seoul's bid for the 1988 Games was its contest of legitimacy with North Korea. Since the division of the peninsula at the end of World War II, the two Koreas had been involved in an extended contest of legitimacy over which entity rightfully represents the Korean nation.[52] This contest manifested itself in many contexts, including at major international sporting events. When South Korea declared its bid for the 1988 Games, North Korea saw this as a threat to its standing in the international system, especially when it became clear (as noted below) that some of its own Cold War allies would not be boycotting the 1988 Seoul Olympics.

While much has been written on the discussions among the IOC, South Korea, and North Korea on cohosting the 1988 Games and/or certain events, such discussions must be understood in the context of the political rivalry between the two Koreas. After Seoul was selected as the host city, North Korea proposed that it would jointly host the 1988 Games, with Pyongyang hosting an equal number of events as Seoul. The IOC and South Korea rejected North Korea's proposal, and the IOC instead proposed that Pyongyang host all or part of five Olympic sports (archery, table tennis, women's volleyball, the soccer preliminary round, and men's individual cycling). South Korea accepted the IOC's proposal, but North Korea did not, ultimately deciding to boycott the Olympics.[53] Many saw North Korean overtures for cohosting the 1988 Games as posturing rather than as a serious attempt to use the Games for political reconciliation between the two Koreas. As one observer noted in 1988, "There is just no way that North Korea wanted to have thousands of journalists roaming around Pyongyang writing stories comparing North and South Korea. . . . It would have made the victory for the South just that much sweeter."[54]

While some student protestors in South Korea called for cohosting with North Korea, the broader public did not fully endorse the anti-Olympic and anti-American rhetoric that formed part of their platform.[55] North Korean threats to disrupt Seoul's preparation for the Games, which materialized in a suspected North Korean bomb that was detonated at the Kimpo airport in September 1986 just as the 1986 Asian Games in Seoul were getting under way, also galvanized the South Korean public to work for a successful Olympic Games in the city.[56]

A final unifying factor was the external context of the Cold War and the emerging détente between the opposing blocs. From the IOC's perspective, it was in its interest to see the Seoul Games succeed by having as many countries participate as possible, which was one of the concerns initially raised when Seoul was chosen because it had boycotted the 1980 Summer Olympics in Moscow, along with many other allies of the United States. In addition, the IOC's institutional interests were aligned. Because the two previous Summer Olympics in Moscow and Los Angeles were subject to large boycotts, it was crucial for Samaranch, when he was elected IOC president in 1980, to ensure that the first Olympics whose selection he oversaw did not precipitate yet another boycott.

Because the Soviet Union and China, North Korea's two main allies, decided that they would participate in the 1988 Seoul Games, there was greater international support for the Games. Opposition voices within South Korea therefore had less salience and less capacity to question the Games. A fractured international community would have provided ammunition for those domestic forces that opposed the Olympics, and the same external interests could have preyed on the local fissures to promote their own interests, especially since there were some concerns about South Korea's preparations and ability to host the 1988 Games. However, détente in the international system during the period ensured that domestic politics and international relations reinforced each other.

When the Soviet Union announced in January 1988 that it would participate, it joined other countries from the Eastern bloc including East Germany, Hungary, Poland, Romania, and Bulgaria.[57] Marat Gramov, chairman
of the Soviet Sport Committee, stated at the time that "As for [North Korea],
it should take its own decision in this respect."[58] The 1988 Seoul Games
included the participation of 159 nations, 8,391 athletes participating in 237
sporting events, 27,221 volunteers, and 11,331 members of the media.[59] It
was the largest Olympics held in the Cold War era in terms of participating nations, and this broadened platform reinforced South Koreans' desire to
ensure that the Games would succeed so they could showcase the country's
arrival on the world stage. As Pound emphasized, "The Koreans would *never*
have countenanced losing face on their own account. If external circumstances intervened to prevent the full accomplishment, that would have been
painful indeed and a matter of national sorrow. But the thought of fouling
their own nest was complete anathema to them."[60]

While the dominant narrative of the 1988 Seoul Games has emphasized
the democratizing effect of the Games on South Korea, this chapter has
argued that the dynamic animating the relationship between the Olympics
and democracy is much more complicated and ambiguous. In South Korea,
the Games amplified preexisting and powerful unifying forces in the country and in the international system, including the South Korean desire to
showcase the country's economic growth, the nationalist sentiments of overcoming Japan, rivalry with North Korea, and growing international détente.
While some of these unifying forces were manipulated by the Chun government for its own ends, the regime quickly found that certain popular forces
were beyond its control. The 1988 Games were not "Chun's Games," and they
were not even the "Seoul Olympics"; they were more appropriately the "South
Korean Games," as the entire country was galvanized to ensure their success.
Even Chun underestimated the undercurrents of change: he badly miscalcu-
lated in April 1987 when he tried to forestall political reform by handpicking
his successor rather than hold direct popular elections. He and Roh Tae-woo
had to quickly backtrack when the move triggered massive street protests.
Chun's April miscalculation, not the Seoul Olympics, was the real catalyst
that tipped the political scales in 1987.

A similar pattern of unifying forces emerged three decades later as South
Korea hosted its second Olympics during the Winter Games in Pyeongchang
in 2018. The effort to host its second Olympics was sustained and hard-fought,
overcoming two disappointing losses. While the level of public support for

Pyeongchang 2018 may not have reached the fervent support for Seoul 1988, the broad dynamics of popular support and adherence to the idea that sport serves as a powerful vehicle for national prestige and international reputation remained very potent in South Korea.

For example, the calls to use the 2018 Games as an olive branch to North Korea appeared once again, resulting in a flurry of high-profile political visits and inter-Korean cultural exchanges aimed at reducing tensions on the peninsula and attempting to secure a diplomatic resolution to the issue of North Korean nuclear weapons.

More generally, the tendency of the Olympics and sport in general to reinforce unifying forces and bring people and interests together holds important implications for the relationship between sport and democracy. Both may share certain values such as an emphasis on rules and competition, which may suggest that the former naturally leads to other in terms of establishing a causal link, but the case of the 1988 Seoul Olympics paints a much more complicated and ambiguous picture. At the heart of democracy is the logic of division; power must be decentralized, ideas must be contested, and interests must be divided. Campaigns to host major sporting events such as the Olympics may indeed produce that effect but usually at the cost of losing the bid itself. That is because as currently structured (and, some may argue, they must practically be required to do so), many of the bid processes for such events prioritize order and consensus of public opinion. There is thus an inherent tension that is not easily reconciled, and in many respects such tensions may precisely be the reason why some adhere so strongly to the belief that sport and politics should not mix. But it may be too late to try to avoid the question altogether. The IOC and other major sporting organizations in the world today face and are forced to face great uncertainty and must come to grips with very difficult normative and political questions, such as human rights and democracy promotion.

Notes

1. See Guillermo O'Donnell, Philippe C. Schmitter, and Lawrence Whitehead, eds., *Transitions from Authoritarian Rule: Tentative Conclusions About Uncertain Democracies* (Baltimore: Johns Hopkins University Press, 1986).

2. Victor Matheson, "Why Democracies Don't Want the Olympics Anymore," *Washington Post*, July 29, 2015, www.washingtonpost.com/posteverything/wp/2015/07/29/why-democracies -dont-want-the-olympics-anymore/?utm_term=.954fac3fe79c.

3. Katherine Q. Seelye, "Boston's Bid for Summer Olympics Is Terminated," *New York Times*, July 27, 2015, www.nytimes.com/2015/07/28/sports/olympics/boston-2024-summer-olympics -bid-terminated.html?_r=0. See also Chris Dempsey and Andrew Zimbalist, *No Boston Olympics: How and Why Smart Cities Are Passing on the Torch* (Lebanon, NH: ForeEdge, 2017).

4. Justin Huggler, "Hamburg Withdraws Bid to Host 2024 Olympics," *The Telegraph*, November 30, 2015, www.telegraph.co.uk/news/worldnews/europe/germany/12025211/Hamburg -withdraws-bid-to-host-2024-Olympics.html.

5. Jeré Longman, "Olympics Officials Move Closer to Giving Bids to Paris and Los Angeles," *New York Times*, July 11, 2017, www.nytimes.com/2017/07/11/sports/olympics-2024-2028 -paris-los-angeles.html.

6. Victor D. Cha, "A Theory of Sport and Politics," *International Journal of the History of Sport* 26, no. 11 (September 2009): 1598.

7. Ibid.

8. Liz Clarke, "Russia's Anti-Gay Law Brings Controversy Ahead of 2014 Sochi Olympics," *Washington Post*, August 18, 2013, www.washingtonpost.com/sports/olympics/russias-anti-gay -law-brings-controversy-ahead-of-2014-sochi-olympics/2013/08/18/b42b5182-076f-11e3-9259 -e2aafe5a5f84_story.html?utm_term=.f4491c9e1715. See also Dmitry Dubrovskiy's chapter in this volume.

9. See Chen Kuide, "Two Historical Turning Points: The Seoul and Beijing Olympics," *China Rights Forum* 3 (2007): 36–40, www.hrichina.org/sites/default/files/PDFs/CRF.3.2007/CRF-2007 -3_Seoul.pdf

10. Chalmers Johnson, "When the Olympics Fostered Democratic Process in Asia," *Los Angeles Times*, July 18, 2001, articles.latimes.com/2001/jul/18/local/me-23429. See also Julie H. Liu, "Lighting the Torch of Human Rights: The Olympic Games as a Vehicle for Human Rights Reform," *Northwestern Journal of International Human Rights* 5, no. 2 (Spring 2007): 213–235.

11. See Donald N. Clark, *The Kwangju Uprising: Shadows over the Regime in South Korea* (Boulder, CO: Westview, 1988).

12. See Olympic Charter (August 2, 2016), stillmed.olympic.org/media/Document%20 Library/OlympicOrg/General/EN-Olympic-Charter.pdf#_ga=1.66151278.1983496735 .1481686955.

13. Ibid.

14. "Human Rights Watch Submission to the 2009 Olympic Congress: Proposal for an IOC Committee on Human Rights," Human Rights Watch, www.hrw.org/news/2009/02/23/human -rights-watch-submission-2009-olympic-congress.

15. "IOC Strengthens Its Stance in Favour of Human Rights and Against Corruption in New Host City Contract," International Olympic Committee, www.olympic.org/news/ioc -strengthens-its-stance-in-favour-of-human-rights-and-against-corruption-in-new-host-city -contract.

16. Ibid.

17. See Andrew Zimbalist, *Circus Maximus: The Economic Gamble Behind Hosting the Olympics and the World Cup* (Washington, DC: Brookings Institution, 2016).

18. IOC, "Candidate Questionnaire Olympic Games 2024" (September 16, 2015), stillmed .olympic.org/Documents/Host_city_elections/Candidature_Questionnaire_Olympic_Games _2024.pdf.

19. Ryan Gauthier, *The International Olympic Committee, Law, and Accountability* (New York: Routledge, 2017), 79.

20. "Jerome Valcke: FIFA Chief Says Too Much Democracy Can be a Hindrance," *BBC News*, April 24, 2013, www.bbc.com/sport/football/22288688.

21. Ibid.

22. Ibid.

23. Samuel Huntington, *Political Order in Changing Societies* (New Haven, CT: Yale University Press, 1968), 1.

24. Malcolm Foley, David McGillivray, and Gayle McPherson, "Events Policy: The Limits of Democracy," *Journal of Policy Research in Tourism, Leisure and Events* 3, no. 3 (November 2011): 322.

25. Quoted in David Miller, *Olympic Revolution: The Biography of Juan Antonio Samaranch* (London: Trafalgar Square, 1992), 138.

26. See Han Sung-joo, "South Korean in 1987: The Politics of Democratization," *Asian Survey* 1, no. 1 (January 1988): 52–61; James M. West and Edward J. Baker, "The 1987 Constitutional Reforms in South Korea: Electoral Processes and Judicial Independence," *Harvard Human Rights Yearbook* 1 (1988): 221–252; Yun Deug Heon, 올림픽의 정치 [*The Politics of the Olympics*] (Seoul: Rainbow Books, 2009); Yoo Ho Geun, 현대 스포츠 외교사: 올림픽 중심으로 [*Modern Sports Diplomatic History: Focus on Olympics* (Seoul: Ingan, 2015)].

27. See Seymour Martin Lipset, *Political Man: The Social Bases of Politics* (Garden City, NY: Doubleday, 1960).

28. Moo-jong Park, "Seoul Olympics Gave Powerful Impetus to Great Changes in South Korea," *Korea Times*, July 7, 2010.

29. Ibid.

30. Ibid.

31. Jarol B. Manheim, "Rites of Passage: The 1988 Seoul Olympics as Public Diplomacy," *Western Political Quarterly* 43, no. 2 (June 1990): 221.

32. See Alice H. Amsden, *Asia's Next Giant: South Korea and Late Industrialization* (New York: Oxford University Press, 1992).

33. See Eun Mee Kim, *Big Business, Strong State: Collusion and Conflict in South Korean Development, 1960–1990* (Stony Brook: State University of New York Press, 1997); Meredith Woo-Cumings, *The Developmental State* (Ithaca, NY: Cornell University Press, 1999).

34. Manheim, "Rites of Passage," 281.

35. David R. Black and Shona Bezanson, "The Olympic Games, Human Rights and Democratisation: Lessons from Seoul and Implications for Beijing," *Third World Quarterly* 25, no. 7 (2004): 1248.

36. Susan Chira, "Alone in Dissent in Korea; Although Student Protests Set the Agenda, This Year They Fail to Gain Wide Backing," *New York Times*, August 17, 1988.

37. Ibid.

38. Quoted in Tracy Dahl, "Award of 1988 Olympics Boosts S. Korea's Effort for Political Security," *Washington Post*, October 4, 1981.

39. Richard Pound, *Five Rings over Korea: The Secret Negotiations Behind the 1988 Olympic Games in Seoul* (New York: Little Brown, 1994), 322.

40. Ibid.

41. Christian Tagsold, "The 1964 Tokyo Olympics as Political Games," *Asia-Pacific Journal* 7, no. 3 (June 2009): 1.

42. See Chalmers A. Johnson, *MITI and the Japanese Miracle: The Growth of Industrial Policy, 1925–1975* (Stanford, CA: Stanford University Press, 1982).

43. Pound, *Five Rings over Korea*, 4.

44. Ibid, 5–6.

45. Ibid, 6.

46. Tagsold, "The 1964 Tokyo Olympics," 5.

47. Pound, *Five Rings over Korea*, 8.

48. Tagsold, "The 1964 Tokyo Olympics," 5.

49. Dahl, "Award of 1988 Olympics."

50. Quoted in ibid.

51. Ibid.

52. See Barry K. Gills, *Korea Versus Korea: A Case of Contested Legitimacy* (London: Routledge, 1996).

53. Woong-yong Ha, "Korean Sports in the 1980s and the Seoul Olympic Games," *Journal of Olympic History* 6, no. 2 (Summer 1998): 12. See the detailed negotiation history in Pound, *Five Rings over Korea*, 87–257.

54. Quoted in Ronald E. Yates, "For S. Korea, Olympics Herald a Brighter Era," *Chicago Tribune*, September 18, 1988.

55. Chira, "Alone in Dissent."

56. Clyde Haberman, "5 Dead, 36 Hurt in an Explosion at Seoul Airport," *New York Times*, September 15, 1988, www.nytimes.com/1986/09/15/world/5-dead-36-hurt-in-an-explosion-at-seoul-airport.html.

57. Celestine Bohlen, "Soviets to Compete in Seoul Olympics," *Washington Post*, January 12, 1988.

58. Ibid.

59. "Seoul 1988—Highlights of the Games," International Olympic Committee, www.olympic.org/seoul-1988.

60. Pound, *Five Rings over Korea*, 322.

CHAPTER 4

Peace

The United Nations, the International Olympic Committee, and the Renovation of the Olympic Truce

Roland Burke

International sport and the pursuit of peace have long been linked. Pierre de Coubertin, founder of the modern Olympic Games at the end of the nineteenth century, described the event's "real aim" as "peace among nations."[1] Coubertin was friends with many members of Western peace movements of that era. Like them, he believed that international congregations such as world's fairs, even when framed in terms of national competition, fostered mutual understanding that would reduce the chances of future wars. In this way, he wrote, international athletics might be "a potent, if indirect factor in securing universal peace."[2] However, it took nearly a century for this vague idealism to be translated into a tangible program.[3]

In 2000 United Nations (UN) secretary-general Kofi Annan declared that "Olympic ideals are also United Nations ideals: tolerance, equality, fair play and, most of all, peace. Together, the Olympics and the United Nations can be a winning team."[4] The remark illustrates a remarkable transformation. By the second decade of the twenty-first century, under the proud gaze of the International Olympic Committee (IOC), now one of a handful of observers permanently represented in the UN General Assembly, Olympism had become synonymous with the most hopeful set of postwar ideals.[5] Dedicated Olympic items had become a perennial feature of the UN's agenda, and almost every

speaker in every session cast the Olympic ideal as a breviary of UN priorities. Traversing from the Millennium Development Goals to the fight against
HIV, Olympism was well on the way to being invoked as part of the solution
to everything.[6] Such resolutions, which typically broke records in terms of
supporting sponsors and affirmative votes, prefixed "a better world through
the Olympic ideal." The satellite initiatives they generated, on development,
human rights, and above all peace, appeared to represent a long-delayed
recognition of the shared ideological basis of the IOC's and the UN's two
brands of internationalism—both, after all, predicated on the idea that the
organizations worked to create a more peaceful world.[7] In reality, the affinity
between the UN and the IOC was a recent phenomenon. The organization,
which had been born as part of "The New Deal for the World" in 1945, was
for half a century in profound tension with the Olympic hierarchy, which had
been closer in orientation to the fascist "New Order in Europe."[8] Both had
exhorted peace as their purpose, but whether it should be after a UN victory
was rather less certain.

The flagship of the alliance between the IOC and the UN was the truce
initiative. In the 1990s, IOC president Juan Antonio Samaranch took up a
commitment to resurrecting the Olympic Truce of ancient Greece—in which
warring parties had agreed to let athletes, their families, and pilgrims travel
to the Games and back without interference—as a manifestation of the IOC's
devotion to building a more peaceful world. Samaranch's initiative was a
response to the Yugoslav wars that broke out in 1991—and specifically to the
UN Security Council's 1992 resolution that imposed sanctions on Yugoslavia,
including on sport. The decision threatened to block Yugoslav athletes from
participating in the 1992 Barcelona Olympics, in Samaranch's home country.
Samaranch turned to the idea of the Olympic Truce to convince the UN to
allow Yugoslav athletes to participate in the Games as individuals. He then
pressed the UN to adopt resolutions in support of the truce and, to mark the
centenary of the IOC, to proclaim 1994 the International Year of Sport and
the Olympic ideal.[9]

As much as an interorganizational negotiated settlement as the crystallization
of a common faith in peace, the joint UN-IOC Olympic Truce was a common
platform for conflicting internationalisms and contested versions of "peace."[10]
As an IOC official noted, "It [was] the first time in the history of the Olympic
Movement that a large-scale operation [had] been launched in favour of peace,"
which would be advanced by promoting "dialogue and reconciliation and the
search for lasting solutions to all armed conflicts." On the day of its launch

a market in Sarajevo was shelled by Serb insurgents, with dozens killed.[11] In 2009 at the Olympic Congress in Copenhagen, UN secretary-general Ban Ki-moon enthused that "together, the IOC and the United Nations have revived the idea of observing an Olympic Truce."[12] Along with joint UN-IOC work on the mélange of programs that fall under the rubric of "sport for development and peace," the truce is the most visible manifestation of the two organizations' joint work toward peace.[13] Yet it would be hard to find tangible evidence that the truce is more than a rhetorical device.

While the 1990s and 2000s created a narrative of perpetual comity between UN and IOC ideals, the history was more prosaic. Interest in the IOC was sparse in the first two decades of UN operation. The most sustained discussion of what the UN could learn from the IOC occurred when Nepal's representative lamented to the 1959 General Assembly how useful then-IOC president Avery Brundage's autocratic spirit would be for resolving the issue of Taiwanese representation.[14] Any alignment with human rights, one of the UN's pillars for building peace, was ambiguous. During the drafting of the UN's Universal Declaration of Human Rights, sport was mentioned barely at all; when it was, it was the ally of public order. Sport's most prominent place was in the discussion on the limits of rights, where it was invoked as one of the few permissible bases for curtailing the normal freedoms of society.[15] In a nearly endless list of philosophers, philosophies, religions, revolutions, reforms, and emancipations, Coubertin and Olympism were nowhere to be found in the Commission on Human Rights. Among the countless procession of nongovernmental organizations (NGOs) large and small that shaped the declaration through their voices, the IOC was silent.[16]

After 1945 and the genesis and consolidation of global institutions such as the Commission on Human Rights, the IOC and its animating faith, "Olympism," operated in a new universe. Dormant for almost a decade due to World War II, the IOC faced an explosion in rival universalistic creeds, all combined under the aegis of the most powerful international organization ever devised, the UN. This formally promulgated international idealism, embodied in the UN's organs, centered on the tripartite formulae of peace, sovereignty, and human rights, subtended by a faith in economic and technical progress. Efforts to defend the IOC's own habitat in this new network of regulations, norms, and organization, along with the countervailing initiatives to consume the space occupied by the IOC, were a testament to how seriously the prize of moral custodianship of sport, youth, and international connection was sought in the second half of the twentieth century.

While narrow nationalism and gauche professionalism were longtime rivals to proclaimed Olympic ideals, the UN ideals born with the postwar world were markedly different despite similar language—being universalistic and conspicuously moralizing. The respective missions of the IOC and the UN carried the same fraught and contradictory pretensions to living either above or outside the political. The crises of 1968 (the massacre at Mexico City before the Olympic Games), 1972 (the terrorist attack at the Munich Games), and 1980 (the Moscow Games) may have been the most dramatic threats to the Olympics, but the most profound political contests for postwar Olympic ideas were not against national and sectional interest but instead were against an alternative internationalism. While commercialism could corrupt and chauvinism could compromise, only another universalist vision of global morality could annex Olympism wholesale.

What neither set of champions, Olympic or UN internationalist, anticipated was the convergence, first evidenced in the early 1990s, between UN and IOC activity and rhetoric along with an emergent symbiosis between the two organizations. This chapter charts the interaction between the UN and the IOC, one that began with indifference, progressed to hostility, and ended with an entente cordiale that elevated the degraded stature of both. With a focus on the contested and eventually shared terrain of "peace," the chapter builds on previous work that places the history of the IOC in the frame of wider postwar internationalism.[17]

By the late 1980s with other moral languages, notably human rights, fiercely contested, the open-ended nature of the values attached to the Olympic Games had become a positive virtue. Released from the impediment of precision, international sport allowed ample evasion of the fundamental conflicts that had attached to most major agenda items that confronted the General Assembly from the 1950s onward. Sporting internationalism was appealing simply because it assembled young people together in an internationalized space and did so without weapons. Olympism was a means by which any contentious element of internationalism could be evacuated, leaving only the forms of global connection under a carapace of platitudinous moralizing. Damaged by years of controversy, neither the UN nor the IOC could erect this edifice alone, but together in the General Assembly chamber, at the United Nations Educational, Scientific, and Cultural Organization (UNESCO) symposia, and in the Games themselves, the helpful and hopeful hallucination could be made real.

The Teflon Internationalism

A voluminous body of work has addressed the provenance, evolution, and operation of Olympic internationalism.[18] As themes that speak to the identity of the organization, they have been well served by research conducted through dedicated Olympic studies programs, typically sponsored by the IOC. Although productive and often pioneering, this scholarship can be limited by the affiliation.[19] The orientation of Olympic studies, which takes the Olympics themselves as the central subject, may well overprivilege the relatively small world of Olympic entities and diminish the importance of their interaction with a much larger and more inclusive and powerful set of global institutions.

As with histories of other value-laden discourses, there is also a degree of self-selection, with a cohort skewed toward to enthusiasm and implied, or candid, activism. History in particular has been singled out by at least one eminent commentator as a disciplinary friend of the IOC, though more recent histories are certainly less celebratory in their inflection.[20] Modern historiography of international sport, with the flourishing subfield of Olympic studies, has moved beyond reciting Olympic illusions and is especially dismissive of the IOC's ostensible freedom from politics.[21] Attention has instead migrated to the more fruitful plane of historicizing the nature of the contention between, on the one hand, the IOC and the extrinsic political world and, on the other hand, the manner in which the political was enacted at particular moments.[22] Much like rights, humanitarianism, health, population, and telecommunications, Olympic internationalism has a political history, complicated only by the dynamics of operating these politics while simultaneously expressing an aversion to them.[23]

Nonetheless, the persistent belief in Olympic ideals as a set of transcendent, suprapolitical verities presents a serious historical question. While so many antipolitical idealisms fell into discredit, Olympism survived seven decades of demolitions, from Hitler's Berlin Olympics to the Hungarian and Suez crises that threatened the 1956 Games, the IOC's obvious lassitude in confronting racism, and major boycotts in the 1980s. In the 1990s and 2000s, a sequence of devastating journalistic salvos on corruption and the ever-escalating, hypocritical, and ultimately futile witch hunt of antidoping paternalism should have been rearranging nothing more than the rubble of Olympia. Yet it was the other larger international institution, the UN, that

ultimately sought to bolster its own credibility by borrowing Olympic prestige. When looking at the fawning paeans to "Olympism" that were aired in
the General Assembly between 1993 and 2013, the exaggerated belief in the
significance, power, and virtues of the Olympic Games seems less a structural
defect in Olympic studies than an observable reality.

Resilient in a way that the UN was not, Olympism failed ethical tests
just as comprehensively but with less visible loss of faith. Samaranch could
cheerfully survive living links with fascism.[24] His UN counterpart, Secretary-
General Kurt Waldheim, was properly placed beyond redemption for a Nazi
past.[25] Across myriad humanitarian crises of the 1990s, trivial aid provisions
in brightly signed IOC trucks won plaudits.[26] The deficiencies of the UN
Office of the High Commissioner for Refugees (UNHCR), which delivered
many orders of magnitude more relief and did so every year under artillery
fire, were seen as evidence of an institutional failure to secure peace and inter-
communal harmony. The UN Human Rights Commission and its rebranded
successor, the Human Rights Council, were ridiculed for seating gross violators of human rights in the chair when they belonged in the dock.[27] The
IOC could disburse its highest reward, status as an Olympic host, to the same
regimes that were prime targets of pressure from human rights NGOs—
Vladimir Putin's Russia and the People's Republic of China—and yet still
have claims to moralism widely credited. If the UN was slated for its limited
success in inducing human rights improvements, there was a credible case for
regarding the IOC as being actively harmful to human rights. Self-evidently,
something was special about Olympism.

The Inadvertent Synthesis: UNESCO, the IOC, and the Future of the Olympic Movement

Lord Killanin was elected leader of the IOC in 1972, at a moment of danger for
the organization. Earlier forays by UNESCO, on the interface between international sport and its own terrain of peace, education, culture, and youth, had
begun to nibble at the edges of the IOC's empire.[28] UNESCO had granted sport
its own subbody, the International Council of Sport and Physical Education
(ICSPE), though given the abundance of UNESCO-affiliated committees, this
was not necessarily a dramatic development.[29] At one of the ICPSE's foundational meetings in October 1963, René Maheu, director-general of UNESCO,
had spoken extensively on the relationship between his organization's ethos

and that of Olympism in terms that suggested co-ownership, most especially because the Olympics engaged in internationalism.[30] UNESCO's award for fair play, established in 1964 under the auspices of the International Committee on Fair Play, already wandered dangerously close to the triptych panels of the IOC: internationalism, sport, and moralizing platitudes on peace.[31]

While these UNESCO initiatives were an organizational curiosity in the 1960s, this measure of safety rapidly disappeared. Even before Brundage's departure, there was at least one public demand for UNESCO to seize the IOC's role, with Finnish president Urho Kekkonen devoting an address to the idea in 1971.[32] UNESCO's drift away from its designated playpen of physical education was visible by 1972.[33] The low ebb for Olympic internationalism began to collide with the king tide of UN activism, infused with the radical spirit of the Third World. UNESCO director René Maheu's address in August 1972 was markedly bolder than the one he delivered nine years earlier. At the seventy-third IOC Congress in Munich, he lectured his Olympic pupils on the need to reflect the wider decolonized world. "Sport," Maheu said, was "a universal phenomenon," and "a distinguished world-wide organization like the Olympic body" was "duty bound to accept the implications of this universality." Having established this premise, one the IOC embraced in its own rhetoric, he drew some unsettling implications. International sport "must recognize and reflect in its structure, and maintain and indeed develop in its action, the manifold variety of cultures which constitutes the richness of mankind's spiritual heritage." Glaring at an audience composed predominantly of Atlantic and Mediterranean aristocrats, Maheu cautioned that "any form of cultural ethnocentrism must be resolutely repudiated."[34]

Animated by the confident spirit of the mid-1970s General Assembly, indifference and halfhearted rivalry were supplanted by a growing mood for the UN to capture the IOC outright and to harmonize Olympism with its closest phylum on the tree of international organization: UNESCO.[35] There was a prospect, somewhere between spectral and real, that the Olympic Games would be acquired wholesale by a UN that had been steadily seeking to incorporate all rivals—including the one major modern internationalism that predated the IOC, the International Commission of the Red Cross (ICRC). The IOC, like the ICRC, seemed on the edge of being assimilated into the proliferating set of "New International Orders," revisionist efforts to reshape global structures in ways more amenable to the Third World.[36] Given its conspicuous exclusivism and Western oligarchic governance, the IOC was a fine target for "New International" crusading.[37]

The first of the New International schemes and the model for all its sequels was the New International Economic Order (NIEO), which was pursued relentlessly by the Group of 77 (G-77) from 1973 onward. Officially codified at the UN in 1974 and 1975, the NIEO proposed a radical shift in the balance of the world economy or, as it was often termed, "the existing, unjust" order.[38] Those "new international orders" that followed, in humanitarianism, information, and health, adhered to the essential proposition of redistributing power within the frame of internationalism and drew upon global institutions to augment the capacity of sovereign states in the developing world.[39] Each order asserted the need for much greater state control, provided a given state was a member of the G-77. A renewed interest in the potential of sport arrived at a UNESCO that was seeking to rewrite internationalism. Cultural power had already been subject to this (re) "New"-al in the New International Information Order (NIIO) and its more complete sibling, the New World Information and Communications Order (NWICO).[40] In this milieu, the prospect of a New International Order in Sport, or New International Sports Order, began to seem like a credible threat.[41]

For his part, Killanin "saw the danger inherent in" UNESCO's "attempting to take over the administration of international sport," but he adopted cosmetic accommodation as the primary line of defense.[42] Killanin's prime interlocutor was René Maheu's successor, Senegal's Amadou-Mahtar M'Bow. M'Bow departed little from Maheu but was more ardent in seeking to control all spheres of human culture and society in ways consistent with the disposition of UNESCO's membership.[43] U.S. diplomats at UNESCO reported that sport had "become a high-priority program in UNESCO because of interest and support by the Director-General."[44] Sufficiently maximalist to fully alienate the last few liberals in the senior leadership, notably his deputy, Richard Hoggart, M'Bow's directorship accelerated the radicalization of UNESCO.[45] The result was a UNESCO dramatically sharpened as an instrument for Third Worldist priorities—opening up a new front for attacking "imperialist" knowledge, culture, education, and sport. As the course of other "New Internationalisms" had shown, assimilation and subversion was a more lethal risk than attack. A direct assault on sport as imperialist, as had been attempted by Indonesian president Sukarno's Games of the New Emerging Forces experiment in the 1960s, was proven to fail. Olympism owned the utopian claim on international sport; the battle was over who owned Olympism.

Across 1977 and 1978, the portents of a concerted UNESCO effort gathered in the form of the draft Charter on Physical Education and Sport.[46] Myriad news stories, including from journalists close to the IOC and Killanin, reported on the forthcoming revolution.[47] At the close of 1976, U.S. representatives observing the direction of the charter had discerned an obvious risk to the IOC and explicitly warned of "another 'Mass Media Declaration' problem," that is, the creation of an NWICO equivalent for international sport.[48] Reporting from the nineteenth UNESCO General Conference in 1977, the U.S. delegation warned that the deliberations "clearly demonstrated that international activity in these areas [sport] could easily be used as a vehicle for political propaganda" and diminish the IOC's authority, with the UNESCO Charter on Sport "an instrument for furthering state control."[49] By 1978, a relayed account from a source in the UN Secretariat observed that although the Soviet officer, Boris Gromov, was skeptical of UNESCO's having real power in the immediate term, he nevertheless envisaged himself head of the future UNESCO-run IOC in little more than a decade.[50] Surveys conducted by UNESCO in preparation for its work on international sport asked troublingly suggestive questions, seemingly as reconnaissance for an invasion of Olympic territory.[51]

Maurice Herzog, IOC chief protocol officer, was alive to the risk and urged preemptive reform "to adapt the IOC to the world of today." "We are vulnerable," he warned. The Soviet bloc in the 1980s would "push the cause of the third world in the IOC."[52] Closing the chasm between IOC and UNESCO positions was urgent. Killanin was less convinced, once protesting that "if the IOC ever becomes anything like the United Nations, I think it would not be in the interest of the youth of the world."[53] Nevertheless, both sides had a history of surviving and ultimately succeeding by the operation of subterranean deals and strategic ambiguity, and open battle was mostly eschewed. The IOC unconvincingly embraced UNESCO's most compelling interest, the nonthreatening realm of physical education.[54] UNESCO pretended that it was not looking to acquire the Olympic Games while steadily extending tendrils further into international sport in the general case.[55]

At the dawn of the 1980s, this configuration of mutual mistrust and superficial cooperation was beginning to change.[56] Both entities were facing a more important threat: moral marginality and monetary distress. The disastrous financial outcomes of the 1976 Montreal Games were now fully manifest, and the IOC was in serious trouble. Reserves of moral capital were arguably more depleted than the nearly bankrupt financial accounts. The damage of the Moscow Games was inescapable, and the ubercommercialism of Peter Ueberroth's forthcoming Los Angeles Games, while it might replete the reservoir of funds, would do so by drawing down moral prestige and organizational autonomy. UNESCO's position was scarcely better. M'Bow's crusade to repartition cultural power had crested and overreached. The extremity of Third World and Soviet politicization had severe reputational consequences, and the notionally specialist body ended up arguably more discredited that its UN parent. U.S. president Ronald Reagan at first disengaged and then withdrew from UNESCO entirely by 1985. For the Reagan administration, already mistrustful of multilateralism, the body seemed as offensive as what it regarded as the worst aspects of the UN proper but without any pressing strategic requirement for ongoing participation. British prime minister Margaret Thatcher's Conservative government was similarly unenthused, along with much of the more centrist democratic world.

The halfway house of stalemate became the arena for pooling moral resources. The overlap in rhetoric and moral claims that had aroused UNESCO's annexationism was also the basis for stumbling toward partnership: the powerful instrument of international sporting moralism could be shared, because both organizations were ostensibly devoted above all to peace.[57] Both organizations had lowered their horizons, a process that was evident in the UNESCO sporting body, and the two major conferences of the Ministers and Senior Officials Responsible for Physical Education and Sport (MINEPS).[58] This new spirit was encapsulated at the 1988 MINEPS II meeting in Moscow. M'Bow's successor, Frederico Mayor, enthused that international sport was the site for "basic ethical values," values that could "transcend the plurality of cultural identities and constitute the very fundament of modern humanism."[59] Like the original Third Worldist crusade of the NIEO, which disintegrated into progressively more attenuated forms of the Right to Development, and eventually the still weaker Millennium Development Goals and the NWICO, which was mostly ignored, Olympism found a nonthreatening alignment with the professions of solidarity, development, and peace that were prominent features of "New Internationalism."[60] By the mid-1980s, it was clear that the IOC would not lose its status. As an IOC member had declared half a century earlier, the organization would "always come out victor."[61]

Solidarity Between Internationalisms:
The IOC-UN Rapprochement of the 1990s

While the IOC and UNESCO recuperated, the promise of a grander alliance migrated to the wider UN system. After the disappointments of the extraordinarily ambitious 1992 Earth Summit in Rio and the 1993 World Conference on Human Rights in Vienna, the short bursts of possibility after the Cold War had closed.[62] After the failures of Somalia, Rwanda, and the former Yugoslavia, the second iteration of a new world of international cooperation and genuine universality had, much like the first, collapsed into national particularism. With its own idealisms once again abraded, the UN had gone prospecting for more secure repositories of idealist illusion. As the Romanian delegate catechized in 1995 when endorsing the draft resolution on what was called the "Olympic ideal," "what other idea could be equally shared" in an utterly divided world?[63] Across the 1990s, an elevated status for the nascent shared Olympism made sense for both parties, not least given that the IOC itself was appearing more tarnished with every journalistic exposé, culminating in a reputation-shredding corruption scandal reported in 1999.[64] One of Olympism's main moralizing pillars, gentlemanly amateurism, had in fact long been dead and was recently disposed of even as usable fiction. In this setting, sharing custodianship of the universal values of peace and humanity burnished the moral credentials of both beleaguered institutions.

Ownership of "youth" and "culture" as the underpinning for a more peaceful world was the key nexus for the IOC and UNESCO. A more elaborate shared platform with the wider UN built on these but with increased emphasis on the previously secondary themes of "peace" and "development." Peace was perhaps the most salient, given the disastrous wave of ethnonationalist conflicts that had accompanied the end of the Cold War. An expedition into Coubertin-era mythology and the pauses in violence that were dictated for the classical Games furnished a discrete focal point and the kind of joint project that engaged the latent power of Olympism. An Olympic-inflected call for (transient) peace refurbished the Cold War category of "peace," which had been damaged by instrumentalist deployment by Soviet, Western, Arab, and Israeli legations. Prospects that the resultant Olympic Truce item would induce a halt to armed conflict in the world were slender, but for the IOC and the UN the initiative served to transition an uneasy interorganizational cease-fire into a durable peace treaty—aptly enough, on "peace" itself.

Introduced with much fanfare in 1993, the annual reinscription of resolutions on the Olympic Truce wrote the Olympic movement into the UN system and brought the IOC into the General Assembly.[65] Paeans to Olympism and its leaders, issued from the secretary-general down, were a welcome respite from the libel cases and investigations that preoccupied the IOC outside the UN chamber. For the UN, hours of ritualized praise were arguably preferable to the normal debate of the General Assembly. The proposal of the truce resolutions and their enthusiastic adoption were a pleasant contrast to agenda items that arrived at the same stasis point every year and to the bloc votes on North-South lines that were virtually determined before anyone had even landed at La Guardia. Lauding the ideals of Olympism, redefined as generic virtues, afforded a unique opportunity to perform the sort of global solidarity that had been so scarce since the late 1940s.

When Secretary-General Boutros Boutros-Ghali took the podium in the final moments of the 1994 session on December 7, 1994, he desperately clung to Olympism. Even without lingering on the greatest failure in the organization's history, the withdrawal of UN forces from Rwanda after reliable warnings of imminent genocide, there was scarce material for celebration. UNHCR efforts in the former Yugoslavia appeared to be providing little more than slightly less malnourished civilians, whom the UN-mandated peacekeeping presence remained unable to protect. The largest official event of the year, the World Conference on Population and Development held in Cairo in September, had been at best a mixed success—compromised by an ecumenical coalition of obstruction agreed between antifeminist reactionaries.

Amid a grim year, "the Olympic ideal," Boutros-Ghali pronounced, was "a hymn to tolerance and understanding between people and culture." In the Olympics, he found "a school for democracy." There was, he proclaimed, "a natural link between the ethics of the Olympic Games and the fundamental principles of the United Nations." The secretary-general concluded that "In the International Olympic Committee, the United Nations has a precious ally in its action in the service of peace and bringing peoples together."[66] Member states themselves found the same salvation in the Olympics.[67] The resolution binding the UN to Olympism was advanced by a then record number of sponsors, a spectacular 141 countries.

Andrew Young, who had represented the United States in the General Assembly in the 1970s, returned in 1996 in a new and much less challenging capacity. Speaking now as cochair of the Atlanta Committee for the Olympic Games, the city's organizing committee, he encountered the kind of consensus that he could not have dreamt of two decades earlier when haplessly trying to advance President Jimmy Carter's human rights agenda. Young reminisced about a bond of friendship forged with the Soviet ambassador via regular tennis matches. The decorousness of split sets purportedly translated to both sides restraining their use of the veto.[68] A vestigial form of détente was preserved on Har Tru and Deco Turf. Speaking to a resolution with more supporters than any that had been "sponsored by the United States in a long, long time," Young saw "the unanimity of the family of peoples on this Earth."[69] A diverse constellation of delegations praised Young, remembering his heroic efforts in the exceptionally polarized climate of the late 1970s. What he had been unable to secure for Carter's human rights universalism could be delivered in sport. After an approving recitation of quotes from Samaranch, the Panamanian representative observed that sport was "the proper arena for the exercise of an active universalism."[70] Speakers gave charitable accounts of the Olympic movement's position on apartheid, and the IOC was refashioned into a volunteer at the vanguard of the anti-apartheid struggle rather than a conscript acting under compulsion. It was a rewarding exercise for all within and an encouraging spectacle for the wider world: the experiment of IOC presence in the UN had proven successful.

In November 1995, almost twelve months on, the condition of the world had not appreciably improved, and recourse to the symbolic theater and pantomime of global harmony under Olympism again served as a much-needed sanctuary. As preparations for Atlanta progressed, IOC efforts assisted Bosnian athletes in competing at the Games, while their cities lay besieged or in ruins. Expressions of sorrow for the assassinated Israeli prime minister Yitzhak Rabin, murdered for his pursuit of peace, rapidly gave way to recitation of the dreams of Olympism. Samaranch was welcomed effusively at the UN.[71] The "international community," in the words of the Japanese representative, owed the IOC "a debt of gratitude."[72]

South Africa's recent transition to multiracial democracy, showcased at the 1995 Rugby World Cup, was cited as a testament to the possibility of transformation by the Jamaican representative. So too was Jamaica's bobsled team, its plucky effort to participate, however uncompetitive, in the Winter Games somehow a worthy pairing to the epochal collapse of apartheid.[73] Interspersed in many speeches were forthright endorsements of the intensified crusade against performance-enhancing drugs, even as the most sophisticated doping agent on the market, recombinant human erythropoietin, had quietly wrought a revolution in endurance sport following its approval for market in 1989.

The Iraqi National Olympic Committee's representative, Major General Maki Khamas, sounded a dissonant note. Observing the numerous hymns to peace, solidarity, and human dignity that had preceded him, Khamas complained bitterly about the suspension of his NOC in 1990—a decision that was apparently inexplicable, the consequence of "narrow political reasons," namely the armed invasion and annexation of another sovereign state.[74] He appealed to the ideals of Olympism as a direct riposte to the UN Security Council, whose actions had "worked against the attainment of these [Olympic] objectives." More poignant was his reference to the appalling impact of sanctions on Iraqi civilians. The shortage of items such as "balls, nets, and training equipment," which seemed to be caught in the promiscuous category of dual use, had severely restricted sporting activity in Saddam Hussein's tyrannical state.[75] Massive shortages of food and medical supplies that were affecting Iraq's most vulnerable were not merely a humanitarian crisis; they were preventing the realization of Olympic values. Khamas nevertheless found solace in Samaranch's "tireless efforts to keep sports independent of the policies of vested interests" or at least vested interests, which were not his own.[76]

Partners in Reciprocal Repair: The IOC and the UN, Rebuilding the Broken Faith in Internationalism

Paired with the millennial UN "Alliance of Civilizations" program, which tried but generally failed to find some kind of common bonds between humanity through intercultural dialogue, the UN-Olympic partnership sought to author a language to transcend the division that had riven all other forums and their lexicons.[77] Ten years after the restoration and modernization of the Olympic Truce, the chair of the London Games organizing committee, Sebastian Coe, enthused that sport was "one of those forces which can still offer real hope." He proudly spoke of the "visionary determination" of Samaranch, who had inspired Coe's own violation of the 1980 Olympic boycott.[78]

Although Mishka the bear, herald of the Moscow Games, had not roamed the city since 1980, the Olympics were healthy in Putin's Russia, which had developed (excessively) close links to IOC and International Association of Amateur Federations (IAAF) leadership. As the 2014 Sochi Winter Games approached, the Russian Federation was energetic. Sergei Naryshkin, president of the Duma who would later assure Syria that provision of Russian weapons would not be curtailed, initiated the 2014 truce resolution in his correspondence to the secretary-general.[79] Russia also proposed sport and the Olympic ideal as a vehicle for drug abuse prevention, a resolution that would sit uneasily with the revelations of an extensive state-sanctioned doping program for Russian athletes, with alleged collaboration from members of the IAAF leadership.[80]

The much-advertised flying of the UN flag at the Olympics and the reciprocal IOC representation within the General Assembly hall and in joint com-
muniqués was the solution to maintaining the idea of international exchange
and dialogue as a virtue that would somehow promote peace. With the existence of continuous dialogue in the normal spaces of the UN no longer an
obvious route to global solutions, the theater of the Olympics preserved the
dream of procedural internationalism as coterminous with international
progress. Olympia furnished a terrarium of peoples and nations united in
peace and unity, individual expression, and cross-cultural interaction. This
imaginary order, transparently delusional in the natural world, was still periodically plausible on the artificial playing fields of Olympic-grade Mondo.

Despite the enormous ellipses that were intrinsic to the international idealism espoused by the UN-IOC alliance, it was a demonstration that some
sort of shared utopian aspiration was still possible. The IOC's ethical deficits
had not destroyed its ability to inspire. Pretensions of an ancient creed hewn
from marble remained convincing enough, despite the proven plasticity of
Olympism's meaning. Equally, the UN's vision of genuinely global humanity,
arranged around universal inclusion and indivisible human rights, remained
appealing even if the organization itself seemed incapable of advancing that
vision. A haphazard synthesis between the two, which only needed to pass
the test of public opinion for a few weeks per decade, was a slender platform
for hope. Yet by the close of the twentieth century, with so many alternative
sites of optimism lost, consensus on a pleasing illusion was the best reality
that could be found. As Australian representative Penelope Wensley, then
looking forward to the Sydney Games, stated at the 1997 General Assembly, the omnibus of hope represented by that year's Olympic resolution was a
rare case where no one, anywhere, could find objection. With the twin flags
of the UN and the IOC, "a visible daily reminder of the shared ideals of the
United Nations and of the International Olympic Committee," the message—
of inchoate solidarity in "international cooperation" that could foster peace—
was one "no country could oppose."[81] Unanimity, even confined within the
platitudes that were modern Olympism, was something to celebrate.

Notes

1. Quoted in Dietrich R. Quanz, "Formatting Power of the IOC Founding: The Birth of a
New Peace Movement," *Citius, Altius, Fortius* 3, no. 1 (Winter 1995): 6.

2. Quoted in ibid., 10.

3. See Jean Harvey et al., *Sport and Social Movements: From the Local to the Global*, 93–113 (London: Bloomsbury, 2014).

4. "Olympic Games a True Celebration of Humanity, Secretary General Says," United Nations, August 31, 2000, www.un.org/press/en/2000/20000831.sgsm7523.doc.html.

5. UN Sixth Committee, Report on the Observer Status for the International Olympic Committee in the General Assembly, October 15, 2009, A/64/458; Regarding Observer status for the International Olympic Committee in the General Assembly, letter from the Permanent Representative of Italy to the United Nations addressed to the Secretary-General, July 14, 2009, A/64/145.

6. IOC (President Samaranch), Report on the International Year of Sport and the Olympic Ideal (United Nations), 1994, A/48/720; Statements from UNESCO Director-General, Pierre Sané, in UNESCO, Sport for Development and Peace: Proceedings of the Kingston International Congress, September 13–16, 2008, and Zanzibar Regional Ministerial Roundtable, September 8–10, 2008; UN Human Rights Council, 12/Promoting Human Rights Through Sport and the Olympic Ideal, February 27, 2014, A/HRC/AC/12/L.4; John Ashe, President, General Assembly, "Remarks on Inaugural International Day of Sport for Development and Peace: Celebrating Sport for Development and Peace," 68th session UN GA, New York, April 28, 2014; UN Human Rights Council, Final Report of the Human Rights Council Advisory Committee on the Possibilities of Using Sport and the Olympic Ideal to Promote Human Rights for All and to Strengthen Universal Respect for Them, August 17, 2015, A/HRC/30/50.

7. Since the mid-1990s, a vast catalog of resolutions, collaborative enterprises, and similar sinews have bound the two internationalisms together. For representative and often florid examples of the relationship, philosophy, and rhetoric, see UN General Assembly, International Year of Sport and the Olympic Ideal, A/RES/48/10, November 2, 1993; UN General Assembly, Observance of the Olympic Truce, November 2, 1993, A/RES/48/11; UN General Assembly Plenary, Statement from George Papandreou on "Sport for Peace and Development," November 3, 2003, A/58/PV.52; UN Secretary-General, "Sport for Development and Peace: Mainstreaming a Versatile Instrument," August 9, 2012, A/67/282; H. E. Nassir Abdulaziz Al Nasser, President of the General Assembly, "Remarks at the International Olympic Truce Foundation," Lausanne, Switzerland, May 7, 2012, www.un.org/sport/sites/www.un.org.sport/files/documents/pdfs/Key%20Speeches/2012-05-07_Speech_GA-President_IOTF_Meeting_Lausanne.pdf.

8. On the fascist disposition of the IOC cohort, see John Hoberman, "Toward a Theory of Olympic Internationalism," *Journal of Sports History* 22, no. 1 (1995): 6. On the foundations of postwar internationalism under U.S. suzerainty, see Elizabeth Borgwardt, *A New Deal for the World: America's Vision for Human Rights* (Cambridge, MA: Harvard University Press, 2005).

9. International Olympic Committee, *Olympic Truce File* (Lausanne: International Olympic Committee, [ca. 1994]), 3–5.

10. UN General Assembly, Building a Peaceful and Better World Through Sport, draft resolution, October 22, 1993, A/48/L.9/Rev.1.

11. Ibid., 4.

12. IOC, *Olympism in Action—Sport Serving Humankind* (Lausanne: IOC, Department of International Cooperation and Development, June 2013), 31.

13. For a brief survey see Ingrid Beutler, "Sport Serving Development and Peace: Achieving the Goals of the United Nations Through Sport," in *Sport and Foreign Policy in a Globalizing World*, ed. Steven J. Jackson and Stephen Haigh (London: Routledge, 2009), 11–21.

14. Shana (Nepal), Verbatim Records of the General Assembly Plenary, September 31, 1959, A/PV.800.

15. Summary Records of the Drafting Committee of the Commission on Human Rights, 22nd Meeting, May 5, 1948, E/CN.4/AC.1/SR.22. An implied right to sport, which was certainly within the framework of the kind of society envisaged by its architects, was later discovered within the UN Universal Declaration of Human Rights; see UNESCO—Institute for Education, "UNESCO's Decade of Commitment to Physical Education and Sport," *International Review of Education* 35, no. 1 (1989): 100.

16. William Korey, *NGOs and the Universal Declaration of Human Rights: A Curious Grapevine* (New York: St. Martin's, 1998).

17. Compared against the ample literature on the politics of the Olympics, there is a paucity of work on the IOC's interrelationship with the UN, with the key exception being Nicolien van Luijk's "A Historical Examination of the IOC and UN Partnership: 1952–1980," University of British Columbia, IOC Olympic Studies Centre, Postgraduate Research Program, 2013.

18. For major survey works, predominantly historical in approach, see Allen Guttmann, *The Olympics: A History of the Modern Olympic Games* (Urbana: University of Illinois Press, 2002); Richard Espy, *The Politics of the Olympic Games* (Berkeley: University of California Press, 1981); David Kanin, *A Political History of the Olympic Games* (Boulder, CO: Westview, 1981); Barbara Keys, *Globalizing Sport: National Rivalry and International Community in the 1930s* (Cambridge, MA: Harvard University Press, 2006); Helen Lenskyj, *Inside the Olympic Industry* (Albany: SUNY Press, 2000); Christopher Hill, *Olympic Politics* (Manchester, UK: Manchester University Press, 1992); Lincoln Allison, ed., *The Global Politics of Sport* (Abingdon, UK: Routledge, 2005); Aaron Beacom, *International Diplomacy and the Olympic Movement* (London: Palgrave, 2012); Dikaia Chatziefstathiou and Ian Henry, *Discourses of Olympism: From the Sorbonne 1894 to London 2012* (London: Palgrave, 2012).

19. Even the fully sanctioned history is magisterial in terms of its research. See David Miller, *Athens to Athens: The Official History of the Olympic Games and the IOC* (London: Mainstream, 2003).

20. Lamartine DaCosta, "The Olympic Scholar: Intellectual Purity or Direct Participation?," in *Olympic Studies: Current Intellectual Crossroads*, ed. Lamartine P. DaCosta (Rio: Group of Research on Olympic Studies University Gama Filho, 2002), 289.

21. Andrew Strenk, "What Price Victory? The World of International Sports and Politics," *Annals of the American Academy of Political and Social Science* 445 (September 1979): 128–140.

22. See especially the approach adopted by Keys, *Globalizing Sport*, and Udo Merkel, "The Politics of Physical Culture and German Nationalism: Turnen versus English Sports and French Olympism, 1871–1914," *German Politics & Society* 21, no. 2 (Summer 2003): 69–96. On the modern historiographical approach to international sport, see Allen Guttmann, "Sport, Politics and the Engaged Historian," *Journal of Contemporary History* 38, no. 3 (July 2003): 363–375.

23. Internationalism as a phenomenon is increasingly a vibrant field of historical inquiry; see, e.g., *Internationalism: A Twentieth-Century History*, ed. Patricia Clavin, Sunil Amrith, and Glenda Sluga (Cambridge: Cambridge University Press, 2016).

24. David Zirin, "Burying Juan Antonio Samaranch," *The Nation*, April 22, 2010.

25. Shirley Hazzard, *Countenance of Truth: The United Nations and the Waldheim Case* (New York: Viking, 1990).

26. The trucks are pictured in "The IOC and the United Nations," *Olympic Review XXVI* (October–November 1995), inset editorial page.

27. Amnesty International, *UN Commission on Human Rights: A Time for Deep Reflection*, 2003, AI Index: IOR 41/025/2002.

28. UNESCO, *The Place of Sport in Education* (Paris, 1956); UNESCO International Conference on Youth, August 23–September 1, 1964, ED/211, Paris, 1964; UNESCO, *In Partnership with Youth* (Paris: UNESCO, 1969).

29. For additional detail on these various UNESCO-associated entities, see M. J. Langeveld, "International Council of Sport and Physical Education Seminar at Wassenaar, September 1962," *International Review of Education* 9, no. 1 (1963): 108–110; August Kirsch, "International Council of Sport Science and Physical Education (ICSSPE)," *International Review of Education* 35:1 (1989): 108–111.

30. René Maheu, "Sport Is Education," *UNESCO Courier* 17 (January 1964): 4–10.

31. *Theme: Fair Play and the Amateur in Sport, UNESCO Courier* 17:1 (January 1964); "International Trophies for Fair Play," *UNESCO Courier* 19 (June 1966): 30.

32. President Kekkonen at Jyvaskyla, October 30, 1971, published as "Olympic Games to UNESCO!," *Peace and Violence* 2, no. 1 (1972): 42.

33. For illustration, see René Bazennerye, "International Commission on the Development of Education: Physical Education, Sport and Open-Air Activities ED/76/C/21" (Paris: UNESCO, 1972).

34. René Maheu, "Sport in the Modern World—Chances and Problems," Scientific Congress on Sport, Organizing Committee for the Games of the XX Olympiad, August 24, 1972, Munich, UNESCO DG/72/15.

35. Lord Killanin, *My Olympic Games* (London: Secker and Warburg, 1983), 67–69.

36. Karl Sauvant, "From Economic to Socio-Cultural Emancipation: The Historical Context of the New International Economic Order and the New International Socio-Cultural Order," *Third World Quarterly* 3, no. 1 (1981): 48–61.

37. This prospect of reform was anathema to some, exemplified by one member of the IOC executive who reportedly complained that "we just can't get into the mess of democratizing the committee." See "Defender of the Faith," *Sports Illustrated*, July 24, 1972.

38. UN General Assembly, *Charter of Economic Rights and Duties of States*, December 12, 1974, Resolution 3281; UN General Assembly, *Declaration on the Establishment of a New International Economic Order*, May 1, 1974, Resolution 3201.

39. For elaboration on the architecture of the NIEO, see UNESCO, "Towards a New International Economic and Social Order," *International Social Science Journal* 28, no. 4 (1976); "The Search for a New World Economic Order," special issue, *UNESCO Courier* 29 (October 1976); UN General Assembly, "New International Humanitarian Order," December 16, 1983, A/RES/38/125; "New International Human Order: Moral Aspects of Development," December 19, 1983, A/RES/38/170.

40. The essence of the NWICO/NIIO and its evolution are well documented in UNESCO and UN, *Final Report of the Round Table on a New World Information and Communication Order*, September 14–19, 1983, Igla, A/AC.198/70; UNESCO, *A Documentary History of a New World Information and Communication Order Seen as an Evolving and Continuous Process, 1975–1986* (UNESCO, Paris, ca. 1988); see also the précis of its implications in Mort Rosenblum, "Reporting from the Third World," *Foreign Affairs* 55, no. 4 (July 1977): 815–835.

41. On the prospects of a "New International" in sport, see Aki Hietanen, "Towards a New International Sports Order?," *Current Research on Peace and Violence* 5 (1982): 159–175.

42. Killanin, *My Olympic Games*, 117.

43. Paul Lewis, "Since 1945 UNESCO Has Been a Political Battleground," *New York Times*, December 30, 1983; see, generally, Lawrence Finkelstein, "The Struggle to Control UNESCO,"

in *The United Nations in the World Political Economy*, ed. David Forsythe, 144–164 (London: Palgrave, 1989). See also Jean-Loup Chappelet, *The International Olympic Committee and the Olympic System: The Governance of World Sport* (New York: Routledge, 2008).

44. U.S. Mission Paris to Washington, December 1976, 36715, National Archives and Records Administration Access to Archival Databases and Archives, aad.archives.gov (hereafter AAD).

45. Richard Hoggart, *An Idea and Its Servants: UNESCO from Within* (Oxford: Oxford University Press, 1978). On the politicization already evident at the end of the Maheu era, see William Korey, "On Restoring UNESCO's Raison d'Etre," *New York Times*, April 27, 1975, 205.

46. Concluded as the *International Charter of Physical Education and Sport* (Paris: UNESCO, 1978). For context, see *Final Report of the First International Conference of Ministers and Senior Officials Responsible for Physical Education and Sport in the Education of Youth* (Paris: UNESCO, 1976).

47. John Hennessy, "UNESCO Should Handle Olympics," *Times*, February 4, 1977, 12; "Olympic Games," *Times*, June 14, 1977, 10; "Britain Takes No Chances with UNESCO Sports Group," *Times*, July 9, 1977, 3; John Rodda, "Denis Howell Addresses UNESCO Tomorrow," *The Guardian*, July 7, 1977, 17; "Fears That UN May Be Trying to Control Games," *Times*, June 10, 1978, 16.

48. U.S. Mission Paris to Washington, December 1976, 36715, AAD.

49. U.S. Mission Paris to Washington, "Soviet Performance at UNESCO 19th Conference in Nairobi, October 26–November 30, 1976," January 1977, 01701, AAD.

50. U.S. Mission Paris to Washington, "UNESCO: Soviet View on the International Olympic Committee," August 1978, 24903, AAD.

51. Washington to U.S. Mission Paris, "UNESCO Questionnaire on Physical Education and Sports Prepared for IICPES," February 1978, 039276, AAD.

52. Sam Abt, "Herzog Disturbs IOC with Bid to Alter Rules," *New York Times*, June 19, 1977, 156.

53. Lord Killanin, "Address to 73rd IOC Congress in Maximilianeum, Munich, August 21–24, 1972," *Olympic Review* 59 (October 1972): 400.

54. John Rodda, "Jaw, Not War for IOC," *The Guardian*, March 21, 1978, 24.

55. "UNESCO Assures IOC on Sport-Control Fear," *New York Times*, May 25, 1978, B14.

56. See Barbara Keys, "Political Protection: The International Olympic Committee's UN Diplomacy in the 1980s," *International Journal of the History of Sport* 34, no. 11 (2017): 1161–1178.

57. For the sorts of formulations that were developing in the early 1980s, see "Report by the Intergovernmental Committee for Physical Education and Sport (1981–1983)," 22 C/68, September 12, 1983, Paris; Recommendation 7, "Teaching the Olympic Ideal," 4; Draft Report, Commission I, General Conference, 4th Extraordinary Session, Paris, 1982, 4 XC/COM.I/3. Item 12.4, Promotion of Physical Education and Sport, 36.

58. For examples of the approach characteristic of this period, see "Report by the Intergovernmental Committee for Physical Education and Sport, General Conference," 23rd session, Sofia, June 24, 1985, 23 C/70; "Report by the Intergovernmental Committee for Physical Education and Sport, General Conference," 24th session, Paris, August 6, 1987, 24 C/76.

59. "Address by Frederico Mayor, Director-General UNESCO, Second International Conference of Ministers and Senior Officials Responsible for Physical Education and Sport (MINEPS II)," Moscow, November 21–25, 1988, DG/88/46.

60. For a very anodyne summary of the relationship, see Don Anthony, "The IOC and UNESCO," *Olympic Review* 25, no. 5 (1995), 42–43; Alexandru Sipercu, "On the Right Road to Co-Operation," *Olympic Review* 263–264 (September–October 1989): 454–456.

61. M. Miklas, June 7, 1933, Vienna, *Official Bulletin of the IOC*, 1933, 7.

62. Report of the United Nations Conference on Environment and Development, Rio, June 3–14, 1992, A/CONF. 151/26/Rev.1 (I & II); Amnesty International, Pierre Sané's Address on the outcome of Vienna Conference, June 29, 1993, Cairo, AI Index: NWS 11/74/93.

63. Manoliu (Romania), November 6, 1995, A/50/PV.51.

64. Vyv Simpson and Andrew Jennings, *Lords of the Rings* (New York: Simon and Schuster, 1992).

65. For a brief statement of the basis of the resolution, see IOC (President Samaranch), "Report on the International Year of Sport and the Olympic Ideal," 1994, A/48/720. In it, Samaranch asserted that "the goal of Olympism" was "to contribute to building a peaceful and better world, concerned with the preservation of human dignity." The report cited "the IOC's moral obligation, humanitarian duty and wish to serve the international community . . . so that peace may reign . . . and human suffering cease" ("Report on the International Year," 3, 6). See also Verbatim Records of the General Assembly Plenary, 36th Session, October 25, 1993, A/48/PV.36.

66. Verbatim Records of the General Assembly Plenary, December 7, 1994, A/49/PV.79.

67. See the extensive coverage of United Nations and IOC features across *Olympic Review XXVI* (February–March 1995): 13–24.

68. Andrew Young (Atlanta OOC/USA), December 7, 1994, A/49/PV.79. For procedural origin of agenda item, see Madeline Albright, Letter of November 22, 1994, from Permanent Representative of the US to the United Nations, appending the report prepared by the President of the IOC, describing activities relating to the UN mandated 1994 International Year of Sport and the Olympic Ideal, A/49/720, November 29, 1994.

69. Young (United States/Atlanta OOC), A/49/PV.79.

70. Illueca (Panama), A/49/PV.79.

71. See also "Samaranch at the United Nations," *Olympic Review* 26 (December 1995–January 1996): 4–7.

72. Murayama (Japan), November 6, 1995, A/50/PV.51.

73. Ibid.

74. Khamas (Iraq), A/50/PV.51.

75. Ibid. For context on the impact of the sanctions in humanitarian terms, see "Explanatory Memorandum Regarding the Comprehensive Embargo on Iraq," Human Rights Watch, January 14, 2000, www.hrw.org/news/2000/01/14/explanatory-memorandum-regarding -comprehensive-embargo-iraq.

76. Khamas (Iraq), A/50/PV.51.

77. United Nations Alliance of Civilizations, www.unaoc.org/.

78. Coe's statements are reproduced in the exultant press release on the 2012 Olympic Truce, UN Department of Public Information, "Record Number of Delegations in General Assembly Back Resolution on Building Peaceful, Better World 'Through Sport and the Olympic Ideal,'" GA/11158, October 17, 2011. The boycott had been strongly encouraged by Thatcher and strongly discouraged by Coe's then ownership of multiple world leading times in the middle-distance events. In terms of personal triumph, the brave decision to eschew Tory policy was vindicated by the receipt of both a gold (1,500 meters) and silver (800 meters) medal in Moscow, ascent to the upper echelons of the Conservative Party, the eventual award of a peerage, and presidency of the IAAF. Sebastian Coe, *Running My Life* (London: Hodder and Stoughton, 2012), 119–139, 309.

79. Regarding "Sport for Peace and Development: Building a Peaceful and Better World Through Sport and the Olympic Ideal," see the letter dated February 7, 2014, from the Permanent

Representative of the Russian Federation to the United Nations to the Secretary-General, February 11, 2014, A/68/744.

80. UN Commission on Narcotic Drugs, Russian Federation: draft resolution, Sport for drug abuse prevention: promoting a drug-free society through sport and the Olympic ideal, February 14, 2014, Vienna, E/CN.7/2014/L.4; cf. Jack Robertson and Richard McLaren, *Independent Commission Investigation Reports I & II, 9 November 2015 & 14 January 2016* (World Anti-Doping Agency), final published version January 27, 2016.

81. Wensley (Australia), November 25, 1997, A/52/PV.54.

PART II

The Rise of Human Rights

CHAPTER 5

Reframing Human Rights

Amnesty International, Human Rights Watch, and International Sport

Barbara J. Keys

In recent years sport mega-events have attracted the attention of the two most influential global human rights organizations, Amnesty International (AI) and Human Rights Watch (HRW). Since the turn of the last century, the two groups have published hundreds of reports, held conferences, staged demonstrations, gathered celebrity endorsements, and intensively lobbied governments, the United Nations (UN), and major sports organizations, all in the name of improving the human rights outcomes of sport mega-events. These large-scale campaigns have exposed many people to ideas and arguments about human rights. By virtue of their huge visibility and impact, sport-related campaigns have had a substantial but unrecognized influence on the ways that human rights are perceived around the world.[1] At the same time, AI and HRW are gatekeepers: because of their prestige and the resources they command, they have considerable power to determine which human rights issues matter at the international level and can expand or constrict the public audience for many thousands of individuals and groups concerned with human rights worldwide.[2]

Although AI and HRW would seem to be antagonists of the International Olympic Committee (IOC) and other sport organizations, the relationship between these two types of nongovernmental organization (NGO)—one devoted to human rights, the other concerned with sport—is not entirely adversarial. Human rights campaigns have often been conducted in an optimistic key that reinforces some of the mythology around international sport, including that major sports events are a force for good (even if they need to do more to fulfill that potential). This stance aligns with the human rights movement's basic strategy. As one HRW staffer described, the goal is to get governments to agree to uphold human rights, even if they have no intention of doing so, and then to "work the gap": pushing governments to bring reality into line with rhetoric.[3] In the view of activists, the IOC has already made such promises in the form of the Olympic Charter's espousal of "universal fundamental ethical values."

This approach creates a conflict. AI and HRW read the IOC's "universal fundamental ethical values" as synonymous with "human rights." The IOC sees its ethical values in an entirely different way: not as specifically enumerated rights but as diffuse philosophical principles related to sport. Despite the clear difference in meaning, the IOC has moved toward greater acceptance of human rights, as both sides have come to recognize that a degree of cooperation can have mutual benefits.

Human rights groups do not represent a united front. AI and HRW have some common aims, but they also compete for status, attention, and resources and have tried to differentiate their approaches to sport mega-events in ways that accentuate their respective "brands."[4] HRW was the first to target sport mega-events, in the early 1990s. AI then tried to play catch-up in the 2000s. In 2008 and 2014 as both mounted extensive Olympic-related campaigns, they competed for attention. More recently, they have sometimes worked together. In early 2015 after the controversies of the Sochi 2014 Winter Olympic Games, AI and HRW banded together with other rights-oriented groups, trade unions, and sports bodies to create the Sport and Rights Alliance, dedicated to putting human rights pressure on sport mega-events.[5]

Sports bodies have reacted to growing human rights pressure in inconsistent and sometimes contradictory ways, combining, as John Hoberman aptly writes, "grandiosity and cluelessness."[6] At first they flatly rejected broad human rights demands, citing long-standing arguments that sport should not be politicized and construing their mandate as relating very narrowly to sport issues. In the 1990s, the growing dominance of human rights language intersected with corruption scandals, commercialization, and skyrocketing hosting costs to push both the IOC and the world soccer federation, the Fédération Internationale de Football Association (FIFA), toward greater alignment with human rights goals, although they typically took refuge in vague assertions that staging major events necessarily leads repressive host countries toward reform.

More recently, AI and HRW have adopted more proactive stances, at least on paper. In 2017 as adverse publicity mounted about deaths of migrant workers constructing World Cup 2022 venues in Qatar, FIFA established a human rights advisory board composed of outside experts.[7] The IOC now meets regularly with human rights groups. Signaling its recognition of human rights as a global moral lingua franca, in the Olympic Agenda 2020 adopted in late 2014, the IOC copied language from Article 2 of the UN Universal Declaration of Human Rights into the Olympic Charter's revised nondiscrimination clause. Beginning in 2024, host city contracts will include a requirement to prohibit discrimination and to "protect and respect human rights."[8] To what extent the IOC might use its leverage with host cities to extract real reforms remains unclear.[9]

Public debates over human rights and sport mega-events in the last three decades have been framed around a recurring debate: one side has argued that hosting sport mega-events is an inducement to reform, while the other side has countered that hosting such events leads to increased repression. After the 2008 Beijing Olympic Games, the weight of opinion began to shift toward the second view. Yet measuring human rights outcomes is difficult. It is always possible to point to some improvements to counter instances of repression.[10] Setting up a simple dichotomy between reform and repression obscures more than it reveals. Another central debate has been over which human rights issues matter most. Some human rights groups have focused on human rights outcomes that are directly tied to the staging of sports events: treatment of workers building the venues, evictions for new construction, removal of "undesirables," and freedom of the press and of speech during the events. Others, though, have made much broader claims, as AI did before the 2008 Games—arguing, for example, that any host country must have a human rights record across the board that makes it "worthy" of hosting an international event. In this case too, an either-or approach is unhelpful. All host cities engage in actions that diminish human rights protections before and during sport mega-events, and all host cities are situated in countries with some human rights problems. The issue is not whether problems exist; it is where to draw the line.

Human rights pressures on sport mega-events began in earnest in the 1990s, but the controversial 1936 Berlin Olympic Games and the 1980 Moscow Olympics set important precedents. Awarded to Berlin before the Nazi takeover, the 1936 Games inspired the first debate about the relationship between the Olympics and human rights. Pressure groups sometimes used the term "human rights" to protest aspects of the Berlin Games and support calls for a boycott. Many of the U.S. and European groups that advocated a boycott limited their concerns to fairness in the selection of teams, specifically the exclusion of Jews from the German team, but others cited broad human rights concerns that extended beyond the playing field. In the United States, the Non-Sectarian Anti-Nazi League to Champion Human Rights argued that American athletes should not participate in the Games because of the "brutalities" of the regime.[11] Among the liberal groups and individuals in the proboycott Committee for Fair Play in Sport, some limited their arguments to sport issues, citing discrimination against Jewish athletes in Germany, while others suggested that regardless of German treatment of athletes, broader patterns of discrimination under the Nazi regime justified nonparticipation in the Games.[12]

This brief efflorescence around the notion that the Olympic Games carried a broader social responsibility to combat repression was not repeated for nearly half a century.[13] The UN's adoption of the Universal Declaration of Human Rights in 1948 seemed irrelevant to sports. No human rights outcry was raised when Mexican police killed hundreds of protesting students on the eve of the 1968 Mexico City Games. As Robert Skinner describes in this volume, the IOC banned South Africa from 1964 to 1988 and anti-apartheid boycott campaigns pressed moral claims on sport mega-events, but the campaigns differed in key respects from later efforts fought under the banner of human rights. South African racism raised issues directly related to athletic competition, because apartheid laws affected black South African athletes directly and visibly in ways that grossly violated the Olympic Charter's stricture, first introduced in 1949, against racial, religious, and political discrimination.[14] Anti-apartheid activists sometimes cited human rights, but they framed claims more often in terms of equality and antiracism.[15]

"Human rights" became a popular slogan in the 1970s, when it became strongly associated with activism against torture and political imprisonment.[16] Soviet dissidents were partly responsible for the rise of human rights language, having adopted it for their own struggles beginning in the late 1960s.[17] Andrei Sakharov, Aleksandr Solzhenitsyn, and others, who were seen in the West as moral heroes, helped spur a global wave of human rights activism. The plight of Soviet Jews, persecuted but often refused the right to emigrate, became a prominent moral cause in the West beginning in the late 1960s, and in 1975 the Soviet Union signed the Helsinki Accords, which included human rights provisions. These circumstances virtually guaranteed that when

Moscow was awarded the 1980 Games, the event would attract human rights-related attention. Already in the mid-1970s after the IOC awarded the Games to Moscow, some Jewish groups in Europe and the United States argued that oppression of dissidents and Jewish and other religious minorities made the country an unfit host.[18] In 1978 the California State Assembly, some members of the U.S. Congress, and a resolution at the European Parliament called for moving the Games on human rights grounds.[19]

Yet AI, which had become the world's most respected human rights organization on the heels of winning the Nobel Peace Prize in 1977, avoided taking a position on the Games and sometimes seemed to go out of its way to avoid even mentioning the event.[20] AI's headquarters adhered to the position articulated in 1977: "Sometimes various organizations ask Amnesty International to support boycott campaigns directed against this or that government. We have always refused to go down this path. We have also refused to advocate reductions in aid to regimes that violate human rights."[21]

AI's London leadership seems to have seen the Games only as a marginal "opportunity . . . to draw public attention to particular human rights abuses in the USSR."[22] In an October 1979 open letter to Soviet premier Leonid Brezhnev timed to coincide with the anniversary of the 1917 Russian Revolution and Olympic preparations, AI briefly suggested that imprisoned dissidents were being transferred away from Moscow to prevent any possible contact with Olympic visitors and that such actions violated "the model of peace and friendship as presented in the ideals of the Olympic movement." But this mild hint that hosting the Games might come with obligations was offset by the group's insistence that it took no position on boycotts and saw the Games, like the soccer World Cup just held in repressive Argentina, simply "as an opportunity to inform public opinion."[23]

AI's 1980 report, issued after a preventive crackdown on dissent that observers had linked to Games preparation, spent eight pages on the Soviet Union without mentioning the Olympics except for a reference to a Soviet (TASS) press bulletin about the Games and without connecting the increase in repression that AI observed with the preparations for the event.[24] Likewise, the April 1980 edition of an AI report on Soviet "prisoners of conscience," though timed to garner more publicity because of the upcoming Games, made no specific reference to the event.[25] (Even so, as Dmitry Dubrovskiy notes in this volume, AI's criticisms were enough to make Soviet intelligence label the group as one of several "anti-Soviet" Olympic saboteurs in the West.)

HRW did not exist at the time of the 1980 Games and so did not take a position on them. It would not be until 1988 that the various watch groups—Helsinki Watch, founded in 1979; its affiliated Americas Watch, founded in 1981; and Asia Watch, founded in 1985—joined together as HRW. But Helsinki Watch used human rights arguments to *oppose* the boycott effort that U.S. president Jimmy Carter inaugurated after the Soviet Union invaded Afghanistan in December 1979. Helsinki Watch argued that Carter's boycott violated the rights of athletes and the Helsinki Accords' provision to work toward "freer movement and contacts."[26]

The stances taken by AI and Helsinki Watch appear timid compared with those of other groups concerned with human rights issues, many of which were much more likely to call for a boycott—even before Carter made his call on the basis of national security issues—and framed Soviet repression as a direct contradiction of Olympic ideals.[27] Jewish groups and individuals made heartfelt appeals, often using human rights language, calling for the Games to be removed on explicitly human rights grounds. As one American wrote to the IOC, the event "should be removed from Moscow to a free country where basic human rights are respected."[28] A resolution presented to the Political Affairs Committee of the European Parliament urged the IOC "to declare that in the future, the Games will not be held in any country in which human rights, as decided in the UN's Universal Declaration of Human Rights of 1948 and in the European Convention of Human Rights, are not adequately respected."[29] But a group in the U.S. Congress took a different point of view: "We do not expect the [IOC] to assure basic human rights to all citizens of its member countries, nor do we expect the IOC to enforce the Helsinki agreement. However, if the Olympics symbolizes anything, it is the notion that the individual surmounts political ideology and international borders, and that the individual should be allowed freedom of expression." On those grounds, the group suggested, "it would seem to be a gross perversion to allow the Soviet government to use the 1980 Games as a means to subvert the true meaning of the Olympics."[30]

The IOC sidestepped this pressure. As hundreds of letters poured in demanding that the Games be taken away from Moscow, the IOC dismissed their concerns as irrelevant because "the Olympic Games were awarded to Moscow purely on a sporting basis in view of the contribution of Soviet sportsmen and administrators to the Olympic Movement."[31] The organization advised letter writers to bring complaints to their national Olympic committees, not the IOC.[32]

In contrast to AI and Helsinki Watch, then, some Westerners did start to demand that Olympic hosts meet human rights criteria. But such concerns waned immediately after 1980. The application of human rights standards to the Moscow Games, though limited, was a product of the high visibility accorded to Soviet human rights issues in the Western press but was also an artifact of the Cold War. The notion that human rights standards might also be applied to host countries that were Western allies in the Cold War seems to have occurred only to a small handful of people. In 1981, only a year after the South Korean dictatorship had massacred hundreds of student demonstrators, the IOC awarded the 1988 Olympic Games to Seoul. No one questioned the decision on human rights grounds. Leading up to the Games, the Chun Doo-hwan regime used arbitrary arrests, torture, strict media censorship, and repeated impositions of martial law to maintain order.[33]

When unrest raised the prospect of repression on the eve of the Games, Western media and politicians expressed concern about security issues, but human rights groups hardly noticed. Reverend Jesse Jackson, a civil rights activist and likely Democratic presidential candidate, declared that he would urge a boycott "while the human rights of students, the labor rights of workers and the political rights of the political opposition in South Korea are being so violently oppressed." He told the press that "We should not be in the position of rewarding violators of human rights with an international sports festival and a political facelift."[34] The North American Coalition for Human Rights, representing forty mostly religious organizations in the United States, campaigned "to make Korea fit for the Olympics."[35] Media coverage, however, was minimal, and the notion that the Olympics should require human rights standards of hosts resonated only with a small handful of people.[36] The IOC received far more protests about Korean treatment of cats and dogs than about human rights.[37]

Neither AI nor Asia Watch, soon to become part of HRW, pressed the Olympic issue. Both organizations issued reports on human rights conditions in South Korea, but neither mentioned the Olympics in more than a peripheral way. AI's April 1988 report on human rights in South Korea did not mention the Olympics.[38] AI considered a suggestion from shoemaker Reebok, which provided a $2 million advance for AI's 1987 Human Rights Now! world rock music tour, to buy half the advertising time for the 1988 Olympic Games to promote human rights and AI simultaneously but quashed the idea out of concerns about associating AI's brand with a corporation.[39] Asia Watch issued reports in 1985 and 1987 detailing continued repression but without calling for the Games to be used as a pressure point.[40] Later asked why, staffer Richard Dicker said, "Maybe we just didn't think of it."[41]

As unrest mounted in South Korea, its leaders chose reform over repression to avoid embarrassment on the eve of the Olympic Games. A visit by IOC president Juan Antonio Samaranch in June 1988 may have played an important role, though we do not know what he said. The end result was a set of sweeping reforms, including the first democratic elections in the country's history.[42]

The Seoul Games, despite the paucity of human rights discussions, would retroactively be lauded as a major human rights breakthrough because the Games catalyzed democratic reforms. But the real watershed moment for human rights and sport mega-events came after the end of the Cold War and was deeply intertwined with Western anxieties about a rising China in the new world order. In 1993, HRW played a substantial role in embedding a link between human rights and international sport in popular consciousness when it mounted a major and ultimately successful campaign against Beijing's bid to host the 2000 Olympic Games.[43] The effort seems to have swayed the narrow vote that awarded the event to Sydney instead of Beijing, making the outcome perhaps the single most consequential case of an NGO's thwarting the ambitions of a major power. The collapse of communist rule in Eastern Europe in 1989 and then in the Soviet Union in 1991 contrasted with a very different outcome in communist China, where the regime sent tanks into Tiananmen Square to crush a student-led prodemocracy movement. With the world watching, horrified, on television, hundreds of demonstrators were killed and thousands arrested.[44] In these conditions, HRW and other human rights groups turned to China with new intensity. The Olympic bidding also coincided with internal shifts in HRW, including new leadership and changes in strategy.[45] In a post-Cold War world in which human rights advocacy needed new audiences and new media-friendly messages, HRW's involvement in Olympic affairs was a savvy way to buttress the group's power and prestige.

What made HRW's 1993 innovation so consequential was that it decisively transformed the debate about the moral responsibilities associated with sport mega-events. Instead of talking about issues directly connected to athletes and sports arenas, HRW widened the lens to encompass a country's treatment of all of its citizens. Previously such talk had been muted and sporadic; now it became widespread. HRW's 1993 campaign addressed a limited set of human rights and targeted only the hosting country, but its implications were dazzlingly broad. Because human rights is an extraordinarily expansive concept, HRW opened the door to a nearly limitless range of moral claims on the Olympics.

The People's Republic of China (PRC) under Jiang Zemin staked enormous prestige on its bid to host the Games.[46] China's leaders saw the 2000 Olympics as a way to cement the country's status as a global power at the beginning of the new millennium and repair the reputational damage inflicted by the Tiananmen Square massacre. Beijing was the clear favorite of IOC president Samaranch, who dreamed of the diplomatic coup of bringing China to the world stage—and, most likely, of the probable financial windfall for the IOC.[47] Quite reasonably, given that human rights had barely surfaced in Olympic discussions since 1980, the PRC failed to anticipate that its bid would provoke an outcry on human rights grounds. Wei Jizhong, secretary-general of the Chinese Olympic Committee, told a reporter in 1993 that "I have looked through all the Olympic charter and there is nothing to do with human rights."[48]

The anti-Beijing campaign began when the IOC announced its short list of candidates in February and gathered steam as the September vote approached. The European Parliament passed a resolution urging that Beijing be rejected on human rights grounds. The Paris-based Alliance for a Democratic China compared the prospect of a Beijing 2000 Olympic Games to the infamous 1936 "Nazi" Olympics.[49] UK foreign minister Douglas Hurd declared that Beijing would be a "bad choice."[50] Within China dissidents split over the issue, with some arguing that the Olympics provided an opportunity to open China and others fearing that it would lead to repression.[51]

The loudest opposition came from the United States, and HRW's sustained campaign to stop Beijing was the largest mounted by any group. Still reluctant to advocate sanctions, AI took a quiet and only implicitly oppositional approach.[52] AI issued reports on human rights abuses in China, and its representatives testified to Congress about a "human rights crisis in China." Before the bid vote, AI warned that a Beijing Olympics might lead to a flood of executions of political prisoners, and an AI delegation also met with the IOC leadership to express concern. But the organization took no public stand in opposition to the bid. In contrast, HRW was "a prime mover" in the push to block Beijing.[53] Smaller U.S.-based groups, such as the International Campaign for Tibet and the Alliance for Democracy in China, also mobilized against Beijing, but HRW's preexisting size, clout, and credibility ensured that its views dominated media attention.[54]

HRW's campaign made the case that broad obligations ought to come with hosting the Games. As HRW staff attorney Richard Dicker told the press, "It's way past due. . . . We want to change the attitude that this is sports and it has nothing to do with politics."[55] Although the Olympic campaign cost far less than other HRW efforts—where China was concerned, HRW devoted more resources to the high-stakes annual review of most favored nation trading status—in some respects it had bigger payoffs. In addition to its likely influence on the IOC's vote, the campaign brought HRW much new and favorable publicity: one in four mentions of HRW in U.S. media outlets in 1993 was about the anti-Beijing campaign.[56] The method, as Dicker described it, was "to move the issue from the sports page to the editorial page to the front page," in the process reaching people not yet drawn to human rights. "Nobody needed any explanation of the Olympic Games," he said, making it "a huge opportunity to engage a very different segment of the population."[57]

HRW's anti-Beijing campaign played to the group's strengths and weaknesses. Because it was not a mass organization, HRW was nimbler than AI, which was constrained through the 1990s by a narrow mandate. In the 1980s, for example, HRW devised a way to apply human rights standards to armed conflicts, effectively inventing a new field for human rights advocacy. In the words of a 1993 external report, HRW staffers viewed their group "as the place where innovative approaches to human rights are conceived and carried out" and valued its "adventurous, pioneering nature [that pushed] the boundaries of the field to stay on the leading edge of human rights."[58]

Although at least one HRW staffer suggested that the Olympics might bring publicity that would deter the government from large-scale arrests and give dissidents some breathing room, the group's position on the 1993 bid was unequivocal—a result, Dicker explained, of the temporal proximity to the Tiananmen Square massacre.[59] But the anti-Beijing campaign was also conditioned by HRW's efforts to secure continued relevance. HRW is concerned with not only promoting values but also, like all organizations, ensuring its own growth and influence. In 1993 HRW was coping with internal upheaval wrought by a post-Cold War enlargement of its ambitions, staff numbers, and scope. The group's chief fund-raiser and executive director, Aryeh Neier, left in May, and his successor Kenneth Roth worked to bring the once-independent watch committees more firmly under a unitary HRW name. The organization was debating how far to internationalize its targets or whether stick to what historian Bart De Sutter calls the "Neier Doctrine": leveraging the power of the United States to promote human rights. An

Olympic campaign offered the chance to do both.[60] In 1993, HRW was also experiencing a revenue shortfall. Unlike AI, with its mass membership base, HRW was precariously dependent on four major funders that tended to measure impact in terms of headlines, giving HRW an incentive to play to issues with strong media appeal.[61]

In targeting China, HRW was choosing a popular target of American ire. For years after the Tiananmen Square events, the dominant emotions in American opinion toward China were hostility, indignation, and disgust. China became a hot-button issue in American politics, with China-bashing again a favored pastime in Congress.[62] As a China specialist described, in the early 1990s the American love-hate relationship with China swung sharply in one direction. "When things are going well with China, and China is being good," he said, "Americans think China is wonderful. It's all panda bears, and rosy-cheeked kindergarten children. . . . And then when China does something bad, like Tiananmen, then China can do no right. There is this overwhelming desire . . . to somehow punish and correct China."[63]

HRW's efforts helped spur unprecedented levels of media coverage on human rights issues connected to the Olympics. In the United States, newspapers ran hundreds of articles; television news gave the issue prime-time coverage.[64] A few dissenting voices chastised HRW for "mixing sports and politics," and a minority argued for holding the Games in Beijing as a spur to reform, but the vast majority of the U.S. media reporting toed the line that HRW took, repeating its arguments, quoting its spokespeople, and playing to the public's desire to "punish" China.[65] Beijing's formal bid application, for example, guaranteed that no organizations would emerge in China to oppose the Olympics, and HRW seized on this "extraordinary assertion" as evidence that the PRC would suppress free speech if awarded the Games. HRW cited the Chinese statement throughout the campaign, turning this element of Beijing's bid into perhaps the single most widely quoted statement in media coverage of the bid.[66] Immediately before the IOC vote, leading voices such as the *New York Times* and *Washington Post* ran editorials urging a "no" vote on Beijing—the *New York Times* no fewer than three editorials in two days. Citing HRW information and echoing its arguments, the *Times* wrote that China did not deserve to sponsor the Olympics because of the "overriding issue" of human rights.[67]

HRW's diplomacy targeted all major stakeholders in the Olympic Games: the media, national governments, the IOC, and Olympic corporate sponsors. Dicker issued press releases, gave interviews, and called sportswriters. HRW wrote to U.S. IOC member Anita DeFrantz to warn that China would suppress free speech at the Games, threatened to pressure athletes to boycott the Games if Beijing won, and kept up a drumbeat of reports on political prisoners.[68] When the IOC met to vote in Monte Carlo, Dicker was there, sitting in hotel lobbies and pressing new stories of Chinese human rights abuses on the nine hundred assembled journalists.[69]

In an unprecedented effort, the organization took aim at the lifeblood of the Olympic Games by drawing into the controversy major Olympic sponsors, including Coca-Cola, Visa International, Eastman Kodak, Xerox, and Time Warner. These advertisers, which under the IOC's marketing model place the Olympic rings on their products and advertisements, were willing to pay large sums to associate their brands with ideals such as excellence, peace, and solidarity, making them sensitive to the tarnishing of those ideals.[70] A month before the IOC vote Bernstein wrote to major sponsors about human rights abuses in China, warning that a Beijing Olympics would tarnish their images.[71] It was a savvy move that hit at one of the Beijing bid's greatest strengths: the desire of Olympic advertisers for privileged access to China's booming market.[72]

HRW's case against the bid was underpinned by the conviction that universal human rights was now firmly established as a global moral standard, and as such they should apply to everyone, including China and the Olympic Games. Impatience courses through many of HRW's statements: it was *time* for human rights. Bernstein wrote that rights had attained fundamental importance in the world today, so "it is past time" that they be part of the Olympic Games. As Deputy Director Kenneth Roth put it in April, the world was now "freed from the highly charged political considerations of the Cold War," so the IOC "can and should" now take human rights into consideration.[73] A *Washington Post* editorial illustrated this brand of human rights triumphalism: "This is 1993. The world is changing. Large-scale systemic human rights violations are incompatible with the conduct of a nation seeking status as a late-20th century Olympics host."[74]

In keeping with HRW's practice of calling for sanctions to punish human rights violators, the organization argued that giving the Games to Beijing was wrong because it would "reward" China for repression. HRW pushed the idea that hosting a major event had to be "earned"; countries had to "deserve" it. Respect for human rights should be a consideration for the IOC, HRW argued, "so that especially abusive governments are not rewarded."[75]

HRW used emotional appeals to paint China's continuing repression as a kind of arrogance toward the West. Dicker, for example, characterized

Chinese statements about a lack of internal opposition to the bid as "astounding" and "boast[ful]."[76] Referring to Chen Xitong's appointment, Dicker claimed: "Here you have a country that just four years ago horrified the world with its human rights policies. . . . The fellow who was out greeting the IOC delegates when they visited Beijing is the same fellow who was in no small part responsible for the events at Tiananmen. That is so insensitive, that is so arrogant, it is astounding."[77]

What did HRW mean by human rights? Although HRW monitored an expansive range of civil and political rights, its Olympic campaign focused on detention and maltreatment of dissidents. When giving examples, HRW cited the Tiananmen Square events and the arrests, imprisonment, and torture of men who opposed the communist dictatorship. The selection of abuses was deliberate. As Dicker explains, the idea was to keep the public eye on the consequences that continued to flow from the 1989 massacre.[78]

Linking human rights to Olympic ideals proved tricky. Like the Chinese, HRW could find no mention of human rights in the Olympic Charter. The most direct argument that HRW could come up with was the weak claim that because China practiced discrimination "on the basis of political ideas," political repression should be considered a violation of the charter's ban on discrimination.[79] Other Olympic ideals were harder to press into service on behalf of human rights protection. Peace and international goodwill were too vague to be used as prohibitions on political imprisonment. But HRW paid homage to Olympic mythology with references to "Olympic values" and "the Olympic spirit."[80] As Dicker recalls, it was not so much that the IOC made claims that could be leveraged to support human rights promotion but that its own self-portrayal as "loftier than the angels in heaven" made it vulnerable to moral claims.[81]

HRW's position aligned with that of the U.S. government. As a presidential candidate, Bill Clinton had criticized the George H. W. Bush administration for "coddling" the "butchers of Beijing," and when Clinton came to office his rhetoric pushed Sino-American relations to a new low.[82] The administration did not come out officially against Beijing's bid signaled opposition with little subtlety. Congress took a more overtly oppositional stand.[83] In the Senate, New Jersey Democrat and former Olympian Bill Bradley led the campaign, declaring that "I don't think it's right to give the games to a country that imprisons and tortures political dissidents. I think it's one way the world can say that we don't approve of the gross disregard of human rights that takes place in China."[84]

The PRC was outraged, and IOC officials resented the "political" pressure. Samaranch commented irritably that he found it "difficult to understand why a country that has given China most favored nation status to develop its trade with it, asks us today not to give it the Games."[85] Several IOC officials, including DeFrantz, suggested that if hosting the Games had been conditioned on meeting human rights standards, Atlanta and Los Angeles might never have been chosen.[86]

The IOC initially underestimated HRW's campaign, as evidenced by its dismissive attitude toward HRW's early appeals. In 1993 the IOC's response to hundreds of letters about human rights in China became more mollifying: by May, with media pressure intensifying, the IOC was assuring letter writers that human rights would be a factor in the vote.[87] The IOC hired a lobbyist to push Congress to water down the protest statements that members were drafting.[88] Samaranch, like many others in the Olympic leadership, professed to believe that China's staging of the Games would lead to reforms.[89] As his close colleague Dick Pound put it, "If you really want to influence a change in the behavior of China, [the Olympics are] a way to do so. It's a made-in-heaven opportunity."[90] But Sydney bid head Rod McGeoch was closer to the mark: he recalls having the impression that the IOC's top brass felt that human rights were simply irrelevant—they were "not part of our world."[91]

In September 1993 when the IOC awarded Sydney the Games by a slender two-vote margin, HRW's press release exulted that "It was impossible for the IOC to ignore China's egregious human rights record. This decision puts the Chinese leadership on notice that they will pay a price for the continued abuse of their own citizens."[92] Although it is impossible to determine what swayed members, whose votes remained secret, the PRC attributed responsibility for its defeat to the human rights campaign. Many Chinese saw a U.S. plot to undermine China, and the loss increased anti-American sentiment.[93] Western media attributed the outcome to human rights concerns, and this explanation for Beijing's failure soon became an entrenched part of the narrative. When Beijing bid again, media reporting almost invariably attributed its earlier loss to human rights concerns.

HRW's 1993 success helped entrench the notion that hosting sport mega-events entailed broad human rights responsibilities, and since then both HRW and AI have campaigned around every Olympic Games and more recently around other sport mega-events, including the soccer World Cup. For example, when Atlanta pressed "the human rights angle" in its successful bid for the 1996 Olympic Games, referring to the U.S. civil rights movement, both AI and HRW jumped on the claim. The groups used the Atlanta Games to draw attention to human rights shortcomings in Georgia: AI especially to the death penalty and its racially discriminatory application and HRW to a broad spectrum of abuses from removal of homeless people to antigay ordinances.[94] HRW acknowledged that "human rights issues may seem unrelated to a sporting event" but argued that "a country that wishes to participate in the world sporting system should also participate in the international human rights system. And strive to meet the standards of that system."[95]

The level of attention that the groups have devoted to hosting by dictatorships is on a distinctively different level, and China in particular has come in for more scrutiny than any other host. In 2001 as Beijing bid for the 2008 Games against Toronto and Paris, human rights assumed a prominent place in discussions around the bid, still with a good deal of confusion and ambiguity. Further removed from the Tiananmen Square massacre and with the PRC's growing economic power and its imminent entry into the World Trade Organization, predictions that Beijing would succeed were borne out when the IOC selected it in a landslide. Bowing to the inevitable, President George W. Bush's administration took a low-key stance toward Beijing's bid, and opposition from Congress was muted. Yet human rights was also more firmly embedded as a global moral lingua franca: U.S. IOC member Anita DeFrantz, for example, said that she had read AI and HRW human rights reports relevant to all bid cities.[96]

Neither AI nor HRW opposed Beijing's new bid outright, even though they concurred that the overall human rights situation was worse than in 1993. HRW took a much more low-key approach to this second bid than it had in 1993, suggesting that the IOC should use the opportunity to push for reform. AI was much more vocal and, while not overtly oppositional, implicitly conveyed the message that China's human rights failings made it unworthy of hosting the Games.[97]

AI and HRW correctly judged that China was unlikely to be voted down a second time and that an oppositional stance would diminish their capacity to press for reforms before and during the Games. They worried that a boycott effort would spur a hypernationalist counterreaction in China.[98] The PRC's approach this time around was quite different. Its representatives had learned their lesson about human rights and now were willing to make necessary gestures. In the oral bid presentation to the IOC voting session, for example, China's representative claimed that the Olympics would help the "development" of human rights.[99] HRW also decided that the most effective strategy for addressing a sport-minded audience was not outright condemnation but instead an optimistic approach that played to sport fans' conviction that sport was a force for good. HRW noted that "There can be a positive impact on a tightly controlled society from hosting an international event."[100] Putting it another way, an HRW official commented that "we didn't want to rain on the parade."[101] Both AI and HRW emphasized the moral value of the Games and the prospect that they would lead to reform as long as the world kept up its pressure.

As HRW had been in 1993, AI in the years around 2001 was in the midst of internal restructuring and soul-searching about its mission. Whereas HRW had a small staff focused on research and writing reports, the older and somewhat better-known AI had developed a mass membership base of about 300,000. HRW and AI's U.S. section competed directly for donors.[102] AI was, as HRW's director acknowledged in 2002, "in a class by itself" when it came to resources. But HRW had responded much more easily than AI to the media-driven climate of the 1990s. Around 2001, the aim of many AI staffers was "institutional change . . . from statis to motion, from organization to movement, from impartiality to advocacy." One of the new ideas put forward was "strategic coverage," which meant that even though human rights were equally important everywhere, but it was necessary to "operationalize them [human rights] in a way that's contemporary and relevant." AI now put more emphasis on impact, as measured by media coverage, and aimed to shift from its primarily country-focused approach to a more thematic one. The challenge was "remaining a relevant and influential international movement within an increasingly complex and sophisticated human rights environment." Part of the solution was "human rights constituency building."[103] Targeting the Olympic Games fit beautifully within this broader reorientation.

As the event drew close, both AI and HRW found that discussing human rights at the Olympics was no longer a choice; the issue was thrust upon them, in the recollection of one HRW staffer. They "had to take it on" because everyone knew the event was going to have human rights implications.[104] It was a testament to the newfound power of this moral language that every major event was now seen through a human rights lens. The number of groups using human rights as a pressure point had vastly expanded. One group listed a dozen major "Olympics Advocacy Campaigns," including the broad campaigns by AI and HRW as well as more focused campaigns by groups and coalitions working for Tibetan autonomy, workers' rights, media freedom in China, an end to Chinese support for Sudanese repression in Darfur, and an end to persecution of the Falun Gong.[105] The capacity of such groups to tarnish the Games was on vivid display during the torch relay. As the Olympic flame traveled from Olympia, Greece, around the world to China, it was met with dramatic protests in London, Paris, India, and elsewhere, creating a public relations crisis for the IOC and the PRC.[106]

AI's reporting on the Games premised its demands on China's alleged promise during the bidding to promote human rights and on the Olympic Charter's "respect for universal fundamental ethical principles." The reports focused on rights problems described as having "direct connection" to hosting the Games, but the demands for reform were wide: abolition of the death penalty, reform of the judicial system, freedom of expression and of association, and justice for victims of the 1989 crackdown, along with "freedom from forced eviction."[107] As the event drew nearer, AI narrowed its demands to "progress" on four issues: the death penalty, detention without trial, freedom of expression, and protection of human rights activists. Writing to the IOC, AI acknowledged that "human rights reforms are the primary responsibility of the Chinese authorities" and offered no specific mechanism for the IOC to bring about reform but said that "the IOC can still make a significant contribution."[108]

AI's 2008 campaign included arresting visual imagery that subverted the viewer's expectations. The images depicted common scenes familiar to any sport fan, but inserted human rights abuses into them in ways to create jarring juxtapositions. By placing torture and executions directly into sporting events, the ads constituted an effective frontal attack on the notion that sport was separate from politics—pushing viewers to see sport and human rights as directly linked. In one ad with the message "Stop the world record of executions," a uniformed Chinese official points a gun to the head of a sprinter at the starting block. In another, the Olympic rings are fashioned out of barbed wire. (Reporters Without Borders made a similar poster, with handcuffs as rings.) Because of concerns about the depiction of violence, AI chose not to use a particularly shocking ad in which a policeman dunks the head of a man into a swimming pool as the victim, hands cuffed behind him, appears to howl in pain, but the media reproduced the image in reporting on AI's decision not to use it, ensuring that it was seen anyway.[109]

HRW targeted a narrower range of issues that could more clearly be attributed to hosting the Games, such as forced evictions. The group published five major reports on human rights in China, a book, and a reporters' guide to covering the Olympics; set up an Olympics-focused website; and put out nearly ninety media releases. In addition to meeting with the IOC and forty-six national Olympic committees, HRW staffers met with heads of state and foreign ministers—and, importantly, all twelve of the major Olympic corporate sponsors. HRW tried to put "a major burden on . . . the Games' corporate sponsors to make the Games a force for change in China."[110]

As one HRW staffer recalled, dealing with the IOC was extremely frustrating because of its constantly shifting positions.[111] Sometimes IOC representatives argued that because the organization was apolitical, it could not be concerned with human rights. Sometimes they said that they were working to improve human rights in China. In 2006, IOC president Jacque Rogge told the press that he had made a request to the Beijing organizing committee: "The values of the IOC are full respect [for] human rights. We ask you to do the best efforts so that leading up to the Games, during the Games and after the Games, you would have the best possible human rights record. . . . They received the message."[112] By 2008, Rogge more often tried to avoid talking about human rights. "History will tell that more good than bad has resulted from hosting the Olympic Games in Beijing," he said.[113]

AI and HRW concluded after the Beijing Games that the event had resulted in an overall increase in repression.[114] When the IOC held a major congress in 2009, it was defensive about human rights. Hein Verbruggen, the IOC's chief liaison with the Beijing organizers, denounced human rights-based criticism of the IOC's conduct around the 2008 Games as an "unfounded" product of "confusion" between human rights and the Olympic ethics. "Whereas the human rights movement is based on the idea of achieving human dignity through individual freedoms and the entitlement to certain rights, Olympism instead is based on the ancient Greek virtues of 'healthy spirit and healthy body.' . . . Olympism, therefore, has its own right of existence as an alternative to the ideals of the human rights movement and must not allow the ideals of politically motivated organisations with political objects to impose on it. It is important for the Olympic movement to understand this distinction and strongly reject the agendas of such organisations." In an apparent misunderstanding, he concluded—in an assessment disputed by AI—that AI now concurred that "political discussion of this nature" should no longer be "directed at the Olympic Games" in ways that hijack them "for purposes other than that of the celebration of sport."[115]

Both the 2014 Sochi Winter Olympics, which saw an authoritarian Russian government under Vladimir Putin implement restrictions on free speech and erupted into heated controversy after the legislature passed an anti-"gay propaganda" law, and the 2016 Rio Summer Olympics, held as Brazil weathered political and economic crises, were sites of continuing mobilization around human rights issues, detailed in this volume. Neither AI and HRW, though they campaigned extensively around both Games, devoted as much attention and resources to Sochi as they had to Beijing in 2008. Both continued to frame arguments for inserting human rights considerations around Olympic ideals.[116] Their pressure has paid off in some respects. The IOC under President Thomas Bach has tried to be more agile in responding to a variety of pressures, as shown in the adoption of a reform-minded Olympic Agenda 2020.[117] In 2017, the IOC made host city contracts public and has included in them a very broadly worded provision to protect human rights. HRW has long pressed the IOC to use outside experts (such as HRW) to evaluate human rights conditions in host cities; thus far, the IOC has resisted this approach.

Beijing will again host an Olympic Games in 2022. The event will likely draw scrutiny nearly as intense as in 2008. But so far it seems that the payoffs of such scrutiny have not resulted in the improvements sought by human rights groups. They have, however, succeeded in generating publicity for human rights causes and organizations and in helping to buttress the moral legitimacy of the IOC—and of bodies such as the UN. In 2016 on the eve of the Rio Games, the UN's Human Rights Council held a panel discussion on the topic "the use of sport and the Olympic ideal to promote human rights for all." Zeid Ra'ad Al Hussein, the UN high commissioner for human rights, praised sport as a force for equality.[118]

Human rights campaigns around sport mega-events have helped shape normative expectations of the global order. Today human rights are the most prominent rubric for framing moral claims around international sport. Moral pressures on sport mega-events, once grounded in issues rooted in the competitions themselves, have spilled over at a dizzying pace into areas with no obvious connection to sport. Human rights advocacy groups now pressure international sports competitions to promote basic freedoms (of press, speech, and religion), judicial reform, and fair employment practices in countries hosting the events. Although many sports fans probably remain indifferent to the cause, the media spotlight on the Olympics reaches such an enormous audience that it would be hard to argue that there has been any arena of contestation over human rights that has had more widespread publicity. There are no sure methods for righting human rights abuses, nor does the international community agree on a universal set of priorities for ranking the multiplicity of rights, so punishing or shaming Olympic hosts and host candidates on human rights grounds offers no guarantee that benefits will result. It seems eminently reasonable to propose that hosting a major sporting event not result in gross human rights abuses such as the deaths of thousands of ill-treated workers. But it is also worth remembering that the mind-boggling sums spent on each transient event may well constitute the most significant human cost of the Games.

Notes

1. Scholars of human rights have ignored international sport, while scholars of international sport have only recently begun to attend to human rights. On HRW and AI in 2008, see Susan Brownell, "Human Rights and the Beijing Olympics: Imagined Global Community and the Transnational Public Sphere," *British Journal of Sociology* 63, no. 2 (2012): 306–327. On recent locally based activism, see Jules Boykoff, *Activism and the Olympics: Dissent and the Games in Vancouver and London* (New Brunswick, NJ: Rutgers University Press, 2014). On the use of sport by peace, women's, environmental, rights, and other movements, see Jean Harvey et al., *Sport and Social Movements: From the Local to the Global* (London: Bloomsbury, 2013). See also Daniel Warner, "Human Rights in International Sports," in *The Sage Handbook of Human Rights*, ed. Anja Mihr and Mark Gibney (Los Angeles: Sage, 2014), 534–552.

2. Wendy Wong, *Internal Affairs: How the Structure of NGOs Transforms Human Rights* (Ithaca, NY: Cornell University Press, 2012), 38.

3. Nicholas Bequelin, Senior Researcher, Human Rights Watch, "The Human Rights Cost of the Beijing Olympics: An Assessment," paper presented at "Human Rights at the Olympic Games" workshop, University of Melbourne, November 2014.

4. Wong, *Internal Affairs*, 55.

5. See "Sport and Rights Alliance," Sport and Human Rights, www.sportandhumanrights .org/wordpress/index.php/2015/07/06/sport-and-rights-alliance/.

6. John Hoberman, "Think Again: The Olympics," *Foreign Policy*, October 7, 2009, foreign policy.com/2009/10/07/think-again-the-olympics/.

7. FIFA Human Rights Advisory Board, business-humanrights.org/en/fifa-human-rights -advisory-board.

8. "Host City Contract Principles," International Olympic Committee, February 28, 2017, stillmed.olympic.org/media/Document%20Library/OlympicOrg/Documents/Host-City -Elections/XXXIII-Olympiad-2024/Host-City-Contract-2024-Principles.pdf#_ga=2.123744906 .1658143164.1527879825--833919830.1527879825. See also "Olympic Agenda 2020: 20+20 Recommendations," International Olympic Committee, bit.ly/1wS3TED; "Olympic Charter: In Force as from 2 August 2015," sixth principle, International Olympic Committee, bit.ly/1fNiL1J; S. Wilson, "Rights Group Praises IOC on Human Rights Clause," *USA Today*, October 24, 2014, www.usatoday.com/story/sports/olympics/2014/10/24/rights-group-praises-ioc-on-human -rights-clause/17831613/.

9. For a general survey of Olympic boosters and critics, see John Horne, "The Politics of Hosting the Olympic Games," in *The Politics of the Olympics: A Survey*, ed. Alan Bairner and Gyozo Molnar, 27–40 (London: Routledge, 2010).

10. See also Susan Brownell's contribution to this volume.

11. "American Acceptance of German Olympics Bid Decried by Untermyer," *Jewish Exponent*, October 5, 1934.

12. Pamphlet, Committee for Fair Play in Sports, Papers of Gustavus Kirby, Box 7, United States Olympic Committee Archives, Colorado Springs, CO.

13. See also Barbara Keys, "The Early Cold War Olympics: Political, Economic, and Human Rights Dimensions, 1952–1960," in *The Palgrave Handbook of Olympic Studies*, ed. Helen Jefferson Lenskyj and Stephen Wagg, 72–87 (New York: Palgrave Macmillan, 2012).

14. Douglas Booth, *The Race Game: Sport and Politics in South Africa* (London: Frank Cass, 1996); Douglas Booth, "Hitting Apartheid for Six? The Politics of the South African Sports Boycott," *Journal of Contemporary History* 38, no. 3 (2003): 477–493.

15. Saul Dubow, *South Africa's Struggle for Human Rights* (Athens: Ohio University Press, 2012); Ryan Irwin, *The Gordian Knot: Apartheid and the Unmaking of the Liberal World Order* (Oxford: Oxford University Press, 2012), 188.

16. See Barbara J. Keys, *Reclaiming American Virtue: The Human Rights Revolution of the 1970s* (Cambridge, MA: Harvard University Press, 2014); Jan Eckel and Samuel Moyn, eds., *The Breakthrough: Human Rights in the 1970s* (Philadelphia: University of Pennsylvania Press, 2013).

17. See the forthcoming book by Benjamin Nathans on the history of Soviet dissidents.

18. For evidence of the campaign, see the hundreds of letters, mostly from individuals and Jewish groups, in Files of President Killanin, Memos Relies, and Jeux Olympiques 1980—Boycott, 205430-20544, International Olympic Committee Archives, Lausanne, Switzerland; the papers of Daniel Patrick Moynihan, II: 1589, 1600, Manuscript Collection, Library of Congress, Washington, DC; the British Foreign Office's reporting in FCO 28/3546 and 28/3548, National Archives, Kew, UK. Umberto Tulli has characterized such calls as influential in contributing to Carter's boycott and argues that the Olympics were "an important field" in an emerging human rights discourse. Umberto Tulli, "'Boicottare le Olimpiadi del Gulag': I diritti umani e la campagna contro le Olimpiadi di Mosca," *Richerche di Storia Politica* 1 (2013): 3. See also Umberto Tulli, "Bringing Human Rights In: The Campaign Against the 1980 Moscow Olympic Games and the Origins of the Nexus Between Human Rights and the Olympic Games," *International Journal of the History of Sport* 33, 16 (2016): 2026–2045.

19. Tulli, "Bringing Human Rights In."

20. See, e.g., L. Downie Jr., "Amnesty Asks Brezhnev to Release Prisoners," *Washington Post*, October 10, 1979.

21. "Amnesty's Position on Boycott Campaigns," Amnesty International Section Française, *Chronique*, no. 29 (July 1978), 19, quoting International Executive Committee chairman Thomas Hammarberg's preface to the 1977 internal annual report (in a section that does not appear in the published version of the report but does appear in substance in the 1978 report).

22. *Amnesty International Report 1980* (London: Amnesty International Publications, 1980), 17.

23. Amnesty International, "Open Letter to President Leonid Brezhnev," October 10, 1979, Amnesty International Documentation, Warwick University Archives.

24. *Amnesty International Report 1980*, 302–310.

25. *Prisoners of Conscience in the USSR: Their Treatment and Conditions*, 2nd ed., April 1980 (London: Amnesty International Publications, 1980). The first edition had appeared in 1975.

26. Draft letter, Robert Bernstein, Orville Schell, and Aryeh Neier to Carter, April 24, 1980, Ser. I.1, Box 67, Human Rights Watch Records: Helsinki Watch, Columbia University, New York.

It is not clear whether the letter was sent, but see also Aryeh Neier, "Right to Travel," *The Nation*, May 3, 1980.

27. See Tulli, "Bringing Human Rights In." The Carter administration framed its postinvasion boycott effort primarily in terms of national security, claiming that standing firm against aggression would help to deter future aggression. See, e.g., Press Release, Office of the White House Press Secretary, April 8, 1980, in 250/9/31 PART 12, National Archives, Canberra, Australia.

28. Iris Edelson to Killanin, October 9, 1978, Memos sent to Michael Killanin (President), Folder ID 8315, Killanin Files, CIO PT-KILLA-MEMO, International Olympic Committee Archives, Lausanne (hereafter Killanin Papers).

29. Memo re Mr. Hamilton's resolution, November 24, 1978, Killanin Papers; see also Tulli, "Bringing Human Rights In," 2033.

30. Congresswoman Patricia Schroeder and 21 others to Killanin, July 27, 1978, Folder ID 8314, in Killanin Papers.

31. Killanin to Novikov, March 4, 1980, Affairs Politiques—Correspondance, Jeux Olympiques 1980, International Olympic Committee Archives, Lausanne, Switzerland.

32. See, e.g., Monique Berlioux to John Roberts, August 7, 1979, Jeux Olympiques 1980 Boycott 205444, IOC Archives.

33. Crystal Nix, "South Korea: United States Policy and the 1987 Presidential Elections," *Human Rights Yearbook* 1 (1988): 251.

34. "Jackson: U.S. Should Boycott in '88 Unless S. Korea Betters Human Rights," *Washington Post*, June 16, 1987, E2. See also "North Korea Willing to Take Over If South Korea Can't Stage Games," *Los Angeles Times*, June 16, 1987, D3. Perhaps thinking of Jackson, Aryeh Neier writes that "There seemed a distinct possibility of a boycott of the 1988 Seoul Olympics over human rights abuses." Because the regime chose reform over a crackdown, it was never brought to a test, but the evidence suggests that a boycott on specifically human rights grounds was not a real possibility. See Aryeh Neier, *The International Human Rights Movement: A History* (Princeton, NJ: Princeton University Press, 2012), 181.

35. North American Coalition for Human Rights in Korea, *Update*, no. 85 (December 1987): 79.

36. For a discussion of various database searches that turned up very few connections between human right and the Olympic Games in 1987–1988, see Barbara Keys, "Harnessing Human Rights to the Olympic Games: Human Rights Watch and the 1993 'Stop Beijing' Campaign," *Journal of Contemporary History* 53, no. 2 (2018): 415–438.

37. See the files titled "Protestations," C-J01-1988/207 and C-J01-1988/208, in Jeux Olympiques 1988, IOC Archives.

38. Amnesty International, "South Korea: Human Rights Developments, January–March 1988," April 1988, Human Rights Documents Online. AI used the occasion of the Games to urge South Korea to release more political prisoners and restore more civil liberties but without linking the Olympics to human rights obligations. "Amnesty International Urges South Korea to Free Prisoners," *Washington Post*, September 9, 1988, A33.

39. Stephen Hopgood, *Keepers of the Flame: Understanding Amnesty International* (Ithaca, NY: Cornell University Press, 2006), 113.

40. Asia Watch, *Human Rights in Korea* (1985); Asia Watch, *Steady Crackdown: Legal Process and Human Rights in South Korea* (1987), Human Rights Documents Online.

41. Telephone interview with Richard Dicker of Human Rights Watch, January 8, 2016.

42. For an IOC insider account, see Richard Pound, *Five Rings over Korea: The Secret Negotiations Behind the 1988 Olympic Games in Seoul* (Boston: Little, Brown, 1994).

43. This section draws on Keys, "Harnessing Human Rights to the Olympic Games." HRW archives dealing with internal decision making are almost entirely closed to researchers, and HRW denied me access to a number of files relating to this topic. HRW's Minky Worden has refused several requests for an interview.

44. On the shift in attention to China, see Jan Eckel, *Die Ambivalenz des Guten: Menschenrechte in der internationalen Politik seit den 1940ern* (Göttingen: Vandenhoeck & Ruprecht, 2014), 828.

45. Aryeh Neier, *The International Human Rights Movement: A History* (Princeton, NJ: Princeton University Press, 2012); Widney Brown, "Human Rights Watch: An Overview," in *NGOs and Human Rights: Promise and Performance*, ed. Claude E. Welch Jr. (Philadelphia: University of Pennsylvania Press, 2001), 79.

46. At the time of the Tiananmen Square massacre, the IOC was already anticipating a Beijing bid for 2000. For IOC vice president Richard Pound's comment that he hoped the unrest would be resolved "positively" in time for Beijing to put in its bid, see "Turmoil in China May Affect Olympics," *Globe and Mail*, June 8, 1989.

47. See the memoirs of China's IOC member and leading figure in the Beijing bid: Liang Lijuan, *He Zhenliang and China's Olympic Dream*, trans. Susan Brownell (Beijing: Foreign Language Press, 2007), 428; Lena Sun, "China Pulls Out Stops in Olympic Bid," *Washington Post*, July 15, 1993.

48. V. Finlay, "China Will Open Up Anyway, Says Beijing Bid Leader," *South China Morning Post*, September 24, 1993.

49. L. Siddons, "China Human Rights," Associated Press, June 3, 1993.

50. D. John and S. Vines, "Hurd Opposes China Olympics," *The Guardian*, September 17, 1993; Cable, London to Washington, "Media Reaction Report, London, Friday September 17, 1993," September 17, 1993, National Security Council Cables, Bill Clinton Presidential Library, Little Rock, Arkansas, FOIA Request.

51. See, e.g., W. Dan, "Give China a Chance," *New York Times*, September 21, 1993.

52. See, e.g., P. Goodspeed, "A Sporting Chance," *Toronto Star*, August 8, 1993; M. Myers, "Olympic Vote Caught in Human Rights Crossfire," United Press International, September 22, 1993.

53. S. Beck, "IOC Hired Lobbyist to Voice Concern over US Campaign," *South China Morning Post*, September 20, 1993.

54. Luke Cyphers, "Scoring Political Points: U.S. Activists Wage Fight Against Olympics in China," *Asian Wall Street Journal*, March 30, 1993; "Chinese in Australia Launch Anti-Beijing Campaign," Reuters News, May 26, 1993.

55. Cyphers, "Scoring Political Points."

56. A comparison of the total results in ProQuest Historical Newspapers for 1993 for keywords "Olympic*" and ("Human Rights Watch" or "Asia Watch"), compared to just ("Human Rights Watch" or "Asia Watch"), and counting only U.S.-based media outlets, yields 241 hits for the former and 1,054 for HRW generally. (In 1993 Asia Watch was a division of HRW, and news reports sometimes refer to "Human Rights Watch" and sometimes to "Asia Watch.") The same search in Lexis-Nexis yields a similar proportion.

57. Interview with Richard Dicker.

58. Management Assistance Group, "Discussion Paper Regarding the Structure, Management and Organizational Development of Human Rights Watch," 1–2, November 5, 1993,

Reel 7311, grant file PA930-0689, Grant Files, Ford Foundation, Rockefeller Archive Center, Tarrytown, NY. I thank Bart De Sutter for providing me with a copy of this document. HRW experimented in other ways with new approaches and issues in these years, such as pursuing an unusually public and collaborative project to ban land mines beginning in 1992. See Wong, *Internal Affairs*, 152–153.

59. Robin Munro to Richard Dicker, "China Olympics Bid," March 30, 1993, Box 402, Asia Watch Records, Human Rights Watch Collection, Columbia University, New York City, NY (hereafter AWR).

60. On the organizational pressures that drove HRW decision making, see Bart De Sutter, "Paradox of Virtue: Helsinki Human Rights Activism during the Cold War (1975–1995)," Ph.D. Dissertation, University of Antwerp, 2015; on the "Neier Doctrine," see ibid., 91.

61. On funding and publicity, see Management Assistance Group, "Discussion Paper," and William Korey, *NGOs and the Universal Declaration of Human Rights* (New York: St. Martin's, 1998), 347–349, 361.

62. R. Greenberger, "U.S., Unhappy with Beijing's Abuse of Human Rights, Focuses on Olympics," *Wall Street Journal*, August 23, 1993; Nancy Bernkopf Tucker, ed., *China Confidential: American Diplomats and Sino-American Relations, 1945–1996* (New York: Columbia University Press, 2001), 437–438, 446.

63. D. Anderson quoted in Tucker, *China Confidential*, 450.

64. See note 56 above regarding ProQuest Historical Newspapers keyword searches. On TV news, see, e.g., ABC Evening News, September 3, 1993, Vanderbilt Television News Archives.

65. For an example of a pro-Beijing argument, see the case made by investment banker Jonathan Kolatch, "Beijing Deserves the 2000 Olympics," *Washington Post*, July 30, 1993.

66. This conclusion is based on a survey of hundreds of media reports from Factiva and the hundreds of newspaper clippings in Asia Watch's archives (Box 402).

67. "China Doesn't Deserve the Olympics," *New York Times*, September 21, 1993. See also Abe Rosenthal's sharp condemnation of Beijing the same day: A. M. Rosenthal, "The Olympic Decision," *New York Times*, September 21, 1993. And see Bernstein's editorial the day before: "China: A Regime That Tortures Doesn't Deserve the Olympics," *New York Times*, September 20, 1993.

68. Letter, Kenneth Roth, Deputy Director, to Anita DeFrantz, April 26, 1993, Box 402, AWR; "IOC Pressured to Make Beijing a Forbidden City," *New York Times*, April 21, 1993, 18. For the IOC's response, which said that although human rights would "undoubtedly be one of many factors" influencing the voting the prime task of the IOC was the evaluate technical issues, see NOC Relations, IOC, to Bernstein, "Bid to Host the Games of the XXVII Olympiad—Human Rights," April 20, 1993, Box 402, AWR.

69. "Human Rights Watch World Report 1994—China and Tibet," Human Rights Watch, January 1, 1994, bit.ly/1OVEeVe; J. Weiner, "2000, An Olympic Odyssey," *Minneapolis Star Tribune*, September 19, 1993.

70. See the account by a former IOC marketing director, Michael Payne, *Olympic Turnaround: How the Olympic Games Stepped Back from the Brink of Extinction to Become the World's Best Known Brand* (New York: Praeger, 2006).

71. Letter, Robert Bernstein to Steven Weisman, *New York Times*, August 16, 1993; Letter Template, Robert Bernstein, August 3, 1993, Box 402, AWR; M. Dodd, "Sponsors Hear Plea to Block Beijing Bid," *USA Today*, August 25, 1993.

72. L. Siddons, "Olympics-China," Associated Press, August 25, 1993.

73. Letter, Roth to DeFrantz.

74. "Olympics of 2004," *Washington Post*, July 16, 1993.

75. Richard Dicker, "Human Rights Would Lose in a Beijing Olympiad," *International Herald Tribune*, June 23, 1993. See also Press release, "Human Rights Watch Welcomes House Resolution 188, July 26, 1993," Box 402, AWR.

76. Dicker, "Human Rights Would Lose."

77. S. Brunt, "IOC Ignores Human Rights When Awarding Games," *Globe and Mail*, June 21, 1993.

78. On which abuses were highlighted, see, e.g., Letter, Roth to Bondy, New York Times Sports, May 19, 1993, Box 402, AWR. In my interview with Richard Dicker, he discussed why these abuses were highlighted.

79. Letter, Bernstein to Samaranch and Leroy Walker, USOC, February 8, 1993, Box 402, AWR.

80. Cyphers, "Scoring Political Points."

81. Interview with Richard Dicker.

82. Michael Schaller, *The United States and China: Into the Twenty-First Century*, 4th ed. (New York 2016), 191–193. On the most favored nation debate, see the detailed account in James Mann, *About Face: A History of America's Curious Relationship with China, from Nixon to Clinton* (New York: Vintage, 2000), 274–297.

83. Beck, "IOC Hired Lobbyist." See also the resolution opposing Beijing by the House Subcommittee on International Security, International Organizations, and Human Rights: S. North, "US Congress Opposes Beijing's Olympic Bid," *Sydney Morning Herald*, June 12, 1993, 9.

84. "Interview: Senator Bill Bradley Discusses His Opposition to Having the Olympic Games in China in 2000," *NBC News: Today*, June 24, 1993.

85. Lena Sun, "China Has Biggest Stake in Olympic Games," *Washington Post*, September 21, 1993.

86. Ibid.; S. Brunt, "IOC Ignores Human Rights When Awarding the Games," *Globe and Mail*, June 21, 1993. On Anita DeFrantz, see "Robert Bernstein Draft for Op-Ed," n.d., Box 402, AWR.

87. See, e.g., Jean-Michel Gunz, Deputy Director, to John Cunningham, May 12, 1993, Villes candidates JO Ete 2000, Beijing: Protestations, 152/011-23A, IOC Archives.

88. Peter S. Knight to Francois Carrard, "Senator Bradley," July 16, 1993; Peter S. Knight to Francois Carrard, "House Foreign Affairs Mark-Up," July 21, 1993, Villes candates JO d'été 2000: Beijing: Protestations, 152/011-23a, IOC Archives.

89. Dicker, "Human Rights Would Lose." Samaranch had sent a telegram of "support and sympathy" to the Chinese Olympic Committee during the Tiananmen Square crackdown and when attending the 1990 Asian Games in Beijing had insisted that sport and politics remain separate. J. Kohut, "Olympic Chief Gave Support During Dissident Crackdown," *South China Morning Post*, April 12, 1991; S. Faison, "Asiad Success Key to China's Olympic Hopes," *South China Morning Post*, September 24, 1990.

90. William Drozdiak, "Sydney Wins 2000 Olympics," *Washington Post*, September 24, 1993. According to McGeoch, Pound voted for Beijing. Interview with Rod McGeoch, June 9, 2016.

91. Interview with McGeoch.

92. Drozdiak, "Sydney Wins 200 Olympics"; Press releases, September 24, 1993, Box 402, AWR.

93. Joseph Fewsmith, "The Impact of WTO/PNTR on Chinese Politics," *NBR Analysis* 11, no. 2 (2000): 50.

94. "Amnesty International Holds Press Conference in Atlanta," Hartford Web Publishing, July 9, 1996, www.hartford-hwp.com/archives/45a/200.html; Human Rights Watch, *Modern Capital of Human Rights? Abuses in the State of Georgia* (New York: Human Rights Watch, July 1996), 1, 146.

95. Human Rights Watch, *Modern Capital of Human Rights*, 1.

96. Amy Shipley, "To Beijing or Not to Beijing," *Washington Post*, July 13, 2001.

97. See "Questions & Answers: China and the Olympic Games 2008," Human Rights Watch, March 1, 2001, bit.ly/1sFCSJB; Amnesty International statement, "Should Beijing Get the Games? The Observer Debate," *The Guardian*, July 1, 2001, www.theguardian.com/world/2001/jul/01/china.sunderkatwala; Jane Perlez, "U.S. Won't Block China's Bid for Olympics," *New York Times*, July 11, 2001. "The Chinese government must prove it is worthy of staging the Games by upholding the Olympic spirit of 'fair play' and extending 'respect for universal fundamental ethical principles' to the people of China," AI stated. "Alarm as China Wins Olympics," *The Guardian*, July 14, 2001.

98. Reflecting after the fact, HRW's Minky Worden told an interviewer that she thought that the 2008 Olympics worsened the human rights situation in China but that boycotting Beijing would have resulted in a counterproductive ultranationalist response from China. Brownell, "Human Rights and the Beijing Olympics," 317, 313.

99. As Susan Brownell notes in this volume, the decision to make the statement came at the last minute and was hotly debated.

100. Frank Ching, "Games Can Only Hasten Reform," *South China Morning Post*, July 14, 2001.

101. Nicholas Bequelin, senior Researcher, human Rights Watch Hong Kong, personal communication.

102. On the relationship between AI and HRW, see Hopgood, *Keepers of the Flame*, 140–141.

103. Ibid., 141, 178, 182, 187, 189, 191.

104. Bequelin, "The Human Rights Cost of the Beijing Olympics."

105. "Resource List: Olympics Advocacy Campaigns," Human Rights in China, *China Rights Forum*, no. 3 (2007): 126–128, www.hrichina.org/en/content/4092.

106. Kingsley Edney, "The 2008 Beijing Olympic Torch Relay: Chinese and Western Narratives," *China Aktuell: Journal of Current Chinese Affairs* 37 (2008): 111–125.

107. AI Report, "People's Republic of China: The Olympics Countdown: Three Years of Human Rights Reform?," August 2005.

108. AI Public Statement, "China Olympics: Amnesty International's Appeal to IOC Executive Board Meeting," December 7, 2007.

109. "The 2008 Beijing Olympics Through Amnesty's Campaigns," Campaigns Worth Sharing, July 25, 2012, campaignsworthsharing.wordpress.com/2012/07/25/the-2008-beijing-olympics-through-amnestys-campaigns/. For the Olympic rings, see "Creative Olympic Rings," N4MB3RS, n4mb3rs.com/creative-olympic-rings/; "Beijing Olympics 2008: Amnesty International Torture Ads Dropped," *Telegraph*, July 16, 2008, www.telegraph.co.uk/news/worldnews/asia/2419191/Beijing-Olympics-2008-Amnesty-International-torture-ads-dropped.html.

110. John Goodbody and Giles Whittell, "Olympic Win Puts China on Probation," *Times* (London), July 14, 2001. For the total list of activities, see Bequelin, "The Human Rights Cost of the Beijing Olympics," and the HRW website.

111. Bequelin, "The Human Rights Cost of the Beijing Olympics."

112. S. L. Price, "The Silent Partner," *Sports Illustrated* 108, no. 7 (February 18, 2008), www.si.com/vault/2008/02/18/103703643/the-silent-partner.

113. Ibid.

114. See, e.g., "Olympic Congress: Monitor Host Countries on Rights," Human Rights Watch, October 1, 2009, www.hrw.org/news/2009/10/01/olympic-congress-monitor-host-countries-rights.

115. IOC, *Proceedings, XIII Olympic Congress, Copenhagen 2009*, 78, International Olympic Committee, www.olympic.org/olympic-congress. Verbruggen was chairman of the Coordination Commission for the Beijing Games. AI's disagreement was confirmed in an e-mail to the author from Kharunya Paramagura, AI communications manager, August 21, 2017.

116. See, e.g., "IOC Urged to Uphold Human Rights," Amnesty International, February 10, 2014, www.amnesty.org/en/latest/news/2014/02/ioc-urged-uphold-human-rights/; "Submission to the 2009 Olympic Congress," Human Rights Watch, February 23, 2009, www.hrw.org/news/2009/02/23/human-rights-watch-submission-2009-olympic-congress.

117. "Olympic Agenda 2020."

118. United Nations Geneva press release, "Council Holds Panel Discussion on the Use of Sport and the Olympic Ideal to Promote Human Rights for All," June 28, 2016, at www.unog.ch/unog/website/news_media.nsf/(httpNewsByYear_en)/9A5AA73D9AEA741CC1257FE000519D14?OpenDocument.

CHAPTER 6

The Moscow 1980 and Sochi 2014 Olympic Games

Dissent and Repression

Dmitry Dubrovskiy

The Olympic Games of 1980 and 2014 present a case study in the hosting of sport mega-events by repressive regimes. In both cases, authoritarian governments sought hosting rights in order to enhance their own legitimacy, an aim that was largely met at home but at the cost of incurring damaging criticism abroad about human rights violations. In both cases, the Games sparked debates about how sporting events could be most effectively used to improve human rights overall. These debates revolved around familiar poles: on the one hand, claims that the events could help spur reform, and on the other hand, the argument that hosting would lead to heightened abuses. In 1980 even before the Soviet invasion of Afghanistan triggered a large-scale boycott, some voices in Western Europe and the United States were arguing that Moscow should be spurned because of the Soviet Union's record of repression. In 2014 though some boycott calls were made, boycotting seemed a less compelling tactic. Instead, reformers hoped to achieve results through public pressure. In the final tally, the results of both Games suggest that sport mega-events in repressive regimes are likely to lead to more repression.

Moscow 1980: The Soviet Olympics

The two sides in the Cold War had opposing interpretations about the link between human rights and the Olympic Games. In the West, advocates of the Olympics believed that such sporting events could bring the world closer to the ideals of democracy and human rights. In contrast, the Soviet Union insisted that the main goal of international contacts was strengthening peace and mutual cooperation. When Moscow was awarded the Games, not long before the 1975 Helsinki Accords that marked the high point of détente, the Soviet regime presented the selection as an indication of international acceptance.[1] Although the Soviet regime had used human rights language to criticize Western deficiencies, especially in the area of race relations in the United States, it considered growing Western attacks on its own human rights record in the years after the signing of the Helsinki Accords as unacceptable interference in its internal affairs. Rather than using the language of human rights, Soviet rhetoric about the benefits of the Olympic Games emphasized instead advancing the ideas of peace and progress. Thus, evaluating the preparations for the 1980 Games, the Moscow Organizing Committee stressed "Olympic ideals of harmonious personal development, of rejecting discrimination on political, racial or religious grounds, of the development through sport of mutual understanding and friendship, of strengthening peace."[2] A manual for political activists involved in Games preparations described the Soviet Union as having earned the right to hold the Olympics in recognition of its peaceful international policies.[3]

The importance of the 1980 Moscow Games to the Soviet regime was heightened because these were the first Olympics to be hosted in a communist country. Due to the enormous propaganda value that the Olympics provide, the regime was intent on preventing "hostile actions" and "anti-Soviet propaganda" at all costs. Preparing for the Games involved suppressing and preventing public protests and contacts between "undesirable elements" and foreigners, especially in the media. The regime was convinced that Western countries had, in the words of a 1978 report, "a well-coordinated plan to use the 1980 Olympics as a means to put pressure on the Soviet Union and to spread lies (*kleveta*) about the Soviet system in general" and specifically about its human rights record.[4] The KGB undertook "preventive measures" such as isolating "mentally ill persons harboring aggressive intentions."[5] "Hostile elements" were purged and the city's population was reduced, both through threats and with violence. For example, the KGB "advised" Iurii Iarym-Agaev, a member of the Soviet human rights body the Moscow Helsinki Group, to leave the country before the start of the Olympics.[6] Gypsies were expelled from Moscow, schoolchildren were sent to compulsory summer camps, and access to Moscow by private vehicles was limited.[7] Moscow resembled a "fortress under siege." Viktor Fainberg recalled that "Moscow was declared 'an exemplar Communist city." Anything that did not comply with this definition was expelled from the capital."[8] "Preventive measures" meant that many activists were permanently expelled from the country, sent into internal exile, or locked up in prisons or mental institutions. In short, the human rights situation in the Soviet Union seriously deteriorated as a result of the Olympics.

To some in and outside of the country, it seemed clear that a country that consistently engaged in major human rights violations should not host the Olympics and that hosting, far from improving the situation, would lead to more human rights violations on the grounds of "enhancing security" and "preventive measures." They called for a boycott, many of them as early as the mid-1970s. Opponents of the boycott, on the other hand, saw the large numbers of foreign tourists and athletes coming to Moscow as a unique opportunity that could be used to boost human rights activities—such as campaigning for the release of political prisoners and importing religious and human rights literature.

For some activists in Western Europe and the United States, the Games presented an opportunity to use the event as a publicity vehicle to call attention to their causes. In Belgium, the Committee Moscow-80 hoped to use the Games to protest against the arms race, demand the removal of Soviet and U.S. troops from Europe, call for respect for human rights in the Soviet Union, condemn punitive psychiatry and political repression, and much more. The group urged the Belgium Olympic team to choose "a particular political prisoner and use the Games as a stage to show their support for him."[9] Amnesty International—by the late 1970s a world-renowned human rights organization—took no stance on the question of boycotting the Games but did write an open letter to Leonid Brezhnev and published a report on prisoners of conscience that angered the Soviet regime, leading it to include Amnesty International as part of the "anti-Olympic campaign."[10]

The KGB was particularly concerned about the activities of the Natsional'no Trudovoi Soiuz (National Labor Alliance, NTS), the oldest and most respected Soviet anticommunist émigré organization in Europe. Initially, the NTS opposed a boycott: "We are against the boycott of the Moscow Olympics because we believe that the more contacts there are between our country and the West the better." After the Soviet invasion of Afghanistan in December 1979 led to a major boycott campaign by U.S. president Jimmy Carter, the NTS came around in support.[11] One author writing in the NTS's magazine called for supporters to boycott the Olympics but at the same time to make a tourist trip to Moscow as "an opportunity to spread ideas."[12] The NTS published special instructions to Olympic tourists, emphasizing information exchange and openness that could be promoted by the Olympic Games and offering advice on what kind of books to bring and how to answer if stopped at the border.[13] *The Economist* offered a similar proposal, suggesting that visitors to the Games help dissidents by wearing T-shirts with pictures of dissidents, waving signs such as "Free Orlov!," shouting anti-Soviet slogans during the award ceremonies, and carrying anti-Soviet banners.[14]

In similar ways, nationalist movements and religious groups saw the Games as an opportunity to use a global spotlight to draw attention to their causes. Religious minorities, such as Estonian Pentacostals, hoped to use the Games to import and disseminate religious literature, while the YMCA proposed a conference in Moscow titled "Religious Youth and Sport," encouraging participants to arrive in Moscow as tourists.[15] The British group Women's Campaign for Soviet Jewry campaigned to remove the Olympics from Moscow. In letters to British and U.S. politicians, the group stated that the campaign was not intended "to spoil the event for genuine athletes but is, we feel, the only course open for any human being to whom the rights of other humans is important."[16] The group warned the International Olympic Committee (IOC) that the free world would consider it responsible for KGB crimes.[17]

The position adopted by most Soviet dissidents was far more radical. Even before the invasion of Afghanistan, most of them favored boycotting the Games. Soviet dissidents in the United States were among the most consistent opponents of the Olympics. The sports pages of the émigré newspaper *Novyi amerikanets* actively promoted the idea of the boycott. Sport journalist Evgenii Rubin, writing in the *New York Times*, declared that the Soviet regime "despises Olympic ideals" and was "waging unrelenting war" against constitutional rights and those who defended them.[18]

In April 1980, dissident Alexander Ginsburg and a group of former Soviet sport journalists appealed for a boycott. Their letter noted that in addition to waging war in Afghanistan, the Soviet regime was also "waging a war against its own people, by sentencing them to lengthy terms of imprisonment for non-violent protests in defense of human rights and for religious activities. In recent years this war has been waged under the Olympic flag." The appeal underscored that the persecution of human rights activists had intensified during preparations for the Games: "While building festive decorations the authorities are [simultaneously] purging Moscow of dissenters so nobody could tell [the story that] we are telling now." The authors urged U.S.

athletes to consider that their Soviet counterparts were directly implicated in the repression: "among others, you will face the Soviet Army team (CSKA)" and "athletes from the Dinamo athletic club representing the KGB and the Ministry of Internal Affairs."[19] Ginzburg said that the boycott would be necessary even without the invasion of Afghanistan, and he drew parallels with the 1936 "Nazi" Olympics.[20] Rubin recalled that he and Ginzburg had a meeting with the American Olympic Committee officials, and though they were not allowed to address the committee directly, their position had an effect on the committee's decision to support the boycott.[21]

The attitudes of human rights activists from Europe were more ambiguous. In late 1978, Radio Liberty hosted a discussion between the writer Anatolii Gladilin and *Kontinent*'s editor, Vladimir Maksimov, which was representative of debates among dissidents inside the Soviet Union. Maksimov insisted that the boycott campaign would generate discussion and momentum and that by "engaging considerable political and social forces, we will thus attract significant public attention to the problems in the Soviet Union." Maksimov was convinced that the boycott would fail and the Games would take place but that even so, the campaign could improve the human rights situation. Gladilin argued that the Soviet media would convey to the Soviet people an impression that the "enemy" wanted to deprive them of a major event that Westerners regularly host.[22]

By the mid-1970s physicist Andrei Sakharov was regarded as the most respected and authoritative human rights activist in the country, indeed the only one inside the Soviet Union who had ready access to international media. His statements about human rights were therefore brought directly to an international audience. Before the invasion of Afghanistan, his position on the Olympic Games was cautious. He knew very well that the Games, like any other Kremlin propaganda event, entailed special security measures, including "purges" of the dissidents, preventive detention, exile, arrests, and charges. In 1974 shortly after Moscow was awarded the Games, Sakharov met with Senator James Buckley in Moscow and expressed concern that the Games would encourage the regime to purge the city of dissidents.[23]

Sakharov later recalled that boycott supporters never believed that the boycott could be implemented in full; instead, they hoped that the wider campaign would strengthen and expand the human rights movement in the West. He considered this position flawed both in tactical terms and in principle. "It was a mistake, I thought, to call for an Olympic boycott simply as a tactical ploy" if it was not going to succeed. "I didn't want . . . millions of innocent people, including the athletes, deprived of the pleasure the games would afford." As he explained, "For me the Olympics were part of the process of détente: the arrival of hundreds of thousands of visitors from the West, even with nothing but sports on their minds, could make a dent in the wall dividing our two worlds." The goal, he said, should be not to "spoil" the Games but instead to use them to spread the word about Soviet human rights violations and to generate support for reform.[24]

In June 1978, Sakharov signed the Moscow Helsinki Group's letter to IOC president Lord Killanin that alleged serious violations of the Olympic principle of openness, including censorship, limitations on the rights of foreign tourists, and the beginning of purges of dissidents from Moscow. The letter demanded a "ceasefire" (a halt to persecution of dissidents) as a nonnegotiable condition for the Olympics to go ahead, the release of specified political prisoners, and an end to arrests for nonviolent human rights protests, religious activity, and attempts to emigrate.[25] However, according to Sakharov, the Moscow Helsinki Group, with one exception, eventually opposed a boycott and instead took the position that the Games offered an opportunity to promote human rights issues.[26]

The Olympics drew the attention of political prisoners at the Mordovskii high-security labor camp, who wrote an open letter to participating athletes. The letter argued that "nothing is outside politics; sport is also politics and big sport is big politics." Though they drew parallels between the Berlin and Moscow Olympics, the authors did not call for a boycott of the Games. Instead, they encouraged athletes not to forget the brutal and hypocritical nature of the Soviet regime and to use the stadium as a stage to call for humane domestic policies and respect for human rights.[27]

Thus, Soviet human rights activists took varying stances toward the Olympics and the prospect of a boycott. Sakharov believed that differences over the boycott issue were the most serious factor that prevented a united position toward the Olympics. He recalled later that even before the invasion of Afghanistan, the divisions were "agonizing" and "did serious harm" after Carter initiated his boycott campaign.[28] In a long interview in September 1978, Sakharov said that he was a true "supporter of détente" and as such called for the Olympics to be held in Moscow "as it would be in any other place" because it would enable outsiders to visit, explore, and meet Soviet citizens. In his words, "to the Games in Moscow—yes; to political amnesty— also yes." According to Sakharov, every Olympic delegation should choose a "mentee" from the ranks of political prisoners and demand his or her release according to the formula "ten athletes to one prisoner." At the same time, Sakharov argued that in order to allow the government to "save face," outsiders should insist on "specific humanitarian measures . . . demanding amnesty or exchange of sick people."[29]

When the Soviet Union invaded Afghanistan just half a year before the opening of the Olympics, the international politics around a boycott changed dramatically. Sakharov now reversed himself. Citing the tradition of the Olympic Truce, he said that unless the Soviet Union withdrew its troops, the IOC should deny it the Games because "the conduct of the Olympic Games in Moscow would contradict the Olympic charter."[30] His widely publicized criticism prompted a crackdown: within days the Soviet regime stripped him of his awards and banished him to Gorky.[31] Sakharov's exile strengthened the boycott campaign, widening its appeal.

In the end, the hopes of those who wanted to use the Games to stage protests proved to be misplaced. Security measures made public protest impossible. The few attempts were promptly stopped by the KGB.[32] A few incidents took place in the Olympic Village, where some shouted "Soviet Union the occupant!" and "Freedom to Afghanistan!" at guards. A member of the Belgian Moscow '80 Committee managed to arrange a meeting with the representatives of a recently created trade union but was detained and deported shortly after.[33]

It is not a coincidence that the forced end of the dissident movement in the Soviet Union coincided with the start of the Moscow Olympics. Preparations for the Games provided the ideal pretext to crush the human rights movement. The boycott campaign failed to achieve its goals: the human rights situation in the Soviet Union deteriorated, and war raged on in Afghanistan. The IOC had essentially ignored human rights complaints as being beyond its purview. The boycott succeeded in diminishing the spectacle; the Soviet regime succeeded in staging a well-organized festival.[34] Those dissidents remaining in the city had to keep their heads down and remain silent.[35]

The Sochi 2014 Winter Olympics: Putin's Games

In July 2007, the IOC awarded Sochi the 2014 Winter Olympics. From the beginning, these were "Putin's Games." The IOC decision came in his second term; the competitions would occur in his third term. Thus, above all the Games were intended as a demonstration of the success of Vladimir Putin's

Russia and proof that Russia had risen "from its knees," overcoming the humiliations of the 1990s.[36]

Like the Moscow Games, the Sochi Olympics exposed the contradictions between human rights ideals and Olympic realities. In both cases, as was standard practice, the IOC ignored the state of democracy and human rights in selecting a host country.[37] Yet the Sochi Games became a major forum for debates about free speech. In response, in an unprecedented effort the IOC put considerable pressure on several National Olympic Committees to suppress "political demonstrations" and enforce "Olympic principles."

Despite major differences in the international climate, the nature of the Russian government and the Putin regime's "nostalgic modernization" meant that there were many similarities between the Games of 2014 and those of 1980. Just as the Soviet regime had used the Moscow Games as propaganda for its values and way of life, the Putin regime used the Sochi Games to legitimize itself internationally and strengthen domestic authoritarianism.[38] Some observers argue that there was a direct translation of security policies from the 1980 Games to the Sochi Olympics that resulted in similar violations of human rights. Like the KGB in the late 1970s, Putin claimed to see a "well-coordinated attempt to derail the preparations for the Olympics and the major Olympic events."[39] Between the selection of Sochi in 2007 and the opening of the events in 2014, human rights conditions in Russia drastically deteriorated.[40] These years saw a de facto permanent President Putin, direct attacks against civil society, a sharp increase in anti-Western rhetoric, and an aggressive push against foreign organizations and foreign funding.[41]

The situation became progressively worse as the Olympics drew near. The Krasnodar region where the Olympics took place was "purged." Olympic construction projects were marked by exceptionally high levels of corruption as well as many violations of workers' rights.[42] Human Rights Watch reported inadequate accommodations and meals for workers, failing to pay agreed wages, delayed payments of wages, failing to provide contracts, demands for excessive working hours, and other forms of exploitation.[43] Environmentalists protested on the grounds that the event would place a heavy burden on the region's natural environment. Their forecasts have proven correct, although their protests were ignored by the IOC.[44] Environmental standards were circumvented, and side effects of the preparations included illegal dumping of waste, polluting the water supply, and damaging a national park. The government also began an assault against local ecological nongovernmental organizations (NGOs), such as Eco-Watch, North Caucasus.[45]

At recent Olympics it has become common to acknowledge the first nations, or indigenous peoples, of the land. Thus, at the Vancouver 2010 Games, the "first nations" of Canada and their cultures were highlighted and celebrated. At Sochi, the status "first nation" was assigned to the Cossacks. The local population who consider themselves the indigenous people of the Krasnodar region are the descendants of Circassians who were conquered and resettled during Russia's late nineteenth-century imperial expansion. Circassian activists launched a boycott campaign, arguing that Sochi is the ancient capital of the Circassians, that the Circassians had suffered genocide at the hands of Russians in 1864, and that genocidal policies were continuing because of the government's refusal to allow Circassians to return to their ancestral lands. Their online petition demanded a minute of silence to honor the victims of genocide, the erection of a monument to the victims, and the exclusion of Cossacks from the opening ceremony.[46]

As in 1980, security practices such as purges of "unreliable elements," "preventive measures," and special border security measures were implemented in preparation for the Sochi Games. Krasnodar's local government has always been exceptionally hostile toward human rights groups and the media.[47] To separate the administration of Sochi from the North Caucasus regional administration, the Kremlin created a separate North Caucasus Federal District from within the existing Southern Federal District.[48] The creation of a special legal regime in which security forces exercised practically unlimited powers dramatically worsened the situation by applying "preventive measures" to activists and journalists.[49] Both civil rights advocates and journalists concluded that these events were directly connected to preparations for the Olympics.[50] Vulnerable groups such as the homeless and the Roma found themselves in similarly difficult circumstances.[51]

Security measures also seriously limited the rights of prospective tourists, who were required to submit personal data in advance to obtain special passes to attend the events.[52] A ban on demonstrations and other public activism during the Olympics was enacted, and the IOC's agreement with the Russian proposal to create special protest zones sealed the image of the Sochi Games prioritizing security over free speech.[53]

Most Russian human rights activists were too busy resisting the ongoing state-sponsored assault on civil society to notice the Olympics or include them in their political agenda. When asked what she thought of a possible Western boycott of the Sochi Olympics, Liudmila Alekseeva, a leading Russian human rights activist, said that she was "against the boycott because for many people, both the athletes and the spectators, sporting events are a cause for celebration, and the NGOs will not score any points by depriving people of a celebration."[54] In June 2014, former Soviet dissident Boris Al'tshuler called on the U.S. Congress and European legislatures to advocate a boycott of the Olympics due to the Russian government's policies of children's rights abuses (including the infamous Dima Yakovlev Law).[55] But in general, Russian human rights activists did not use the Olympics as a tool in their human rights agenda, apart from a few local protests against human rights violations in Krasnodar. Two factors account for this disinterest: first, a general impression that the Olympic movement and human rights were disconnected, and second, broader constraints on free speech and concerns that the government would use any criticism of the Olympics to further its assault against civil society.[56] The famed feminist punk rock band Pussy Riot represented the only consistent and fervent opposition to the Olympics, but even this provocative group called only for a civil boycott.[57]

But in June 2013 the Russian government enacted an administrative law that dramatically weakened LGBT rights and triggered a sea change in attitudes toward the upcoming Games.[58] The Russian move came in the context of a surge in transnational activism on behalf of LGBT rights that had wrought significant changes in Western democracies. The global gay rights boom can be explained by policy contagion, in which policies in one country rapidly spread to others, and the socialization of countries in international society, along with the influence of U.S. popular culture. Even as gay rights deepened in some countries, however, they regressed in others, sharpening a divide between liberal Western democracies and poorer non-democratic society. The Sochi Olympics thus pitted the forces of reaction against a transnational tidal wave, triggering an international debate about how to protest the Russian law.[59] As sociologist Helen Lenskyj explains, opponents of sanctions argued that a boycott would be ineffective and that greater effect would be achieved through civil protests, refusing to watch or attend the Games, boycotting Russian products, or openly displaying the LGBT movement's symbols. They also suggested that a boycott violated the rights of athletes, that the Olympics was no place for human rights protests, and that the IOC and the Russian government should be held accountable rather than punishing athletes. Lenskyj suggests that a "magic mindset" prevailed among this group: a belief that sport unites people and breaks down barriers and that LGBT athletes could fight prejudice by performing well and winning medals.[60]

Both supporters and opponents of a boycott cited the Olympic Charter's sixth principle to demonstrate the incompatibility of Russia's discriminatory anti-LGBT law and Olympic ideals: "The enjoyment of the rights and freedoms set forth in this Olympic Charter shall be secured without discrimination of any kind, such as race, colour, sex, sexual orientation, language, religion, political or other opinion, national or social origin, property, birth or other status."[61] The IOC's reaction was predictable, stating that every country's legislation was its own business and that the charter was intended to protect athletes, not the population in general, while also assuring the world that Russia would not discriminate against athletes on the basis of their gender or sexual orientation.[62]

In Russia a few organizations and activists, such as RUSA LGBT, called for an Olympic boycott immediately after the law was passed.[63] A group of twenty-three activists, with Masha Gessen in the lead, called for an economic boycott of both Russian products and those of Olympic sponsors.[64] Most activists, however, argued against a boycott on the grounds that it would not solve the community's problems and would impinge on the rights of athletes. Well-known LGBT activist Nikolai Alekseev, for example, urged activists to attend the Olympics, to protest against the discriminatory law, and to wear the gay pride signs to attract attention to LGBT rights violations in Russia.[65] The president of the LGBT Sport Federation, Konstantin Yablotskii, followed suit: "Someone is breaking his back to get this Olympic medal, he could not care less about all these human rights, he came to break the record and get the medal, and the rest of it can burn in hell."[66] Igor Kochetkov, chair of the Russian LGBT Network, also argued against a boycott. "The decision where to host the Olympics was made by people who could not care less about human rights; we came to this realization when we talked to them," he said. The Olympic movement's agenda was closely intertwined with business interests, he noted, and "unfortunately the Olympics are not held to defend human rights."[67]

No international boycott campaign on the scale of the 1980 effort materialized, but there were scattered appeals. In Georgia, leaders advocated a boycott because of Sochi's proximity to the disputed region of Abkhazia.[68] In Britain, actor and writer Stephen Fry became the most ardent supporter of a boycott. In an open letter to the IOC and to British prime minister David Cameron, Fry cited violations of LGBT rights as the main reason for boycotting the Games. He likened Putin to Hitler, because "[Putin] is making scapegoats of gay people, just as Hitler did Jews."[69] Cameron's response, delivered by Twitter, was "we can better challenge prejudice as we attend, rather than boycotting the Winter Olympics."[70]

In the lead-up to the Games, athletes around the world actively participated in a campaign against the "LGBT law." They demonstrated their solidarity with the Russian LGBT movement by posting on social media pictures of themselves wearing red T-shirts with "6" on it (referring to the Olympic Charter's sixth principle).[71] On the other hand, official representatives of Russian athletes, such as Yelena Isinbaeva, openly defended Russian law as non-discriminatory and merely protecting "Russian traditions."[72] Despite foreign commentators' sniping comments about the juxtaposition of the "normal" and the "LGBT" in the famous gymnast's speech, sporting officials showed no particular interest in the Russian situation.[73]

Once the Olympics began, however, the athletes were silent.[74] As one commentator noted, there seemed to be as few human rights activists among the athletes as among the general population.[75] The IOC played a crucial role in ensuring this silence, as it explicitly banned all actions in support of the LGBT community during the Games as constituting "political propaganda" that contradicted the Olympic Charter. This statement was elicited by the actions of two Swedish athletes who posted an Instagram photo of their fingernails in rainbow colors in support of the Russian LGBT community. The Swedish National Olympic Committee reacted immediately and banned the use of such symbols during the Olympics because "political propaganda is forbidden."[76] Indeed, Rule 50 of the Olympic Charter states that "No kind of demonstration or political, religious or racial propaganda is permitted in any Olympic sites, venues or other areas."[77]

Without significant participation by athletes or Russian human rights groups, it was left to an international coalition of LGBT organizations and human rights bodies such as Human Rights Watch and Amnesty International to carry the banner of human rights, with the former focusing specifically on LGBT issues and the latter on broader rights issues. Human Rights Watch's position was consistent: it argued that a boycott impinged on the rights of spectators and athletes who, under international law, had no obligation to protect human rights.[78] Therefore, athletes should not be blamed for being unwilling to take up the cause of human rights.[79] But the group refused to comment on the most controversial issues, such as the application of the Olympic Charter's fiftieth principle to rainbow nail polish. As one staffer commented, "On the one hand we never called for athletes to express their support for human rights and we do not believe that they are obliged to do so[;] . . . however, the athletes like all people should have a right to self-expression and freedom of speech that has to be protected as one of the basic human rights."[80] Amnesty International was also active, among other activities collecting 200,000 signatures on a petition calling for discarding laws that restricted freedom of speech and association.[81]

The international campaign aimed first and foremost at changing the rules of the Olympic movement, including the demand for Olympic cities to follow the principle of nondiscrimination on the basis of gender and sexual orientation. The aim was that if in the future any discriminatory law, such as the Russian statute, was passed, the IOC would invoke strict sanctions, including a change in the Games' venue.

At the same time, a coalition of forty-four Russian and international NGOs addressed Olympic sponsors with a letter in which they attempted to link corporate reputations with violations of human rights. The letter pointed out that "you can expect that your brands will be indelibly linked to events and occurrences in Russia. . . . Silence in the face of discrimination also carries reputational risks."[82] This campaign was unsuccessful; no sponsor spoke out against discrimination in Russia with the exception of AT&T, which criticized the discriminatory law on its corporate blog.[83]

The Sochi Games became a platform for broadcasting LGBT topics worldwide, as some countries chose alternative ways of celebrating the opening of the Olympic Games. Instead of attending the opening ceremony, the Swedish delegation, for example, decided to meet with civil rights and LGBT activists in Moscow. Many countries sent low-level government officials to the Games instead of heads of state, a snub that dealt a severe blow to the political importance of the Olympics. German president Joachim Gauck cancelled his visit and explained his decision by citing the spirit of imperialism and the violation of the rule of law in Russia.[84] Other nonattendees such as the French, Georgian, and Polish presidents cited busy schedules. Many other European countries and the United States simply sent low-level officials.[85] President Barack Obama sent an Olympic delegation staffed by LGBT representatives.[86] Bukovskii has cited the refusal of many heads of state to attend the Sochi Games as evidence that the scale of human rights protest has expanded in recent years. Because the Olympics were intended in part to improve Russia's international image, the attendance issue was of critical importance: the huge investment in the Games risked being turned into a loss.[87]

In Russia, the LGBT Sport Federation attempted to host alternative LGBT Games in Moscow, which took place in five sports despite a virtual absence of publicity as well as pressure from the security apparatus.[88] Konstantin Yablotskii noted that this event "aimed at drawing attention to violations of human rights."[89] As another activist explained, "The campaign's main aim was to uplift the spirit of the community, and the campaign did help to unite and boost the community"; this became the campaign's main achievement.[90]

The fight for LGBT rights demonstrated that the IOC was unable to defend its position that human rights outside of sport should be ignored. An international movement of solidarity arose and succeeded in expressing sympathy with the LGBT community as well as in forcing the IOC to make modest changes to the rules of the Games. Under pressure, the IOC agreed to reforms in selection of host cities and explicit language prohibiting discrimination on the basis of sexual orientation in the Olympic Charter.[91] These achievements were brought about not by the efforts of the Olympic athletes but instead by the transnational movement in defense of LGBT rights, a movement that represents yet another step toward establishing "transnational rights."[92]

Activism in defense of human rights in Russia before the Sochi Olympics demonstrated that most of the actors in this process, including the world's great powers, no longer viewed sport boycotts as a useful means of achieving political goals, as had been the case in 1980. Nor did many human right activists see the Olympics as a means for improving a country's human rights situation; they did not expect athletes to abstain from participating in events hosted by undemocratic or openly autocratic countries. Human rights still constitute no meaningful part of the IOC's vision. Like Russian law, the IOC sees any action in support of human rights at the Games as "political."[93] But activism does make a difference: the LGBT movement, which was very active, was partially successful in fighting homophobia, whereas economic migrants, who were less able to mount a public campaign, found little help in fighting violations of their rights. Violations of human rights that occurred in direct connection with Olympic construction and preparations failed to attract the international public's attention to anywhere near the degree as violations of LGBT rights, even though the former were directly connected to the Games and the latter were not. That Putin ordered the "peaceful annexation" of the Crimea to begin the night after the Sochi closing ceremony is fascinating in its improbable timing. It seems that the lessons of the Soviet invasion of Afghanistan had been taken to heart. Two scholars even consider the annexation of Crimea just weeks after the Games as a logical step after the success of Sochi 2014—a legacy of Putin's Olympics.[94]

Overall, one can draw a line between the human rights discourse in Moscow 1980 and in Sochi 2014: both events had been planned during periods of détente in international relations, and both ended up taking place in the context of rising tensions in the international arena—first in a renewed Cold War and then in what has been called a new Cold War. As a result, human rights concerns in both cases were sacrificed to keep dialogue alive, thanks to assumptions that international events promote peaceful coexistence. And in both cases, hosting the Olympic Games resulted in opportunities for repressive governments to tighten their repression.

Notes

1. Robert Edelman, "Moscow 1980: Stalinism or Good, Clean Fun?," in *National Identity and Global Sport Events: Culture, Politics, and Spectacle in the Olympics and the Football World Cup*, ed. Alan Tomlinson and Christopher Young (Albany: SUNY Press, 2012), 149.

2. Organizing Committee to the Central Committee, memorandum, "Ob osnovnykh napravleniiakh raboty s natsionalinymi sportivnymi organizatsiiami stran Azii, Afriki i Latinskoi Ameriki v sviazi s provedeniem Olympiiskiikh igr v Moskve" [On the Main Directions of Work with National Sporting Organizations of the Countries of Asia, Africa, and Latin American in Connection with the Olympic Games in Moscow], August 31, 1976, in *Piat' kolets pod kremlevskimi zvezdami: Dokumental'naia khronika Olimpiady-80 v Moskve* [Five Rings Under the Kremlin Stars: A Documentary Chronicle of the 1980 Olympics in Moscow], ed. N. G. Tomilina (Moscow: Demokratiia, 2011), 117.

3. Nicolas Evan Sarantakes, *Dropping the Torch: Jimmy Carter, the Olympic Boycott, and the Cold War* (Cambridge: Cambridge University Press, 2011), 97.

4. Novosti Press Agency to Central Committee, information note, "Osnovnye tezisy vrazhdebnoi propagandy v sviazi c Olimpiadoi-80 i predlozheniia po kontrpropagande" [Main Theses of Hostile Propaganda in Connection with the 1980 Olympics and Proposals for Counterpropaganda], September 13, 1978, in *Piat' kolets*, 187.

5. Yuri Andropov, "On the Main Measures to Guarantee Security During the Preparation and Implementation of the XXII Olympic Games in Moscow," May 12, 1980, psi.ece.jhu.edu/~sasha/IRUSS/BUK/GBARC/pdfs/sovter75/kgb-ol80.pdf.

6. It is telling that leaving for the United States was "not recommended"; he left the country on an invitation from Israel even though he was not a Jew, and the Soviet authorities did not object to his departure. "Uezhaite ili podaete v tiurmu," *Novyi amerikanets*, June 11–16, 1980, 4.

7. Vardan E. Bardasarian, "Olimpiada-80 i olimpiiskii turizm cherez prizmu 'kholodnoi voiny'" [The 1980 Olympiad and Olympic tourism Through the Prism of the Cold War], *Sovremennye problem servisa i turizma* 3 (2008): 15.

8. Viktor Fainberg, "Odna zhizn' v pokushenie v Parizhe," *My zdes'*, no. 520, February 4–17, 2016, www.newswe.com/index.php?go=Pages&in=view&id=37.

9. Memo by the Committee for Physical Culture and Sport, "O sozdanii v Belgii provokatsionnoi organizatsii 'Komitet Moskva-80'" [On the Formation of the Propagandist Organization "Moscow-80 Committee" in Belgium], April 16, 1979, in *Piat' kolets*, 215.

10. Samuil Zivs, *The Anatomy of Lies*, trans. Nadezhda Burova (Moscow: Progress, 1982), 22–25. For more on Amnesty International's position, see Barbara Keys's chapter in this collection.

11. E. Romanov [R. Redlikh], "Olimpiiskaia bitva," *Posev* (February 1980): 10. On the NTS, see Sergei Levitsky, "The Ideology of NTS," *Russian Review* 31, no. 4 (1972): 398–405.

12. K. Bedov, "Olimpiada—dlia turistov," *Posev* (June 1980): 2.

13. "Dlia edushchikh na Olimpiadu 'Moskva-80,'" *Posev* (June 1980): 3–4.

14. Novosti Press Agency to Central Committee, analytical note, "Nekotorye osobennosti vystuplenii burzhuaznoi propagandy vokrug Olimpiady-80 i predlozheniia no kontrpropagande" [Some Features of the Speeches of Bourgeois Propaganda Around the 1980 Olympics and Proposals for Counterpropaganda], March 21, 1979, in *Piat' kolets*, 210.

15. *Piat' kolets*, 178.

16. Women's Campaign for Soviet Jewry to Harold Wilson, July 17, 1978, FCO 28/3546, National Archives of the United Kingdom, Kew.

17. Letter to the International Olympic Committee, in *Piat' kolets*, 184–185. See also Daphne Gerlis, *Those Wonderful Women in Black: Story of the Women's Campaign for Soviet Jewry* (London: Minerva, 1996).

18. Yevgeny Rubin, "The Soviet System: A Better Life for Better Athletes; Glaring Part of Facade," *New York Times*, November 12, 1978.

19. A. Ginzburg, P. Dembo, Iu. Egorov, A. Orlov, V. Reison, E. Rubin, E. Faibusovich, "Olimpiiskomny komitety SShA," *Novyi amerikanets*, no. 9 (April 11–17, 1980): 22.

20. Evgenii Rubin, "Boikot," *Novyi amerikanets* 1, no. 10 (April 18–24, 1980): 12.

21. Ivan Tolstoi, "Dovlatov protiv Olimpiadi," Radio Svoboda, February 6, 2014, www.svoboda.org/a/25255350.html.

22. Transcript, "Vokrug bylykh igr. Olimpiada i zhurnalistika. Peredacha tret'ia," Radio Svoboda [1978], www.svoboda.org/content/transcript/25224454.html.

23. John Hoberman, *The Olympic Crisis: Sport, Politics and Moral Order* (New Rochelle, NY: A. D. Caratzas, 1986), 70. I have found no reference to this statement in either Associated Press reports or Sakharov's memoirs. Perhaps because the meeting was long and primarily about the right to emigrate, the Olympics was a secondary issue that escaped Sakharov's attention in his memoirs.

24. Andrei Sakharov, *Memoirs*, trans. Richard Lourie (New York: Knopf, 1990), 496.

25. A. D. Sakharov, *Dnevniki*, Vol. 1 (Moscow: Vremia, 2006), 720–721.

26. Sakharov, *Memoirs*, 496.

27. E. Kyznetsov et al., "Obrashchenie 12 pollitizakliuchennykh lageria osobogo rezhima k Sportsmenam—Uchastnikam Olimpiiskikh igr c prizyvom trebovat' ot sovetskogo pravitel'stva sobliudeniia prav cheloveka, Sosnovka, MordASSR" [Appeal by 12 Political Prisoners in Special Prison Camps to Sportsmen Participating in the Olympics with an Appeal to Demand Respect for Human Rights from the Soviet Government, Mordovskaia ASSR], Arkhiv Samizdata no. 3759, Open Society Archive, January 15, 1979, osaarchivum.org/files/fa/300-85-9-9.htm.

28. Sakharov, *Memoirs*, 496.

29. "Boikot ne mozhet byt' panatseei," Sakharov interview in *Le Matin*, reproduced in *Posev*, no. 10 (1978): 24–25.

30. Quoted in *The KGB File of Andrei Sakharov*, eds. Joshua Rubenstein and Alexander Gribanov (New Haven, CT: Yale University Press, 2005), 36; see also 241.

31. Ibid., 37.

32. "Olimpiada-80. Podebit' liuboi tsenoi," at www.youtube.com/watch?v=Qz9IHKYrDrA.

33. N. Besslavnaiia, "Olimpiada: Ot spetsial'nogo korrespondenta 'Poseva,'" *Posev* (September 1980): 9–10.

34. Edelman, "Moscow 1980," 153.

35. Ibid., 159.

36. Richard Arnold and Andrew Foxall, "Lord of the (Five) Rings," *Problems of Post-Communism* 61, no. 1 (2014): 3–12.

37. Adam Wittenberg Cox, *The International Olympic Committee, Transnational Human Rights and the Conundrum of Political Neutrality: Examining the Impact of the LGBT Controversy on the Sochi Winter Games and the IOC*. Kindle version.

38. See Ilia Kalinin, "Nostalgic Modernization: The Soviet Past as 'Historical Horizon,'" *Slavonica* 17, no. 2 (2011): 156–166; Natalia Gronskaya and Andrey Makarychev, "The 2014 Sochi Olympics and 'Sovereign Power,'" *Problems of Post-Communism* 61, no. 1 (2014): 41–51.

39. "'Eto ne rasplata za Krym,' 20 kliuchevykh tsitat iz press-konferentsii Putina," RBC, December 18, 2014, www.rbc.ru/politics/18/12/2014/5492d9bc9a79476a76c691c1.

40. "Approaching the 2014 Sochi Olympics: Human Rights in Russia," Amnesty International, 2013, www.amnestyusa.org/sites/default/files/ai_brief_-_human_rights_in_russia_2013_0.pdf.

41. For details, see Helen Jefferson Lenskyj, *Sexual Diversity and the Sochi 2014 Olympics: No More Rainbows* (London: Palgrave Macmillan, 2014), 48–53.

42. Sufian Zhemukhov, "Migrant Workers and the Sochi Olympics," *Russian Analytical Digest*, no. 143 (February 9, 2014): 10.

43. "Race to the Bottom," Human Rights Watch, February 6, 2013, www.hrw.org/report/2013/02/06/race-bottom/exploitation-migrant-workers-ahead-russias-2014-winter-olympic-games.

44. Robert W. Orttung and Sufian Zhemukhov, *Putin's Olympics: The Sochi Games and the Evolution of Twenty-First Century Russia* (New York: Routledge, 2017), 45–50.

45. "Four Reasons Why Sochi Olympics Is Environmental Disaster," EcoWatch, February 12, 2014, www.ecowatch.com/4-reasons-the-sochi-olympics-are-an-environmental-disaster-1881859802.html; Andrew Foxall, "Russia's Olympic Shame: Corruption, Human Rights and Security at 'Sochi 2014'" (London: Henry Jackson Society, 2014), 24–32, henryjacksonsociety.org/wp-content/uploads/2014/02/Russias-Olympic-Shame.pdf.

46. "Why Boycott the Sochi Olympics?," Internet Archive, 2014, web.archive.org/web/20140227052103/http://petition.nosochi2014.com/.

47. Foxall, "Russia's Olympic Shame," 12. See, e.g., "Olimpiiskaia zachistka," Novaia gazeta, December 2013, www.novayagazeta.ru/articles/2013/12/14/57653-olimpiyskaya-171-zachistka-187.

48. Orttung and Zhemukhov, *Putin's Olympics*, 72–74.

49. On persecution of activists before the Olympics, see Sochi Watch, sochi2014watch-en.blogspot.com.au/.

50. Svetlana Bolotnikova, "Zachistka kuban pered olimpiadoi," Big Caucasus, May 30, 2013, www.bigcaucasus.com/events/actual/30-05-2013/83422-kimaev-0/.

51. "Mer Sochi predlagaet prinyditel'no otpravliat' bezrabotnykh i tsygan no stroike goroda," Interfaks, October 19, 2009, www.interfax.ru/russia/105968.

52. Orttung and Zhemukhov, *Putin's Olympics*, 73.

53. Steve Gutterman, "Critics Say Putin's Olympic Security Decree Violates Rights," Reuters, August 24, 2013, www.reuters.com/article/2013/08/24/olympics-russia-decree-idUSL6N0GP02520130824.

54. "Liudmila Alekseeva: Ia protiv boikota Olimpiada v Sochi," Regnum, June 10, 2013, regnum.ru/news/polit/1669604.html.

55. Boris Al'tshuler, "Sochi: Mnogodetnaia sem'ia v garazhe kak simvol Olimpiadi," ROO "Prava pebenka," right-child.ru/94-sohi.html.

56. See, e.g., Alexander Podrabinek, "Games Olympic and Political," Institute of Modern Russia, August 27, 2013, www.imrussia.org/en/analysis/politics/540-games-olympic-and -political.

57. Eliana Dockterman, "Pussy Riot Turns Watching the Sochi Games into a Moral Dilemma," *Time*, February 6, 2014, world.time.com/2014/02/06/pussy-riot-turns-watching-the -sochi-games-into-a-moral-dilemma/.

58. On the history of this law, see Lucas Paoli Itaborahy and Jingshu Zhu, *State-Sponsored Homophobia: A World Survey of Laws; Criminalisation, Protection and Recognition of Same-Sex Love*, May 2013, 8th ed., ILGA-Europe, old.ilga.org/Statehomophobia/ILGA_State_Sponsored _Homophobia_2013.pdf. For a detailed analysis of the increase in homophobic sentiments, see Cai Wilkinson, "Putting 'Traditional Values' into Practice: The Rise and Contestation of Anti-Homopropaganda Laws in Russia," *Journal of Human Rights* 13, no. 3 (2014): 363–379.

59. See Omar G. Encarnación, "Gay Rights: Why Democracy Matters," *Journal of Democracy* 25, no. 3 (July 2014): 90–95.

60. Lenskyj, *Sexual Diversity and the Sochi 2014 Olympics*, 77–78. For a political analysis of LGBT issues, human rights, and the Olympics, see Adam Wittenberg Cox, *The International Olympic Committee, Transnational Human Rights and the Conundrum of Political Neutrality: Examining the Impact of the LGBT Controversy on the Sochi Winter Games and the IOC* (Amazon Digital Services, 2015).

61. "Olympic Charter: In Force as from 2 August 2015," International Olympic Committee, stillmed.olympic.org/Documents/olympic_charter_en.pdf.

62. IOC chairman Jean-Claude Killy said that "The IOC doesn't really have the right to discuss the laws in the country where the Olympic Games are organized. As long as the Olympic Charter is respected, we are satisfied, and that is the case." Kathy Lally, "IOC: No Grounds to Challenge Russian Anti-Gay Law as Sochi Olympic Games Approach," *Washington Post*, September 26, 2013.

63. "Boycotting Anti-Gay Russia," Erasing 76 Crimes, July 30, 2013, 76crimes.com/2013/07 /30/boycotting-anti-gay-russia-vodka-maybe-olympics-too/.

64. "Russian LGBT Activists and Supporters Call for Boycott of Russian Products and Winter Olympics," International Lesbian, Gay, Bisexual, Trans and Intersex Association, July 29, 2013, ilga.org/russian-lgbt-activists-and-supporters-call-for-boycott-of-russian-products-and -winter-olympics/.

65. "Should the World Boycott the Sochi Olympics in Defense of Gay Rights?" *Russia Today*, August 8, 2013, www.rt.com/op-edge/gay-olympics-fry-ioc-sochi-245/.

66. Author interview with Konstantin Iablotskii, president of the Russian LGBT Sport Federation, June 21, 2016.

67. Author interview with Igor Kochetkov, May 26, 2016.

68. See, e.g., "Burdzhanadze grozit sorvat' sochinskuiu Olimpiadu," July 27, 2007, Lenta.ru, lenta.ru/news/2007/07/26/olympic.

69. Stephen Fry, "Open Letter to David Cameron and IOC," The Old Friary, August 7, 2013, www.stephenfry.com/2013/08/an-open-letter-to-david-cameron-and-the-ioc/.

70. "Cameron Rejects Stephen Fry's Call for Russian Winter Olympics Boycott," *The Guardian*, August 10, 2013, www.theguardian.com/sport/2013/aug/10/cameron-rejects-stephen-fry -russia-winter-games-boycott.

71. See the official site of "Principle 6" at www.principle6.org/.

72. "Yelena Isinbayeva Defends Russia's Anti-Gay Propaganda Law," CNN, August 13, 2013, www.cnn.com/2013/08/15/sport/world-championships/.

73. "IAAF President Lamine Diack: 'No Problem' with Russia's Anti-Gay Law," CNN, August 9, 2013, www.cnn.com/2013/08/09/sport/russia-anti-gay-diack-athletics/index.html; Matt Brigidi, "Sochi 2014: Brian Burke Calls Russia's Anti-Gay Law 'Repugnant,'" SB Nation, August 27, 2013, www.sbnation.com/nhl/2013/8/27/4664566/brian-burke-russia-anti-gay-law-olympics-2014.

74. One exception was track-and-field athlete Nick Symmonds who, having won a medal in Moscow, used the opportunity to protest the homophobic law. See "Russia: US Track and Field Star Dedicates Moscow Silver Medal to Gay and Lesbian Friends," PINK News, August 14, 2013, www.pinknews.co.uk/2013/08/14/russia-us-track-and-field-star-dedicates-moscow-silver-medal-to-gay-and-lesbian-friends/.

75. Cyd Zeigler, "How We Blew It in Sochi: The LGBT Community Took a Shot at Anti-Gay Laws in Russia and Missed the Olympic-Sized Target," *QED: A Journal in GLBTQ Worldmaking* 1, no. 3 (Fall 2014): 36.

76. Sara Gates, "Athletes' Rainbow Nails Will Not Be Tolerated at the Olympics, Sweden Warns," Huffington Post, August 20, 2013, www.huffingtonpost.com/2013/08/20/rainbow-nails-olympics-sweden_n_3785418.html.

77. Olympic Charter.

78. Author interview with Jane M. Buchanan, May 24, 2016, author's audio archive.

79. See the above-mentioned Human Rights Watch reports regarding human rights violations on Sochi Olympic premises.

80. Interview with Jane Buchanan.

81. Press release, "Amnesty International Directors to Deliver Global Petition to Russian President Ahead of Sochi Olympics," Amnesty International, January 27, 2014, www.amnesty.org/en/press-releases/2014/01/amnesty-international-directors-deliver-global-petition-russian-president-a/.

82. LGBT Coalition to Corporate Leaders, January 31, 2014, Freedom House, freedomhouse.org/sites/default/files/Sochi%20letter.pdf.

83. "AT&T Becomes First Major U.S. Corporation to Condemn Russia's Anti-LGBT Law," Human Rights Campaign, February 4, 2014, www.hrc.org/blog/att-condemns-anti-lgbt-law-in-russia-sets-example-for-other-olympic-sponsor.

84. Philipp Oltermann, "German President Boycotts Sochi Winter Olympics," *The Guardian*, December 8, 2013, www.theguardian.com/world/2013/dec/08/german-president-boycotts-sochi-winter-olympics.

85. "Chernyshenko podvel itogi Olimpiady v Sochi," Mail.ru, April 7, 2014, sport.mail.ru/news/olympics/17729424/?frommail=1.

86. Josh Leberman, "President Obama Selects Athletes for Sochi Delegation," *Mercury News*, January 30, 2014, www.mercurynews.com/national-sports-news/ci_25025987/president-obama-selects-gay-athletes-sochi-delegation.

87. Ol'ga Khvorostova, "Vladimir Bukovskii: Chem bol'she protestov v zashchitu politicheskikh zakliuchennykh, tem veroiatnee ikh osvobozhdenie," Institut sovremennoi Rossii, February 20, 2014, bit.ly/2n5q0ul.

88. Egor Vinogradov, "Otkrytye igry v Moskve: Malen'kaia pobeda bol'shogo sporta," Deutsche Welle, March 3, 2013, bit.ly/2nRDnBH.

89. Interview with Konstantin Iablotskii.

90. Author interview with Anastasiia Smirnova, coordinator, LGBT protest campaign against the Sochi Olympics, June 28, 2016.

91. Olympic Agenda 2020 (2014), International Olympic Committee, stillmed.olympic.org /Documents/Olympic_Agenda_2020/Olympic_Agenda_2020-20-20_Recommendations-ENG .pdf.

92. Susan Brownell, "Human Rights and the Beijing Olympics: Imagined Global Community and the Transnational Public Sphere," *British Journal of Sociology* 63, no. 2 (2012): 306–327.

93. Dmitry Dubrovskiy, "Undesirable Organizations and Foreign Agent Law," *IWMpost*, no. 116 (Fall–Winter 2015): 21–22, www.iwm.at/publications/iwmpost/iwmpost-archive /iwmpost-116/.

94. Orttung and Zhemukhov, *Putin's Olympics*, 97–98.

CHAPTER 7

Hosting the Olympic Games in Developed Countries

Debating the Human Rights Ideals of Sport

Jules Boykoff

In July 2015, the International Olympic Committee (IOC) selected Beijing to host the 2022 Winter Games. In reality, the IOC had few options. Voters in Stockholm, Munich, Kraków, and Switzerland had categorically rejected hosting the 2022 Games. Norwegian politicians followed suit, throttling Oslo's bid and leaving only Beijing and Almaty, Kazakhstan, in the running. Both China and Kazakhstan are human rights bête noires. No matter which city won, the Olympic movement was destined to receive criticism. In choosing Beijing, the IOC not only made the Chinese city the first to host both the Summer and Winter Games but also demonstrated its tendency to select cities with questionable human rights records that clashed with the principles of Olympism. After all, the Olympic Charter trumpets "social responsibility and respect for universal fundamental ethical principles."[1] Such principles vis-à-vis human rights and civil liberties were in short supply in the two finalists for the 2022 Winter Games.

In coronating Beijing, the contradiction bit doubly deep, as back in 2001 Beijing Summer Games bidders vowed that awarding the Chinese the Olympics would speed up the process toward a more democratic future for the country. As Beijing bid committee luminary Wang Wei had claimed, "We are confident that, with the Games coming to China, not only are they going to promote the economy, but also enhance all the social sectors, including education, medical care and human rights."[2] Jacques Rogge, then president of the IOC, spoke from a similar script, stating that "It is clear that the staging of the Olympic Games will do a lot for the improvement of human rights and social relations in China."[3] Longtime Olympic power broker Richard Pound created an uproar in defending Beijing as a viable Olympic host despite its problematic human rights profile. He told *La Presse* that "We must not forget that 400 years ago, Canada was a land of savages, with scarcely 10,000 inhabitants of European descent, while in China, we're talking about a 5,000-year-old civilization."[4] In short, he tried to paper over serious human rights problems by crudely harkening to a genocidal campaign against First Nations peoples. Pound later apologized. As it turned out, however, predictions of Olympics-induced human rights progress in China were greatly exaggerated. Sophie Richardson of Human Rights Watch even argued that "The reality is that the Chinese government's hosting of the Games has been *a catalyst* for abuses."[5]

When it comes to civil liberties and due process, hosting the Olympics in the modern era has been "a catalyst for abuses" in Western democracies as well. In fact, objections similar to those lodged over the awarding of Olympic Games to human rights violators such as China and Russia also apply to developed country hosts such as the United States, Greece, Canada, and England. It is a relatively straightforward enterprise to single out Olympic hosts Russia and China as major human rights violators that do not merit hosting the world's top-flight Olympic athletes. However, other hosts deserve similar scrutiny. In hosting the Games, democratic governments tend to adopt authoritarian practices that have deleterious effects on civil liberties and the democratic practice of dissident citizenship.

In this chapter I examine how these suppressive dynamics played out in the context of recent Olympic Games. I analyze the tensions between human rights rhetoric and on-the-ground reality at recent Olympic Games in Western countries: Atlanta 1996, Salt Lake City 2002, Athens 2004, Vancouver 2010, and London 2012. In evaluating these Olympic Games transpiring in Western democracies, it becomes apparent that it is not just authoritarian regimes that use the Olympic Games to catalyze repression: something similar, albeit qualitatively different, happens in the democratic context. When it comes to Olympic protest groups in democratic countries, particular rights come under fire—civil and political rights, especially free speech and the right to assemble—while we also see affronts to individual liberty, such as forced evictions, to make way for the Games as well as the impingement of civil rights related to due process and property. Long-term targeted political imprisonment and torture remain the purview of authoritarian states hosting the Olympic Games. In short, in the context of the Olympics, host cities in democratic countries tend to rely on the *suppression* of political dissent and civil liberties, while authoritarian hosts exhibit a tendency toward political *repression* through direct violence.[6]

Human rights are rooted in principles of equality, freedom, and dignity. In the 1970s, U.S. president Jimmy Carter's administration embraced rights rhetoric, but as Barbara J. Keys points out, "human rights became a way of directing attention elsewhere—a program for improving the rest of the world rather than rectifying deficiencies at home." Human rights talk emerged as "the new mantra" because the idea "resonated with extraordinary power among a public eager to reclaim American virtue" after the tumultuous 1960s.[7] In reality, human rights scholars have noted that "the United States is far from the 'gold standard' for international human rights practice."[8] Examining recent Olympic Games held in Canada and England shows that this gap between rhetoric and reality is not limited to the United States.[9]

The Olympics and Human Rights

The Olympic Charter is brimming with optimistic possibilities expressed through universalistic language. For instance, the second "fundamental principle of Olympism" intones that "The goal of Olympism is to place sport at the service of the harmonious development of humankind, with a view to promoting a peaceful society concerned with the preservation of human dignity." The fourth "fundamental principle" directly states that "The practice of sport is a human right. Every individual must have the possibility of practising sport, without discrimination of any kind and in the Olympic spirit, which requires mutual understanding with a spirit of friendship, solidarity and fair play."[10]

Yet the Olympic Charter also circumscribes political dissent. While on one hand it forbids discrimination based on politics and reprimands "any political or commercial abuse of sport and athletes," on the other hand it proffers Rule 50, which explicitly squelches political speech: "No kind of demonstration or political, religious or racial propaganda is permitted in any Olympic sites, venues or other areas."[11] Prohibiting free political speech in "other areas" is a strikingly broad spatial stroke.

Rule 50 exemplifies the wider state of exception that predominates in the lead-up to and during the Games. Carl Schmitt offered an influential iteration of the concept, asserting that being able to name the state of exception nestles into the core of sovereignty: "Sovereign is he who decides on the exception."[12] Giorgio Agamben took this further in *State of Exception*, describing how an exceptional moment, as defined by those in power, can galvanize a slew of extrajudicial actions, judicial decrees, and state measures that the powerful create to maintain their advantageous political positioning, claiming necessity all the while. He writes that "In truth, the state of exception is neither internal nor external to the juridical order, and the problem of defining it concerns precisely a threshold, or a zone of indifference, where inside and outside do not exclude each other but rather blur with each other."[13] Local Olympic organizing committees embrace the state of exception, leveraging it into special laws and rules as well as a justification for bypassing normal procedures. This sets up an internal tension within the Olympic Games. Human rights are meant to be universal—in theory there are no exceptions. Yet the Olympic Games occur in a state of exception whereby the normal rules of politics—and sometimes actual rules and laws—do not apply. The Olympic context demonstrates that despite the putative universality of human rights, there are exceptions made all the time, even with democratic hosts.

Scholars William T. Armaline, Davita Silfen Glasberg, and Bandana Purkayastha emphasize the importance of the concept of the "human rights enterprise," which they define as "any and all efforts to define or realize fundamental dignity and 'right' for all human beings." Human rights instruments such as the force of international law can help advance this "human rights enterprise," although the implementation and consistent enforcement of human rights standards often falls short. They argue that today "the role and relative power of corporations and other significant private actors are crucial to an analysis of the contemporary human rights enterprise." This is certainly the case in the context of the Olympics, where private sponsors and the IOC play key roles that guide power relations in the host city. Armaline, Glasberg, and Purkayastha delineate different types of rights—economic, social, cultural, political, and civil—while recognizing their interdependency.[14] Economic, social, and cultural rights are not typically attached to or directly affected by the Olympics Games, whereas political and civil rights are often impinged upon by the Olympic machine. Scholars have long recognized the multivalent nature of rights regimes and the emergent gaps between rhetoric and reality.[15] In addition, the term "human rights" suffers from definitional promiscuity and conceptual squishiness. Furthermore, as Dominique Clement puts it, human rights "principles are not easily translated into practice."[16]

In the context of sport, scholars Andrew Adams and Mark Piekarz recognize that tethering abstract human rights principles to the earth into actual policies replete with accountability and oversight is where matters get complicated. They have identified "key points" where human rights intersect with sporting events such as the Olympics: land use involving the construction of sports venues and requisite mega-event infrastructure and employment standards and practices affecting workers in and around sporting events.[17] Land-use issues link laterally to displacement through either forced removals or gentrification. Sport-related activity can foster positive expressions of solidarity as well as hypernationalism and xenophobia. Mega-events are becoming infamous for substandard work environments, often with temporary jobs that end with the Games. Discrimination based on race, gender, and sexuality can also emerge in the context of the Games.

At the 2014 Sochi Winter Games, United Nations (UN) secretary-general Ban Ki-moon proclaimed that the UN and the IOC were "a team" that was "joining forces for our shared ideals. Sustainability. Universality. Solidarity. Non-discrimination. The fundamental equality of all people."[18] This was hardly the beginning of the UN and the IOC "joining forces." The relationship between the two supranational behemoths extends back to the 1950s when the United Nations Educational, Scientific, and Cultural Organization (UNESCO)—the UN agency for education, culture, science, and free expression—became interested in the power of sport as an educational tool. The path was not always smooth. Skirmishes erupted in the 1950s when the IOC's notoriously prickly President Avery Brundage became convinced that UNESCO was critiquing the Olympic Games to an unfair degree over the undemocratic organizational practices of international sports organizations such as the IOC.[19] By the 1990s the IOC had firmed up its relations with the UN, based on a concern for the importance of human rights and environmental sustainability. In 1993, the UN General Assembly approved the revival of the Olympic Truce whereby countries affiliated with the IOC would cease bellicose combat during the Games. The timing was designed to encourage a truce in the besieged city of Sarajevo (host of the 1984 Winter Games), which was caught in the conflicts that erupted on the disintegration of Yugoslavia. Since then, the UN General Assembly routinely adopts resolutions to honor the Olympic Truce.[20] Despite the ideal, numerous countries have flouted the truce. For example, the United States did not curtail wars or occupations in Afghanistan or Iraq during the Olympics. During the 2008 Beijing Summer Games, Russia and Georgia continued to fight over South Ossetia.[21] In 2009 the IOC capped its relationship with the UN by securing permanent observer status, a rarity for nongovernmental organizations.

It should be noted that there are significant trade-offs involved in making human rights the focus in sport-related activities. Sport scholar Richard Gruneau argues:

> A focus on improving human rights . . . promises to open up opportunities for marginalized individuals but also risks deflecting attention from less immediately evident social and organizational features that reproduce broader inequalities in condition. When this latter situation occurs, rights-based approaches to development can become disconnected from the structural changes that many community groups argue are necessary to improve the lives of the world's poorest citizens.[22]

As Gruneau readily acknowledges, asking sports organizations to solve entrenched, multifarious sociopolitical problems is extremely ambitious. In addition, as Stuart Hall notes, the term "human rights"—especially individual rights predicated on the existence of a strong state—is often freighted with class privilege. "Whenever one sees that [rights] language appear in the ideological field, one has to be quite careful about the persistence of its articulation to certain bourgeois positions" that are sympathetic to the very capitalism that gives rise to—or at least contributes to—human rights violations. Although "human rights" is a complicated concept and we ought not set expectations for its use value too high, Hall points out that "the language of rights cannot belong *only* to the bourgeoisie."[23] Strategically asking sport bodies such as the IOC to ensure that human rights and civil liberties are respected in the host city is judicious; after all, such ethics are enmeshed in the Olympic Charter. In particular, political and civil rights are key to maintaining democracy during the state of exception brought on by the Olympics. Political rights such as the freedom to assemble, freedom of speech, and freedom of association are vital to activists keen to challenge the Games. Civil rights related to the consistent rule of law as well as property rights become relevant at times.

Dissent and Western Democratic Hosts

Relatively uncontroversial human rights lingo freely flows from the mouths of IOC barons each time the Olympics approach. But how well are civil liberties and human rights protected in the lead-up to and during the Olympics in countries with strong democratic traditions? A careful look at the following Olympiads will help us better understand the intrinsic tensions: Atlanta 1996, Salt Lake City 2002, Athens 2004, Vancouver 2010, and London 2012.

Political scientist E. E. Schattschneider famously asserted that *"the definition of the alternatives is the supreme instrument of power."* He focused on the importance of agenda setting insofar as "the definition of alternatives is the choice of conflicts, and the choice of conflicts allocates power."[24] The IOC wields immense—critics say inordinate—power in the Olympic Games host city, setting rules and norms within the state of exception that stultifies sociopolitical conflict or channels it into less threatening space. Through its organizational style it engages in what Schattschneider calls *"the mobilization of bias."* Under this scenario, "some issues are organized into politics while others are organized out." As he notes, "all forms of political organization have a bias in favor of the exploitation of some kinds of conflict and the suppression of others."[25] Through the Olympic Charter as well as a variety of outsourced means, the IOC and the local organizing committee suppress conflict in the Olympic city. Free expression is often sacrificed on the altar of frictionless Olympic Games.

Atlanta Summer Games, 1996

Many remember the 1996 Atlanta Games as the "Coca-Cola Olympics." The Atlanta-based corporation, which had been an Olympic sponsor since the 1928 Amsterdam Games, invested more than half a billion dollars into marketing and sponsorship, funded the Olympic Torch relay, and provided nearly 1,000 volunteers at Olympic venues. The Coca-Cola Company also snapped up land on which it built a $20 million Coke theme park in downtown Atlanta.[26]

Yet others recall the Games as the spur for their displacement and the justification for the squelching of their free speech rights. Coca-Cola's ability to grab land for a theme park symbolized the widespread gentrification spurred on by the Atlanta Games. Fulton County commissioner Martin King III, the oldest son of the Atlanta-born civil and human rights icon Martin Luther King Jr., railed against a high-profile deal for an Olympic-stadium pact that benefited local power brokers such as the Ted Turner-owned Atlanta Braves baseball team. Commissioner King thundered that

We really have two Atlantas. One for the rich and prosperous and another for the poor and downtrodden. One group who can afford the luxuries that Atlanta has to offer. The other who can barely make it through the month. . . . The way I see it, the stadium deal is a one-sided deal. Not only does it place an unknown liability on the tax-payers of this county and city, but it allows the rich to get richer. . . . This is on top of the fact that the last stadium displaced many members of the same community, with little or no positive effect on the lives of the people who still live in the impacted neighborhoods.[27]

King concluded with a bang: "Greed, exclusivity and elitism have become the symbols of Atlanta's Olympic movement—all things that my father fought against—and they are all reflected in the deal proposed before us, the rich and affluent on one side, the poor and hopeless on the other side."[28] Corporate sponsor exclusivity was the order of the day, with Atlanta organizers orchestrating a municipal sign ordinance meant to dissuade ambush marketers and local vendors who might hope to angle in on the five-ring action. Within the restrictive measure, which limited the size of advertisements, a special concession allowed Olympic sponsors to erect massive ten-story-tall billboards around town. Coke carried out the necessary "political arm-twisting" behind the scenes to win the exemption.[29]

In the lead-up to the Games gentrification ran rampant, with rents near the Olympic Park catapulting so high as to leave some residents no choice but to leave. One aggressive property manager—Intown Properties—aimed to cash in on inflated prices during the Olympic period by telling tenants that they either had to vacate or pay $3,000 per month. To make way for Games venues, public housing was demolished including Techwood Homes, the country's first federally subsidized public housing project. The New Deal-era development was bulldozed in 1995. Techwood and Clark Howell Homes were replaced by the Olympic Village. Urban planning scholar Lawrence Vale described the process of purging the poor as "from Techwood Flats to Techwood Flattened," with the main beneficiaries being Georgia Tech University and Coca-Cola.[30] While the poor were being displaced, Billy Payne, president of the Atlanta Committee for the Olympic Games, scooped up a salary of more than $669,000.[31]

Meanwhile, the homeless were targeted for forced removal. In 1995 and 1996 alone more than 9,000 homeless people were arrested—often without probable cause—as part of a state program that attracted the attention of federal authorities who ultimately issued a cease and desist order.[32] Some homeless and poor people were even issued one-way bus tickets to Alabama and Florida.[33] According to the Center on Housing Rights and Evictions, "the demonizing of poor and homeless Atlantans by the moneyed power elite did not begin with the Olympics, but hosting the 1996 Summer Olympic Games gave that practice the adrenaline it needed to become the city's prevailing, even blatant, public policy."[34]

Salt Lake City Winter Olympics, 2002

Protesters had similar concerns regarding the 2002 Winter Games. Activism around the Salt Lake City Olympics was blunted by two key factors: the bribery scandal that consumed a majority of the critical media oxygen afforded to the Games and the terrorist attacks of September 11, 2001, that in the eyes of many Americans made protest appear uncouth. Yet the fact that the Salt Lake City Winter Olympics were the first staged after the attacks of 9/11 meant that security costs were significantly augmented, which exacerbated fiscal concerns among the citizenry. Olympic organizers requested a whopping $4 billion in government funds, according to Mitt Romney, the former Massachusetts governor who helped nudge the Games across the finish line in the wake of the bid scandal.[35] In the end, taxpayers contributed $1.5 billion, about $335 million of it for security measures—one and a half times the amount that the U.S. Treasury spent on all seven previous U.S. Olympics combined. In the end, a 12,000-strong security force policed the Games, replete with biometric surveillance technologies, chemical weapons, riot gear, and paint-pellet weapons for dispersing crowds.[36]

Before the September 11 attacks, local organizers had been planning sizable protests. In response, the Salt Lake City Organizing Committee created "designated forums" where protesters could demonstrate as long as they secured permits. Romney teamed up with Salt Lake City mayor Rocky Anderson to rebrand these areas "public forum zones." Two weeks before the Games commenced, the city council passed an ordinance that forbade activists from wearing masks in public during the Games. Despite these repressive measures, activists staged scattershot protests in parks, on the streets, and in "public forum zones" on an array of issues: environmental concerns, using taxpayer funds on high-profile Games rather than local problems, and animal rights.[37] Their efforts to raise critical questions about the effects of the Olympics foreshadowed future dissent at subsequent Winter Games.

Athens Summer Olympics, 2004

The Athens Games of 2004 highlight a key dynamic in the suppression of political dissent in the context of the Olympics: the intimidation effect. As with Salt Lake City, Olympic security officials amassed an arsenal of weapons and special laws. The result was the intensified militarization of public space. As host of the first Summer Games after the attacks of 9/11, Athens expended around $1.5 billion on security measures, nearly $143,000 per athlete. This was an increase of more than 700 percent over the prior Summer Games in Sydney.[38]

Greek security forces took full advantage of the Olympic state of exception, laminating another layer onto its burgeoning surveillance capacity. Athens created what Minas Samatas calls an "Olympic superpanopticon" made up of surveillance cameras, vehicle tracking devices, satellites, and more. The U.S.-based security firm Science Applications International Corporation created the centralized C4I (command, control, communication, computer, and integration) security system to filter the data derived from surveillance. The system was originally developed for military use. In this instance it was used to monitor terrorist threats but also political dissent.[39]

The intimidation effect was fully evident in Athens. According to Samatas:

> The military security umbrella was activated on July 27, 2004, just before the Olympic Games were to start. Hundreds of CCTV cameras swept the main avenues and squares of Athens, whereas three police helicopters and a zeppelin, equipped with more surveillance cameras, hovered overhead. The helicopters and the zeppelin were flying almost around the clock throughout the games. Dozens of new PAC 3 (Patriot Advanced Capability) missiles were armed and in position at three locations around the capital, including the Tatoi Military Base near the athletes' Olympic Village, to provide a defense umbrella over Athens. Security forces also received 11 state-of-the-art surveillance vans that received and monitored images from around the city. . . . By the August 13 opening ceremony, authorities had installed thousands of CCTV cameras and deployed all over Greece more than 70,000 military and security staff on patrol.[40]

In addition, the security apparatus included around 40 explosives detection devices, more than 4,000 automatic vehicle locators, and chemical and radiological detection systems.[41]

This was expensive: at the time the Games were the priciest peacetime operation ever.[42] It is vital to note that the security hardware and systems were not only expensive but also enduring. The security architecture procured during the Olympic state of exception becomes tomorrow's mechanism for everyday policing. Security officials in Athens were well aware of this dynamic: former minister of public order George Floridis wrote that "This great expenditure is not concerned only with the duration of the Olympics. It is an investment for the future." He went on to note that "The special training, technical know-how, and ultramodern equipment will turn the Hellenic Police into one of the best and most professional in the world, for the benefit of the Greek people."[43]

Although the Athens 2004 official report overstated the Olympics-induced "uninhibited enthusiasm" shown by people across the country, the Games did not see as much dissent as one might have expected.[44] One group, the Anti-2004 Campaign, created and submitted to the IOC "an anti-bid book" that outlined its critiques of the Games, from environmental concerns to fiscal issues.[45] Beyond that, anti-Olympics campaigners organized a number of demonstrations, educational public forums, and press conferences but refrained from confrontation during the Games so as to avoid being labeled anti-Greek or being violently repressed.[46]

Vancouver Winter Games, 2010

Activists in Vancouver adopted a militant approach, taking to the streets in protest before and during the 2010 Winter Olympics. Activists fomented a complex coalition of direct-action activists, environmentalists, civil liberties groups, leftists, professors, and poets. Much leadership came from First Nations activists fully rooted in the community, who along with their allies hammered home the point that the Olympics were being staged on unceded Coast Salish land. Although Olympic organizers folded in the Four Host First Nations—Lil'wat, Musqueam, Squamish, and Tsleil-Waututh peoples—as partners in both the initial bid and the actual Games, their inclusion also generated fierce criticism. Critical sport historians have long problematized the relationship between indigenous peoples and the Olympics.[47] Janice Forsyth, Western University professor and member of the Fisher River Cree First Nation, wrote that "The constructed celebration of Indigenous cultures for only brief periods in host nations has yet to shift the historical patterns of unequal access to power between Olympic organizers and Indigenous people." Vancouver 2010 did little to alter this history, a failure that generated significant political dissent.[48]

The state did not sit by idly as the activism took shape. To harmonize local laws with IOC dictates, the City of Vancouver passed the 2010 Winter Games By-Law ahead of the Olympics. This bylaw forbade placards, posters, and banners that were not "celebratory," although Vancouverites were allowed to display "a sign that celebrates the 2010 Winter Games, and creates or enhances a festive environment and atmosphere." Essentially the ordinance criminalized anti-Olympics political dissent. In the state of exception, Canadian authorities garnered the right to remove signs lacking proper celebratory zeal, even if that meant breaching private property.[49]

Activists were relatively successful in pushing back against repressive laws. Still, in the lead-up to the Games, the Vancouver Integrated Security Unit (VISU)—a force created specially for the Games, headed by the Royal Canadian Mounted Police (RCMP), and composed of more than twenty policing agencies—purchased a military-grade medium-range acoustic device (MRAD) for crowd control, although because of negative press and intense pressure from activists, the MRAD was not deployed as a weapon during the Games. Canadian officials promised "safe assembly areas"—what activists derisively dubbed "protest pens"—but abandoned this repressive measure in response to public uproar. Still, the dialectic of resistance and restriction in the context of the Vancouver Games conforms to Neil Smith and Deborah Cowen's description of "the intensified *weaponization* of social control."[50]

This "weaponization" was readily evident. Authorities spent more than $1 billion on security, well over the initial estimate of $175 million. Officials expended those funds to choreograph a massive policing force, employing 17,000 security agents, including people from the RCMP, the Canadian Border Services Agency, the Canadian Security Intelligence Service, city police forces, and private security officers. According to the Office of the Privacy Commissioner of Canada, around 1,000 surveillance cameras were installed across greater Vancouver.[51] The state also infiltrated activists groups. Victoria police chief Jamie Graham bragged at the Vancouver International Security Conference that a police infiltrator had wormed his way into the movement, becoming a bus driver who carted around activists attending a protest of the Olympic torch relay.[52] VISU aggressively pursued anti-Olympics activists, haranguing them on the streets. Vancouver 2010 critic Christopher Shaw, who wrote *Five Ring Circus: Myths and Realities of the Olympic Games*, was a prime VISU target. Agents visited him at home, at work, and even on the street. Sometimes VISU personnel would flash a copy of his book, mentioning that they found "disturbing information" in it that they wanted to discuss with him. Shaw reported that by 2010 these visits occurred almost daily. VISU also questioned his friends, girlfriend, and ex-wife. State security officials even tried to flip him into becoming an informant, an offer he categorically declined. VISU visited nearly every major anti-Olympics activist during the lead-up to the Games.[53] The wider point is that in the name of the Olympics, the state security apparatus was willing to engage in dissent-squelching activity that sliced mightily against the Canadian Charter of Rights and Freedoms.

London Summer Games, 2012

According to the Olympic Charter that was in effect during the London 2012 Games, "The IOC Executive Board determines the principles and conditions under which any form of advertising or other publicity may be authorised."[54] Under this IOC-imported state of exception, Britain aligned domestic law with this rule: elected officials passed the London Olympic Games and Paralympic Games Act of 2006. The law took a strict stance on trademark infringement, delimiting specific words that could not be used in close proximity "in relation to goods or services." To use two of the following words or terms together—"games," "Two Thousand and Twelve," "2012," and "twenty twelve"—meant violating the law. The act also prohibited using those four terms in combination with any of these seven words: "gold," "silver," "bronze," "London," "medals," "sponsor," and "summer."[55] The Olympic Delivery Authority (ODA)—a public body—engaged in aggressive brand policing, forcing one café to delete the "flaming torch breakfast baguette" from its menu and making a flower shop disassemble a decorative tissue-paper window display in the shape of the Olympic rings. Even former IOC marketing official Michael Payne accused the ODA of being overzealous, calling the actions an "own goal" that went "too far."[56]

While anti-Games activism in Vancouver trended toward the militant and the serious, relying on more traditional mobilizations, activism in London tended to go with the celebratory flow, deploying comedy and wit in an effort to connect with a wider audience and deflect repression. Heavy-handed police actions ahead of the Olympics informed this strategic path. "Given the police crackdown that there already has been and will continue to be in the run-up to the Olympics," Jess Worth of the UK Tar Sands Network and the Reclaim Shakespeare Company told me before the Games began that "I think as activists we're having to be quite creative as to how and where and when we do our interventions. We're looking at other ways to do this, through subvertising, culture jamming, greenwash-exposing—stuff that isn't running into the path of the Olympic torch run because that's going to be incredibly tough."[57] In fact, most of the Olympics-induced activism in London occurred *before* the Olympics, while only a few actions were carried out during the duration of the Games.

As with previous Games, security amassed an arsenal but also deployed quieter, cagier tactics to quell dissent. A prime target was environmental activism in the Greenwash Gold campaign. A week before the Games commenced, activists went to Trafalgar Square to stage a mock award ceremony to award the gold, silver, and bronze for corporate greenwashing. As mock representatives from Olympics sponsors Rio Tinto, BP, and Dow stood on the stand to receive their medals—determined via online voting—they were splashed with lime-green custard. Police swooped in and arrested seven participants on suspicion of criminal damage, apparently for littering the public square with custard. No one from what became known as the Custard 7 was actually charged with any crime. Yet their bail conditions restricted their movement and thus curtailed their political freedom. One activist who shared their bail conditions with me was prohibited entrance into Trafalgar Square, Wimbledon, Wembley Football Stadium, Horseguards Parade, Hyde Park, and Lords Cricket Ground because "it is feared that" the individual "will attend these sites to commit further offences due to the fact that they are being used for Olympic venues." The Custard 7 was mandated to return to the police station in late September after the Paralympics concluded. In the end, officials dropped their case just before the activists were due to be charged, but the bail conditions had done their job of keeping them away from most Olympic-related venues. The police tactic of arresting activists on questionable grounds without leveling formal charges temporarily demobilized some of the most committed campaigners at a vital moment, forcing them to restrict their movements. Not only did this limit their free expression, but it also surreptitiously squelched the possibility of doing solidarity work.

Aggressive, preemptive policing also quashed Critical Mass, a group of bicyclists who had been peaceably convening in London since April 1994. On the night of the opening ceremony, Critical Mass cyclists took to the streets for their comparably low-budget monthly ride. However, partway through the jaunt, police trotted out Section 12 of Public Order Act 1986 to prevent the bikers from crossing north of the Thames River. The law allows police to intervene to stop a public procession if they reasonably believe that it "may result in serious public disorder, serious damage to property or serious disruption to the life of the community."[58] The Met did this despite the fact that the House of Lords ruled in 2008 that the relevant sections of the Public Order Act requiring prior notice did not apply to Critical Mass. Witnesses assert that the ride was peaceful and not a threat to public order or the "life of the community."[59] Ironically, the cyclists were enacting the very health legacy that the Games aimed to create.

Police kettled and arrested 182 people. They even sprayed CS gas at the cyclists. Again, activists were arrested but not charged (only a few of the 182 received formal charges). And again, draconian bail conditions were imposed that forbade the arrestees from going within one hundred yards of any Olympic venues and from entering the borough of Newham with a bicycle.[60] Kerry-anne Mendoza, who was arrested, called this trend of preemptive suppression "political policing." She said that "I'm not charged with any criminal offense, yet the police are able to restrict my freedom to move, my freedom to assemble, my freedom to partake in peaceful protest, and without ever having put me before a court to decide if those infringements on my civil liberties are justified based on law." She added that "the police are getting into the habit now of using bail conditions without charge as a means of restricting the ability of people to dissent."[61] In March 2013, 5 of the 9 cyclists who went to trial were found guilty, receiving minor penalties and fines after the activists expended their time and resources in a defensive stance.[62]

All of this repression stems from the Olympics-inspired state of exception. Kevin Blowe of the civil liberties group Newham Monitoring Project voiced concern: "The rights of free speech shouldn't disappear just because of a sporting event." He added that "The paranoia around the Olympics and the broader sense of wanting to have this almost sterile, incident-free, entirely orchestrated Olympic Games is driving the use of those policing powers."[63]

In October 2016, the European Olympic Committees picked Minsk to host the 2019 European Games, a sort of mini-Olympics for Europe's athletes. In selecting the Belarusian capital, the European Olympic Committees extended its ghastly practice of relying on major human rights violators (all countries violate human rights; to call a country a human rights violator is in itself not a meaningful description) to stage its flagship event. In 2015, Baku hosted the inaugural European Games even though Azerbaijan was openly squelching dissent and censoring journalism.[64] After the Baku debacle, choosing Minsk throws into serious doubt the proclaimed commitment of European Olympic luminaries to human rights.

Alexander Lukashenko, the president of Belarus, is a notorious human rights violator. Amnesty International recently noted that under Lukashenko, "the Belarusian government has cracked down on opposition leaders and movements, and abused civil rights to freedom of assembly and association."[65] Lukashenko, who was elected president back in 1994, has a gruesome track record of repressing activists through violence, arbitrary detention, and "enforced disappearance."[66] In 2012, Britain even rejected granting him a visa to attend the 2012 Summer Olympics in London.[67]

But as we have seen, authoritarian hosts of Olympic events do not hold a monopoly on repressive practices. The state of exception that the Olympics inevitably brings becomes magnified. Laws are flouted. Pet projects with Olympic tags affixed to them are prioritized. Rio mayor Eduardo Paes put it this way: "The Olympics pretext is awesome; I need to use it as an excuse for everything." He added, "Some things could be really related to the games, others have nothing to do with them." He later claimed to be joking, but his words ripple with veracity.[68]

In December 2014 the IOC unanimously passed Olympic Agenda 2020, a slate of recommendations designed to get the Olympic movement on more solid footing after the slew of potential host cities mentioned above said thanks but no thanks to the Games. In a speech that IOC president Thomas Bach gave at the time, he harkened to the importance of integrity and human rights: "The Olympic Agenda 2020 clearly demonstrates our determination to live up to our values and principles," he said. He even alluded to the positive influence of UN human rights language. "The new wording of the 6th Fundamental Principle of Olympism," he asserted, "is derived from the United Nations Universal Declaration of Human Rights."[69] Bach was referencing the fourteenth recommendation in the document: "The IOC to include non-discrimination on sexual orientation in the 6th Fundamental Principle of Olympism." The revamped sixth principle reads "The enjoyment of the rights and freedoms set forth in this Olympic Charter shall be secured without discrimination of any kind, such as race, colour, sex, sexual orientation, language, religion, political or other opinion, national or social origin, property, birth or other status." This echoes what is now standard UN human rights language, enshrined in Article 2 of the Universal Declaration of Human Rights: "Everyone is entitled to all the rights and freedoms set forth in this Declaration, without distinction of any kind, such as race, colour, sex, language, religion, political or other opinion, national or social origin, property, birth or other status."[70]

The revision of the Olympic Charter was a direct response to the furor over Russia's anti-LGBT law passed just ahead of the 2014 Sochi Winter Games. Although this seems like a step in the right direction, the principle already covered sexuality, at least implicitly: "Any form of discrimination . . . on grounds of race, religion, politics, gender *or otherwise* is incompatible with belonging to the Olympic Movement."[71] In short, the IOC already had an ethics platform it could have used to openly criticize Russia's antigay law. The IOC held the Olympics as a trump card and could have even threatened to relocate the Games. However, it opted to remain silent.

The IOC frequently deploys catchall terms such as "equality," "freedom," and "nondiscrimination" in its official rhetoric. However, the organization has a long way to go when it comes to meaningfully installing human rights principles in its everyday practices. The IOC trumpets admirable principles, but its follow-though is often questionable at best. It is fair to assert that the group has conformed to what Gruneau has called "unreflective evangelism."[72] Nevertheless, groups such as the Sports and Rights Alliance—a coalition of human rights groups including Amnesty International, Human Rights Watch, Terre des Hommes, and Transparency International Germany—are working hard behind the scenes to embed more human rights systems of accountability into IOC documents. In January 2017 the group convinced the IOC to revise its host city contract to include human rights principles, beginning with the 2024 Summer Games. The host city, the National Olympic Committee, and the local organizing committee will be obligated to "protect and respect human rights and ensure any violation of human rights is remedied in a manner consistent with international agreements, laws and regulations applicable in the Host Country and in a manner consistent with all internationally recognised human rights standards and principles, including the United Nations Guiding Principles on Business and Human Rights, applicable in the Host Country."[73] However, the execution of the revamped standard may prove to be complicated and prone to stalling tactics by Olympic power brokers in the face of what they perceive to be more immediate, pressing concerns. Plus, numerous covenants and documents already exist, many of them with the imprimatur of the UN, but as we have seen, this does not automatically compel compliance or enforcement.

For the Olympics to truly embody their stated ideals, leaders in the Olympic movement need to sync up their sentiments and actions regarding human rights in all host cities. As we have seen, it is not uncommon for local security officials in democratic host cities to impinge on activists' freedom to assemble and voice their grievances. Special rules and laws curtail the freedom of association. In addition, civil rights related to due process and property are suspended during the Olympic period. Sometimes such processes ripple with irony. Part of the IOC's stated mission is "to encourage and support a responsible concern for environmental issues, to promote sustainable development in sport and to require that the Olympic Games are held accordingly."[74] And yet, the organization stood idly by when local authorities in the host city trampled the civil and political rights of activists pressing environmental causes. Although the civil liberties and political rights of everyday people in democratic host cities are frequently violated in the name of preserving order, we see neither long-term prison sentences nor physically abusive evictions or even torture carried out by police officials against anti-Olympics activists, as we see in more authoritarian contexts such as China.[75] The deployment of human rights in the context of the Olympics is not a straightforward enterprise. As Clement notes, sometimes "even an expansive approach to human rights can function as a camouflage for inequality."[76] Michael Ignatieff asserts that the strategic use of rights discourse "can capture civil and political inequalities, but it can't capture more basic economic inequalities."[77] This observation chimes with what we have seen on the ground in five recent Olympics in Western countries: Atlanta 1996, Salt Lake City 2002, Athens 2004, Vancouver 2010, and London 2012. The civil and political rights of protesters are often violated, while economic rights—as well as cultural and social rights—typically remain off the discursive table.

Notes

1. *Olympic Charter*, International Olympic Committee, August 2, 2015, stillmed.olympic .org/Documents/olympic_charter_en.pdf.

2. Amy Shipley, "To Beijing or Not to Beijing?," *Washington Post*, July 13, 2001, D1.

3. Quoted in "China: The Olympics Countdown—Crackdown on Activists Threatens Olympic Legacy," Amnesty International, April 2008, www.amnesty.org/download/Documents /52000/asa170502008eng.pdf.

4. Rod Mickleburgh, "B.C. Premier Slams Pound's 'Savages' Remark," *Globe and Mail*, October 22, 2008, www.theglobeandmail.com/news/national/bc-premier-slams-pounds-savages -remark/article1064181/.

5. Human Rights Watch, "China: Hosting Olympics a Catalyst for Human Rights Abuses," August 23, 2008, www.hrw.org/news/2008/08/21/china-hosting-olympics-catalyst-human-rights -abuses, emphasis added.

6. Jules Boykoff, *The Suppression of Dissent: How the State and Mass Media Squelch USAmerican Social Movements* (New York: Routledge, 2006), 6–12.

7. Barbara J. Keys, *Reclaiming American Virtue: The Human Rights Revolution of the 1970s* (Cambridge, MA: Harvard University Press, 2014), 7, 10.

8. William T. Armaline, Davita Silfen Glasberg, and Bandana Purkayastha, "Human Rights in the United States: The 'Gold Standard' and the Human Rights Enterprise," in *Human Rights in Our Own Backyard: Injustice and Resistance in the United States*, ed. William T. Armaline, Davita Silfen Glasberg, and Bandana Purkayastha (Philadelphia: University of Pennsylvania Press, 2011), 251.

9. On the emergence of human rights in Canada, see Dominique Clement, *Canada's Rights Revolution: Social Movements and Social Change, 1937–82* (Vancouver: UBC Press, 2008).

10. *Olympic Charter*, August 2, 2015.

11. Ibid.

12. Carl Schmitt, *Political Theology: Four Chapters on the Concept of Sovereignty*, trans. George Schwab (London: MIT Press, 1985 [1922]), 5.

13. Giorgio Agamben, *State of Exception*, trans. Kevin Attell (Chicago: University of Chicago Press, 2005), 23.

14. William T. Armaline, Davita Silfen Glasberg, and Bandana Purkayastha, "Introduction: Human Rights in the United States," in *Human Rights in Our Own Backyard*, 2, 3–4.

15. As David Carleton and Michael Stohl write, "The most significant problem faced by all analysts of human rights is the development of a valid means of measuring violations. Even when one has clearly delineated what is meant by human rights violations, reliable information is often hard to come by." See David Carleton and Michael Stohl, "The Foreign Policy of Human Rights: Rhetoric and Reality from Jimmy Carter to Ronald Reagan," *Human Rights Quarterly* 7, no. 2 (May 1985): 211.

16. Clement, *Canada's Rights Revolution*, 6.

17. Andrew Adams and Mark Piekarz, "Sport Events and Human Rights: Positive Promotion or Negative Erosion?," *Journal of Policy Research in Tourism, Leisure and Events* 7, no. 3 (2015): 222, 227.

18. Ban Ki-moon, "Secretary-General's Remarks at the 126th Session of the International Olympic Committee Session," Sochi, Russia, February 6, 2014, www.un.org/sg/statements/index .asp?nid=7446.

19. Nicolien van Luijk, "A Historical Examination of the IOC and UN Partnership: 1952–1980," IOC Olympic Studies Centre, December 31, 2013, doc.rero.ch/record/209680/files/A _Historical_examination_of_the_IOC_and_UN_Partnership_March_6_Version_II_VAN _LUIJK.pdf.

20. International Olympic Committee, "Olympic Truce," www.olympic.org/content/the-ioc /commissions/public-affairs-and-social-development-through-sport/olympic-truce/.

21. Jules Boykoff and Dave Zirin, "The Sochi Paralympics, Ukraine, and the Olympic Truce," *The Nation*, March 16, 2014, www.thenation.com/blog/178865/sochi-paralympics-ukraine-and -olympic-truce.

22. Richard Gruneau, "Sport, Development, and the Challenge of Slums," in *Playing for Change: The Continuing Struggle for Sport and Recreation*, ed. Russell Field (Toronto: University of Toronto Press, 2015), 33–66, quotation at 44.

23. Stuart Hall, *Cultural Studies 1983: A Theoretical History* (Durham: Duke University Press, 2016), 181, emphasis in original.

24. E.E. Schattschneider, *The Semisovereign People: A Realist's View of Democracy in America* (New York: Holt, Rinehart and Winston, 1960), 68, emphasis in original.

25. Ibid., 71, emphasis in original.

26. Glenn Collins, "Coke's Hometown Olympics," *New York Times*, March 28, 1996, D1.

27. "The Olympic Stadium Debate: The King Speech," *Atlanta Journal and Constitution*, March 4, 1993, C4.

28. Ibid.

29. Michelle Hiskey and Melissa Turner, "ACOG Wins with New Ordinance," *Atlanta Journal-Constitution*, September 1, 1994, F4.

30. Lawrence J. Vale, *Purging the Poorest: Public Housing and the Design Politics of Twice-Cleared Communities* (Chicago: University of Chicago Press, 2013), 150. See also Charles Rutheiser, *Imagineering Atlanta: The Politics of Place in the City of Dreams* (London: Verso, 1996); Center on Housing Rights and Evictions, "Atlanta's Olympic Legacy" (Geneva, 2007); Larry Keating and Carol A. Flores, "Sixty and Out: Techwood Homes Transformed by Enemies and Friends," *Journal of Urban History* 26, no. 3 (2000): 275–311.

31. Melissa Turner, "Olympic Paychecks Increase," *Atlanta Journal-Constitution*, October 12, 1995, A1. This salary made Payne the highest-paid head of a nonprofit in the United States.

32. Rutheiser, *Imagineering Atlanta*, 178; Center on Housing Rights and Evictions, "Atlanta's Olympic Legacy"; Keating and Flores, "Sixty and Out."

33. Center on Housing Rights and Evictions, "Atlanta's Olympic Legacy," 32.

34. Ibid., 7.

35. Mitt Romney with Timothy Robinson, *Turnaround: Crisis, Leadership, and the Olympic Games* (Washington, DC: Regnery Publishing, 2004), 226, 234.

36. Donald L. Bartlett and James B. Steele, "Snow Job," *Sports Illustrated*, December 10, 2001; Larry Gerlach, "An Uneasy Discourse: Salt Lake 2002 and Olympic Protest," *Pathways: Critiques and Discourse in Olympic Research* (2008): 141–150, esp. 144.

37. Gerlach, "An Uneasy Discourse"; "New Salt Lake Law Bans Masks During Olympics," *Deseret News*, January 23, 2002, www.deseretnews.com/article/891161/New-Salt-Lake-law-bans-masks-during-Olympics.html.

38. Minas Samatas, "Security and Surveillance in the Athens 2004 Olympics: Some Lessons from a Troubled Story," *International Criminal Justice Review* 17 (2007): 220–238, esp. 225; John Sugden, "Watched by the Games: Surveillance and Security at the Olympics," in *Watching the Olympics: Politics, Power and Representation*, ed. John Sugden and Alan Tomlinson (London: Routledge, 2012), 231–232; Philip Boyle, "Securing the Olympic Games: Exemplifications of Global Governance," in *The Palgrave Handbook of Olympic Studies*, ed. Helen Jefferson Lenskyj and Stephen Wagg (Basingstoke: Palgrave Macmillan, 2012), 394.

39. Samatas, "Security and Surveillance," 224, 221.

40. Ibid., 224.

41. Athens 2004 Organizing Committee for the Olympic Games, "Official Report of the XXVIII Olympiad, Vol. 1," November 2005, 190, www.la84foundation.org/6oic/OfficialReports/2004/or2004ap1.pdf.

42. John Horne and Garry Whannel, *Understanding the Olympics* (London: Routledge, 2012), 136.

43. George Floridis, "Security for the 2004 Athens Olympic Games," *Mediterranean Quarterly* 15, no. 2 (Spring 2004): 5. He also noted that "The same applies to the Firefighting Corps and to other forces that are being similarly equipped and modernized" (4).

44. Athens 2004 Organizing Committee for the Olympic Games, "Official Report of the XXVIII Olympiad," 1:68.

45. Konstantinos Zervas, "Anti-Olympic Campaigns," in *Palgrave Handbook of Olympic Studies*, 533–548.

46. John Karamichas, "A Source of Crisis? Assessing Athens 2004," in *Palgrave Handbook of Olympic Studies*, 168.

47. Christine M. O'Bonsawin, "'No Olympics on Stolen Native Land': Contesting Olympic Narratives and Asserting Indigenous Rights Within the Discourse of the 2010 Vancouver Games," *Sport in Society* 13 (2010): 143–156; Janice Forsyth, "Teepees and Tomahawks: Aboriginal Cultural Representation at the 1976 Olympic Games," in *The Global Nexus Engaged: Past, Present, Future Interdisciplinary Olympic Studies; Sixth International Symposium for Olympic Research*, ed. Kevin Wamsley, Robert K. Barney, and Scott G. Martyn (London, Ontario: International Centre for Olympic Studies, 2002), 71–75.

48. Janice Forsyth, "The Illusion of Inclusion: Agenda 21 and the Commodification of Indigenous Culture in the Olympic Games," *Public* 53 (Spring 2016): 31–32. See also Jules Boykoff, *Activism and the Olympics: Dissent at the Games in Vancouver and London* (New Brunswick, NJ: Rutgers University Press, 2014), 58–90.

49. Boykoff, *Activism and the Olympics*, 58–59.

50. Neil Smith and Deborah Cowen, "'Martial Law in the Streets of Toronto': G20 Security and State Violence," *Human Geography* 3, no. 3 (2010): 38 (emphasis in original).

51. "Privacy and Security at the Vancouver 2010 Winter Games," Office of the Privacy Commissioner of Canada, August 2009, www.priv.gc.ca/fs-fi/02_05_d_42_ol_e.cfm#004.

52. Darah Hansen, "Victoria Cop Infiltrated Anti-Games Group, Jamie Graham Says," *Vancouver Sun*, December 2, 2009.

53. Boykoff, *Activism and the Olympics*, 73–74.

54. *Olympic Charter*, International Olympic Committee, July 8, 2011, stillmed.olympic .org/media/Document%20Library/OlympicOrg/Olympic-Studies-Centre/List-of-Resources /Official-Publications/Olympic-Charters/EN-2011-Olympic-Charter.pdf#_ga=2.16316918 .1951922994.1527966597–1843477295.1527966597.

55. London Olympic Games and Paralympic Games Act 2006, 47–48, www.legislation.gov .uk/ukpga/2006/12/pdfs/ukpga_20060012_en.pdf.

56. Tom Peck, "Father of Olympic Branding: My Rules Are Being Abused," *Independent*, July 20, 2012, www.independent.co.uk/sport/olympics/news/father-of-olympic-branding-my -rules-are-being-abused-7962593.html.

57. Boykoff, *Activism and the Olympics*, 94.

58. Public Order Act 1986, Part II, Section 12, www.legislation.gov.uk/ukpga/1986/64 /section/12.

59. "Critical Mass Police Ban Blocked by Law Lords," *The Guardian*, November 26, 2008, www.guardian.co.uk/uk/2008/nov/26/critical-mass-london-police.

60. See, e.g., the image at i.imgur.com/3NcgA.jpg.

61. Boykoff, *Activism and the Olympics*, 123.

62. Tom Richards, "How the Met Police Criminalised the Critical Mass Bike Ride," *The Guardian*, March 18, 2013, www.guardian.co.uk/environment/bike-blog/2013/mar/18/police -activism.

63. Boykoff, *Activism and the Olympics*, 124.

64. Jules Boykoff, "Europe's Leaders Should Boycott Autocratic Azerbaijan's Mini-Olympics," *The Guardian*, June 3, 2015, www.theguardian.com/commentisfree/2015/jun/03 /azerbaijan-european-games-human-rights.

65. "Belarus Human Rights," Amnesty International, www.amnestyusa.org/our-work
/countries/europe/belarus.

66. "16 Years of Silence: Enforced Disappearances in Belarus Must Be Investigated,"
Amnesty International, September 18, 2015, log.amnestyusa.org/europe/16-years-of-silence
-enforced-disappearances-in-belarus-must-be-investigated/.

67. Duncan Mackay, "Minsk to Host 2019 European Games After Belarus President Con-
firms They Will Organise It," Inside the Games, October 21, 2016, www.insidethegames.biz
/articles/1042849/minsk-to-host-2019-european-games-after-belarus-president-confirms-they
-will-organise-it.

68. Vanessa Barbara, "An Olympic Catastrophe," *New York Times*, July 3, 2016, SR1.

69. "Olympic Agenda 2020: 20+20 Recommendations," International Olympic Committee,   stillmed.olympic.org/Documents/Olympic_Agenda_2020/Olympic_Agenda_2020-20-20
_Recommendations-ENG.pdf.

70. "The Universal Declaration of Human Rights," United Nations, December 10, 1948,
www.un.org/en/universal-declaration-human-rights/.

71. *Olympic Charter*, July 8, 2011, 11 (my emphasis).

72. Gruneau, "Sport, Development, and the Challenge of Slums," 43.

73. "Olympics: Host City Contract Requires Human Rights," Human Rights Watch, February 28, 2017, www.hrw.org/news/2017/02/28/olympics-host-city-contract-requires-human
-rights.

74. *Olympic Charter*, August 2, 2015.

75. "China: Olympics Countdown—Time Running Out for Improvement in Human
Rights," Amnesty International, April 1, 2008, www.amnesty.org/en/press-releases/2008/04
/china-olympics-countdown-time-running-out-improvement-human-rights-20080/.

76. Clement, *Canada's Rights Revolution*, 210.

77. Quoted in ibid., 210.

CHAPTER 8

The View from China

Two Olympic Bids, One Olympic Games, and China's Changing Rights Consciousness

Susan Brownell

"Human Rights": A Constructed and Unresearchable Category

The Olympic Games held in Beijing August 8–24, 2008, sparked a broad and heated international public debate about the effects of the Olympic Games on the political structure and citizenry of the host country. On one side of the debate were critics who drew parallels with the 1936 "Hitler Games" in Berlin to argue that awarding the Olympics to an authoritarian regime emboldens it by giving it a seal of international approval and providing it with a grand symbolic tool for mobilizing its populace behind a false vision of unity. On the other side were the International Olympic Committee (IOC), the Beijing Organizing Committee for the XXIX Olympic Games (BOCOG), and the defenders of the Games who drew parallels with the 1988 Seoul Olympic Games to argue that the tremendous media scrutiny and the intensified interaction with the outside world entailed in hosting the Olympics would facilitate peaceful integration into the international community and advance progress toward democracy. For the seven years following the successful bid for the Games in 2001, a vast number of words were expended on the question "will the Olympics change China?" Postmortem analysis of the role of the Olympic Games in social change in China continued for several years afterward.

However, there is still no consensus about how the Games might have changed China. Indeed, as the rest of this volume demonstrates, there is no consensus on whether sport mega-events actually possess the capability to improve human rights in any country or push forward peaceful international relations. In short, there has been little progress among scholars toward producing convincing arguments about the role of sport in human rights, whether positive or negative. In the absence of compelling scholarly arguments, the popular debates have raged on, fueled by ideology and stereotypes.

The research on which this chapter is based was motivated by a belief that a major reason for the deficit of satisfactory theories is an inadequate research method. The highly politicized label "human rights" does not name a single unified, objective category that can be isolated from other social phenomena.[1] Popular media, politicians, and human rights advocacy groups lump together a broad spectrum of human behaviors and government actions into one catch-all category of "human rights," in the name of which they generate huge numbers of "reports" and media coverage. This discursive production forms the biggest part of the human rights-related activities that surround sport mega-events, and any research on the effects of mega-events must take into account the part of the question that is a communications problem. The second part of the question is to examine whether this body of communications—which I will call "human rights discourse"—has any impact on the on-the-ground reality.

Between the two realms of discourse and practice there is a tricky part of the question, and that is to pinpoint the mechanisms by which human rights discourse could have an impact if there was one. That is the focus of this chapter. It is my contention that we need more social scientific, empirical research to identify the concrete social actions that surround the Games and track the impact of those actions. This approach produces the obvious but all too often ignored observation that Olympic Games primarily function as a channel for the increase of "mutual understanding" (however limited) between people of different nations and other social groupings via the exchange of ideas, whereas it is difficult to document any broad-based effects—whether positive or negative—on practices in society as a whole. Concentrating, then, on the realm of ideas, this chapter finds ample evidence that the process of bidding for two Olympic Games and organizing one between 1991 and 2008 compelled Chinese decision makers and leaders of public opinion to engage with the concept of human rights and pushed them toward fuller participation in international human rights discourse. This is despite there being only a very limited band of communication through which the Western ideas made their way into Chinese minds, mainly consisting of members of the IOC, university academics, and communications consulting firms.

This chapter uses an interdisciplinary approach with ethnographic methods at its core, supplemented by an analysis of communications. Ethnography, seldom used in Olympic studies, is the only method that can reveal which people in the network of social relationships are actually exchanging ideas and what ideas they are exchanging. Narrowing down the *where* and the *what* transforms a politically motivated rhetorical question into an empirical question that can actually be answered, toward the goal of pushing forward a more accurate understanding of the social phenomenon of the Olympic Games. This might make possible not only a more accurate understanding of the impact of Olympic Games on human rights but also more effective social action in the context of the Games.

The History of "Rights Consciousness"—or Its Lack—in China

In the mid-eighteenth century, China's legal system, a fusion of the legal developments of the late Ming (1368–1644) and Qing (1644–1911) dynasties, was the envy of leading thinkers of the European Enlightenment. Therefore, a question that has occupied scholars is to understand how a well-developed and effective legal system could lack the concept of rights that has been so central to modern Western legal systems. Prior to the last third of the nineteenth century, the concept of rights was not found in China until *quanli* ("power and benefit") was used to translate the concept in Western legal texts.[2] One explanation for the lack of a rights consciousness is that the legal code of the imperial system had presumed that the power of the ruler was total and that the relationship of government to its subjects was like that between parents with total power and young children: there was no need for civil rights to protect subjects from the state, because like parents and children, the interests of government and subject were shared and not opposed.[3] The modern constitutions created since the fall of the Qing dynasty in 1911 were drafted on the Western model and all minimally recognized the modern Western concepts of rights, but the commitment to implementing them was superficial. The patrimonial conception of the central government as a benevolent father persists today, posing an obstacle to the emergence of rights consciousness among the populace, who still tend to believe that if only the leaders of the central government knew about the abuses by local officials, they would step in to fix things.[4]

After the founding of the People's Republic of China in 1949, the attitude toward rights was influenced by China's "socialist big brother," the Soviet Union, and based on an interpretation of the writing of Karl Marx and Friedrich Engels. Marx and Engels were said to be opposed to the concept of human rights; so the concept was rejected. Since the Western powers embargoed and diplomatically isolated the new China, China had minimal engagement with the new human rights discourse emerging out of the United Nations (UN) after World War II. This isolation contributed to China's nearly complete withdrawal into itself during the first three years of the disastrous Cultural Revolution (1966–1976). Sports helped draw China back out through ping pong diplomacy (1971–1973). The People's Republic of China was admitted into the UN in 1971, and diplomatic relations with the United States were restored in 1979, enabling China's readmission into the IOC the same year after three decades of exclusion. In 1981, He Zhenliang became the first Chinese member co-opted in China after its readmission. It is worth noting that during its years of exclusion the Chinese never criticized the Olympic ideals, although letters sent in the name of IOC member Dong Shouyi (drafted by He) hurled many invectives at the IOC's anticommunist president, the American Avery Brundage.[5] It would have been an easy step to denounce Olympism as a bourgeois ideology when almost anything connected with the United States and the developed West (including the human rights concept) was so denounced, but China's sport diplomats did not take it. I once asked He, China's senior sport diplomat, why they did not (more on him below). He answered, "You want to join them, why would you do that?" It was this strong and constant desire to be a part of the international sport world that underpinned the history that follows.

Human Rights and the Bid for the 2000 Olympics

Over the next fifty-five years, the phrase "human rights" went from taboo to inclusion in the Chinese Constitution in 2004. Since this appeared to be a reversal of a half century of principled Marxist rejection of the concept, it required a lengthy official explanation. An article in the *People's Daily*, the newspaper of the central Communist Party, provided that explanation with the following version of history: Marx and Engels opposed the concept of human rights because they envisioned that in a classless society there is no need for a coercive state or coercive laws. There is no need for a principle of human rights to adjudicate a free union of people, that is, the communist society. Particularly during the Cultural Revolution (1966–1976), the "extreme leftist" position, as it later came to be labeled, held that the words "human rights" were a "slogan of the capitalist class" unnecessary in a nation headed by the Communist Party, whose interests were one with the vanguard working class. Bringing up the phrase could be seen as a protest against the party, and the two words "human rights," or *renquan*, became taboo. The attack continued into the beginning of the era of reform (1978). In the 1980s new voices began to contest the old leftist position, spurred by the obvious connection in the Cultural Revolution period, when the concept of human rights had been denounced in theory and in practice human rights had been ignored and violated.[6]

The Cold War was still going on when China began to rejoin the outside world. Human rights had already been politicized in the battle between the Soviet bloc and the United States and its allies inside the UN. In 1966 the International Covenant on Economic, Social and Cultural Rights had been the Soviet bloc's counterpoint to the emphasis of the International Covenant on Political and Civil Rights, which had reflected the West's concerns. China signed the first covenant in 1997 and ratified it in 2001 and signed the second in 1998 but has never ratified it.

Deng Xiaoping was the paramount leader who initiated China's opening up to the outside world, and he did not perceive the world as welcoming. In 1985 he asked, "What are human rights? First, are they the rights of the majority? Are they the rights of the minority, or the rights of the majority, the rights of the people of the entire nation? The so-called 'human rights' of the Western world and the human rights that we speak of are fundamentally two different things, our viewpoints are different."[7] This statement is still considered foundational to the party orthodoxy. However, the *People's Daily* article about the introduction of "human rights" into the Chinese Constitution emphasized an important point that might escape a Western reader, because Deng's naming at all "human rights" opened up the topic for debate: "Deng Xiaoping, from the angle of the difference between our concept of human rights and that of the West, indirectly suggested that socialist China could talk about human rights and what human rights could be talked about."[8]

After the dissolution of the Soviet Union and the Tiananmen Square incident in 1989 (known in China as June Fourth), China was diplomatically isolated. *People's Daily* explained that Deng's successor Jiang Zemin posed the challenge of how to "explain that our democracy is the most extensive people's democracy, explain that socialist China is the most respectful of human rights." At the same time, sport was one of the main ways in which China countered its isolation. Beijing hosted the 1990 Asian Games, and in February 1991 the decision was made to bid for the 2000 Olympic Games, on which the IOC would vote in 1993. The bid committee's task was to persuade the IOC to put June Fourth behind and move forward to a Chinese Olympic Games.

In November 1991, the State Council Information Office issued its first ever white paper, itself indicative of a move toward using Western-style communications. The paper was titled "Human Rights in China." The Information Office is simultaneously the Office of Foreign Propaganda of the Central Committee of the Communist Party. Its function is to act as the communications conduit between China and the outside world, and one of its official responsibilities is to introduce "the state of affairs of the development of China's human rights endeavor to the outside world."[9] Dong Yunhu's 2004 *People's Daily* article assessed the white paper's historical significance: it broke through the extreme leftist taboo against the phrase "human rights"; affirmed human rights as a long-term ideal of humanity, a noble goal of Chinese socialism, and a long-term responsibility of the Chinese government; and was the first document to affirm the place of human rights in Chinese government, "rightly and boldly holding up the banner of human rights." In addition, the article set forth the "Chinese view" of human rights, in particular the position that the right to subsistence is the most basic human right. As the *People's Daily* article put it, "Human rights became an important theme in China's foreign communications."[10]

The close link between human rights and national sovereignty in the 1991 white paper revealed that colonial history is a significant factor in the Chinese view. An oft-repeated argument is that only a nation that controls its own destiny is in a position to protect the rights of its citizens. Therefore, the sovereign rights of the nation are higher than the human rights of individuals; this is considered to be the reverse of the Western position.[11] The white paper got right to this point in its preface, asserting that the real violators of Chinese people's human rights were the imperialist Western powers: "In old China, aggression by imperialism and oppression by feudalism and bureaucrat-capitalism deprived the people of all guarantee for their lives, and an uncountable number of them perished in war and famine. To solve their human rights problems, the first thing for the Chinese people to do is, for historical reasons, to secure the right to subsistence."[12]

By the time he became a member of the 2000 Olympics bid committee, He Zhenliang had become one of the most influential members of the IOC, having been a vice president on the Executive Board from 1989 to 1995. His wife and close partner in his diplomatic work, Liang Lijuan, was a journalist and the author of his autobiography, published in 2000, along with a book about the Olympic bids.[13] He's diaries from the two bids have also been published. From 2002 to 2006 I worked with the two of them to translate the autobiography into English, and it was published under the title *He Zhenliang and China's Olympic Dream*.[14] My conversations with He and Liang over the years shape my following descriptions of their attitude toward human rights.

In 1993 as the IOC vote on the host city for the 2000 Olympics pressed near, the pressure on China ratcheted up. The U.S. House of Representatives passed a resolution expressing opposition to Beijing's hosting of the Olympic Games on the grounds of China's "massive violations of human rights." The European Parliament followed with a similar resolution. As Liang described the political tension,

> No past Olympic bid had had such a thick political atmosphere as the bid for the 2000 Olympic Games, none of them involved an attack from all sides on one bid city as this one did, none had so many feelings of malice and hostility, none had so much government interference, none had so many dirty tricks. They used "human rights," "democracy," "Tibet," and other anti-Chinese subjects to attack Beijing's bid, in the vain hope that China would compromise on the question of principle in order to win the bid. Naturally this was a vain hope.[15]

Despite this intense pressure, it does not appear that the bid committee attempted to engage in dialogues about human rights to any substantive degree. The accounts in the books by Liang are unapologetic and uncompromising and describe no internal debates among committee members such as those that occurred during the second bid in 2001, described below. Canadian Dick Pound, an IOC member who was ineligible to vote because Toronto was a candidate city, recalled in an interview that in 1993 the Chinese were "still very defensive and surly about what happened in Tiananmen." He said that "when they bid for the Games in 2000, not long after the Tiananmen Square issue, it was a very—in quotation marks—'Chinese' bid in the sense that they had few if any outside advisers. And they were very edgy and defensive about the human rights issue and the whole massacre."[16]

It was not until four years later, in 1997, that human rights was listed as a theme in Jiang Zemin's report to the 15th Party Congress—the first time they were written into an important party document. As mentioned, in 1997 and 1998 China signed the two international covenants on human rights.

The Chinese word for "sovereignty" has rather different implications and cultural roots than the English word. The term is rooted in a fundamental distinction in Chinese culture, the host/guest relationship, expressed in the Chinese characters *zhu/ke*. To be a "master (*zhu*) of own's own home" (*dangjia zuo zhu*) is a Chinese phrase for self-determination. The term can be used to express the Chinese version of human rights when government officials have judged the explicit phrase "human rights" too sensitive for inclusion in an official document.[17] Months after China won the hosting rights, "the people as masters of their own home" was put forward at the 16th Party Congress in 2002 as one of the three principles of a socialist democracy, along with the leadership of the party and the rule of law.[18]

The chronological sequence outlined here has shown that human rights discourse cannot be evaluated separately from the bid process, which was drawing China into ever closer relationships with the international community and drawing down upon it an unprecedented level of scrutiny. While they might have been pushed to consider human rights issues, at the time of the second Olympic bid in 2001, the Chinese leadership still insisted on employing a Chinese vocabulary and interpretation of "human rights."

Human Rights and the Bid for the 2008 Olympics

From "People-Orientation" to "People's Olympics" to "Human Rights"

The second bid proposed three main themes for the Olympic Games: the High-tech Olympics, the Green Olympics, and the *renwen* Olympics. *Renwen*, typically the translation for the academic "humanities," is formed of the characters for *ren* (human) and *wen* (literature, culture). It was sometimes translated as the "humanistic Olympics," but after some debate, the "People's Olympics" was fixed as the official translation. Of course, to a native English

speaker this choice transformed the name from a reference to Enlightenment humanism into stereotypical socialist language. In conversations with
intellectuals, I was told that this theme was originally intended as a response
to the West's criticism of China's human rights. However, the response was
delivered in the realm of symbols, not direct verbal discourse, in the "look
and image" of the Games and the "branding" of China: the "dancing seal"
logo, the Fuwa mascots, the Auspicious Clouds torch, the display of "Chinese
traditional culture" in the opening ceremony, and so on. Many intellectuals
considered the People's Olympics to indicate an important change in thinking. Lu Yuanzhen, a leading intellectual in sport studies known for his radical
criticism, told me that

> I think the most incredible thing is the People's Olympics. Before, we
> were not allowed to talk about individual people. . . . We were a society
> without people. People were the means and not the end. The "People's
> Olympics" was a big philosophical breakthrough. No one knows what
> it is. This proves that when it was proposed it was empty. It was pro-
> posed because of the West's criticism, to respond to the West's doubts.
> But after it was proposed it magnified. Its value surpassed the Olym-
> pic Games themselves. A people-orientation [yi ren wei ben] was new.
> It says that Chinese people's values have undergone a great change.[19]

In 2002 Wei Jizhong, a member of the bid committee and an important liaison with the international community (in 2008 he would become president
of the International Volleyball Federation), wrote an essay that began by asking "What in the devil is meant by 'people's Olympics'?" (pardon my col-
loquial translation of jiujing).[20] He answered that the bid committee started
with the idea of yi ren wei ben meaning "take people as the root" or "people-
orientation," inspired by the Olympic ideal of the well-rounded development
of the individual.[21] Fundamental Principle 3 in the 2001 Olympic Charter placed sport "at the service of the harmonious development of man."[22]
It is easy to understand that this phrase would appeal to Chinese speakers,
because it resonated with the party's fixation on "development" and also with
the foundational Taoist and Confucian concept of he (harmony). The entry
for "people-orientation" on Baidu (the Chinese Wikipedia) stated that it was
learned from international lessons.[23]

A sports editor at the Xinhua news agency told me that when the phrase
"people-orientation" was introduced, "No one knew what the words meant.

But then people picked them up, liked them, and started using them." In 2003 Chinese president and Communist Party chairman Hu Jintao employed the phrase in his address to the Third Plenum of the 16th Party Congress in which he proposed a shift in the party's focus toward the "all-around development of people" and the recognition that economic development should serve the people, not the other way around.

The Debate About Mentioning "Human Rights" in the Bid Presentation

In her memoir of the 2008 Olympic bid, Liang wrote that "'Human rights problems' were always an issue that governments of Western countries and public opinion liked to use to attack China."[24] He Zhenliang always advocated proactively addressing sensitive problems such as human rights and the Tibet issue and supported mentioning "human rights" in the official bid presentation. He asserted to foreign friends and media that China's human rights situation was currently the best it had ever been, although of course much work remained to be done—as it did in the United States, France, and Japan. No nation is perfect. According to Liang, IOC president Juan Antonio Samaranch frequently told them that Britain, the North European nations, and the United States—especially the latter—did not really care about human rights but used them as an excuse to oppose China's Olympic bid because they did not want to see China's hosting of the Olympic Games facilitate its rapid development.[25]

Yuan Weimin, director of the State Sport General Administration and executive president of the Beijing Olympic Games Bid Committee (BOBICO), stated in his memoir that the bid committee's view was that human rights in China had achieved great progress, the Olympic Games would help them better solve human rights problems, and the IOC had repeatedly urged that the Olympics be kept separate from politics.[26]

The IOC did not request specific information on human rights during the evaluation of the bid cities beyond what was required in Theme 1 in the candidature file, "National, Regional, and Candidate City Characteristics," under which point 1.1 was "political structure."[27] Beijing's bid book provided a straightforward description of China's political structure; the IOC's Evaluation Commission concluded in its report that "The political system is classed as 'working for China.'" Beijing was in short not requested to make any promises related to human rights in its candidature file and did not make any promises.[28]

BOBICO's leading small group debated about whether to proactively mention "human rights" in the bid presentation before the IOC session.[29] Yuan and He supported mentioning it, but there was a stubborn faction of the bid committee that opposed it, and Yuan recognized that they had a point: "If we proactively spoke about this problem, it was possible that it would 'draw fire upon us' and bring trouble."[30] The question was not easily resolved. Forty-eight hours before the bid presentation it still hung in the balance, and the discussions among the leading small group became increasingly heated to the point that someone asked, "If we can't even dare to mention the two words 'human rights,' then what are we bidding for?"[31] Vice Premier Li Lanqing felt that it was enough for him to state that the Games would promote "social progress" and that a statement about human rights would not change anyone's mind. He Zhenliang then proposed that Mayor Liu Qi could mention it, and Liu was finally able to persuade Li to acquiesce. The decision had already been made when, at the IOC session's lunch break before Beijing's bid presentation, a European IOC member approached one of the BOBICO members, International Badminton Federation president Lü Shengrong, and told her that she represented twenty-five IOC members who were friendly toward China and sincerely wanted it to win the hosting rights. She informed the BOBICO member that they "definitely must express a position on human rights issues."[32]

In his speech to the Moscow session Liu Qi said, "I want to say that the Beijing 2008 Olympic Games . . . will help promote our economic and social progress and will also benefit the further development of our human rights cause."[33] In the entire body of statements in the candidature file and the bid presentation, all considered to be legally binding, this statement was the only mention of human rights.

These accounts leave the reader with the impression that BOBICO members did not believe that China had "human rights" problems, nor did they believe that IOC members felt genuine concern about improving human rights in China—even less so did they believe that the American and European governments felt genuine concern. They interpreted the pressure from many IOC members as coming from a need to be able to justify their support of Beijing to themselves and their countrymen. Of course, the books on which my account is based were published in China, so the authors probably wrote in the formulaic way that is necessary to avoid censorship. It is acceptable to name "human rights" when they are presented inside scare quotes and in contexts that imply that no real human rights violations exist inside China. At the same time, in my conversations with He, Liang Lijuan, and staff from BOCOG's Marketing and Communications Department, they expressed the same sentiments.

The Rectification of Names

Words are extremely important in Chinese politics. New vocabulary is carefully considered before it is introduced in such settings as the Party Congress and is carefully analyzed by the audience after it is introduced. One reason is that in an authoritarian regime, people are always second-guessing what the leaders are thinking. Equally important is a cultural tradition that harks back to Confucius's "rectification of names." Confucius said, "When names are not correct, speech gets no response; when speech gets no response, tasks are not completed[;] . . . therefore the names used by the gentleman must be spoken, and his speech must be acted upon."[34]

This cultural background is the key to appreciating the importance of the above history. In my experience, many intellectuals and organizers were very concerned about what to my Western mind seemed to be mere words. They complained about the lack of clarity of "people-orientation" and "peoples'/ humanistic Olympics" and felt that it was terribly important that these concepts should be fleshed out. In hindsight, looking back over the sequence of events from 1991 to 2004, it is thought-provoking to wonder whether this fetishism of words might not have been so trivial after all.

Reviewing the above discussion, we can see the following sequence of events.

In 1991 in the wake of the isolation of China that followed June Fourth, the central leadership decided to bid for the 2000 Olympics. Accounts of the strategies and deliberations that surrounded the bid process do not indicate a sincere effort by BOBICO to engage in anything that might be called a "dialogue" with the international community about human rights. However, the white paper on China's human rights followed nine months after the decision to put forward a bid.

In April 2001, the United States proposed to the UN Human Rights Commission a resolution calling attention to China's violations of political, religious, and civil rights. China mustered a vote of 23 to 17 (with 12 abstentions) to kill the resolution. While this was going on, the crafting of the Olympic bid report, a document completely oriented toward the goal of marketing China to the Western-dominated IOC, generated two empty neologisms, "people-orientation" and "people's/humanistic Olympics."

In 2002, the phrase "masters of their own house" (*dangjia zuo zhu*) was listed as one of the three principles of a socialist democracy at the 16th Party Congress.

In 2003, "people-orientation" was mentioned by the party chairman at that year's most important party meeting. In this same time frame "human rights" was also undergoing rehabilitation, and the explicit phrase "human rights" (*renquan*) was finally added to the Chinese Constitution in 2004.

It is as if the Chinese concepts "people-orientation," "people's/humanistic Olympics," and "masters of their own house," which referenced traditional Chinese thought, had eased the path toward finally naming "human rights." It seems reasonable to conclude that the pressure surrounding the Olympic Games resulted in increased attention to the words "human rights" and ultimately to official acceptance, perhaps much faster than would have been the case without the Games. In accord with the Confucian notion of the "rectification of names," naming "human rights" implies that they actually exist—which was originally denied by party orthodoxy. If human rights are correctly named, then this means that they actually exist—and then they can serve as a call to action. Therefore, granting a name to "human rights" is by no means trivial. This explains why many observers described the changes of vocabulary as momentous events.

If one were to situate these events within Western theory rather than Confucian theory, one might observe that it is not possible to be a full member of a discursive community when one refuses to use a word that is central to the discourse. China could not be a participant in what is sometimes called "rights talk" until the taboo on the phrase "human rights" was lifted. The two Olympic bid processes played a major role in eliminating the taboo.

The War of Words in 2008

The political debates surrounding the Beijing Games were unlike those in previous eras in that they were led by nongovernmental organizations (NGOs), not national governments. Some thirty groups announced that they planned actions in the year before the Games. The two NGOs with the strongest public voices were London-based Amnesty International (AI) and New York-based Human Rights Watch (HRW). In addition, the various groups coordinated by the International Tibet Support Network, working in concert with the Tibetan Central Authority (the so-called government in exile in Dharamsala, India), were very media-savvy. These groups published reports and books, issued press releases, placed op-eds in major media, gave interviews to journalists, maintained web pages, wrote letters to world leaders, and met with national Olympic committees, teams, and sponsors, numerous heads of state, and foreign ministers.[35]

None of the NGOs that generated so many reports and headlines surrounding the Beijing Olympics had a public presence in China or a direct conduit to Chinese decision makers. AI is organized into national sections, and the Chinese government did not permit a section in mainland China. China researchers for HRW traveled regularly to China on tourist visas, and its staff members met in the United States with embassy staff, government officials, and journalists, but these meetings were not open and friendly dialogues; the organization was tolerated but disliked by the Chinese government. Although dialogues with representatives of the Dalai Lama were restarted after the riots in Tibet in March 2008, the Chinese government considered the Central Tibetan Authority an antagonist and believed that it had secretly organized the riots. In the absence of a grassroots organization and access to decision makers, NGOs were left with two strategies. The first was to try to use "naming and shaming" in the international media to pressure the Chinese government and perhaps influence U.S. and other governments to do the same. The second was to pressure the IOC itself, believing that it had leverage over the Chinese government and that its leaders had direct access to China's top leaders.

The headlines used the universalistic concept of human rights, but the issues were narrower. The cause of ethnic Tibetans occupied a major role after the March riots; in fact, public attention compelled AI to take up the cause even though it was not originally included in the organization's Beijing campaign plan.[36] The original plan targeted four issues: respect for defenders of human rights, the end of Internet censorship, the closing of so-called centers for reeducation, and abolition of the death penalty. HRW highlighted forced evictions and school closures, labor rights abuses, repression of ethnic minorities, controls on religious freedom, the death penalty and executions, obstruction of HIV/AIDS rights advocacy, use of the house arrest system, and China's ties with rights violators (such as Sudan).[37]

The Chinese domestic media rarely covered the attacks on China's human rights record, and when they did so it was to criticize the West's hypocrisy. A search for the phrases "Beijing Olympics" and "human rights" in the Chinese CNKI database turned up only twenty newspaper articles in August 2008, most of them short essays addressing a vague concept of human rights.[38] Chinese media ignored the case studies of specific individuals whose rights had reportedly been violated, which were used by AI and HRW to make abuses concrete for their audiences. Therefore, the furor in the Western media largely consisted of the West talking to itself about the human rights problems in China, occasionally with the aid of Chinese dissidents and intellectuals residing in the West. It was my impression that those Chinese who were aware of the Western criticism had only a vague sense of its concrete content; they were familiar with housing evictions and the unrest in Tibet but had little knowledge about or interest in, for example, imprisoned dissidents, journalists, or Falungong practitioners.

In reality, there were few channels for substantive dialogue about human rights. One channel was informal conversations among the international and Chinese people who were brought together in the years surrounding the Games for the preparatory work or for academic conferences, forums, exchanges, and other such meetings. The number of people involved in such interactions and meetings was very large, probably in the tens of thousands. However, such forums almost never dealt with human rights on the official program.

The several dozen university academics with whom I interacted in those years typically interpreted the issues within the framework of the party orthodoxy. It seemed to them that the "rights" advocated by NGOs were the rights of the minority against the majority. For example, mass evictions to build the Bird's Nest Stadium and the Olympic Park were an issue that received a great deal of attention. A homeowner who holds out against eviction was a well-known phenomenon in urban China; the holdouts are called "nail houses" because of the way they stick to their position among the bulldozers like a nail protruding from a piece of wood. It may be necessary to explain here that while undoubtedly many people have been forcefully and/or illegally evicted from their homes, the more common situation is that homeowners are eagerly hoping that their homes will be scheduled for demolition so they can collect the financial compensation, meaning that there is a built-in incentive to hold out for greater compensation. Demolition is a process by which the collectively owned assets formerly provided by the work unit are liquidated and put into the pockets of private individuals, known as *huagong weisi* (converting the public into the private). My university colleagues in both Beijing and Shanghai argued that when Western NGOs pick up nail houses as a cause célèbre, they are privileging the rights of the minority over the rights of the majority; this reinforces their general perception that this is what Western human rights are all about.

Furthermore, Chinese intellectuals and organizing committee members linked the Western criticism with the issue of national sovereignty, which in turn is linked with the highly refined host/guest (*zhu/ke*) protocol. He Zhenliang spoke passionately to me about sporting events as part of the cycle of host-guest reciprocity. He explained that when a city hosts a major sport event, it is as if he, He Zhenliang, had invited you to his home as his guest, and there he puts you in the seat of honor, feeds you the special foods, and gives you the special gifts unique to his hometown. The cultural performances in the Olympic opening ceremonies are like the unique foods that you receive as his guest, which are not available in your own hometown. The Beijing Olympics were China's opportunity to return the hospitality of the other host nations that had previously invited China into their homes. The West's criticism of China was as if the host invited a guest to his home, and the guest responded by criticizing the host before he even arrived. As Jin Yuanpu, director of the Humanistic Olympic Studies Centre at the People's University, put it, "The Olympics are a party to which we have invited the world. If you don't want to come, then don't! No one is forcing you. But don't criticize us after you have accepted our invitation."[39]

The Chinese term *zhubanquan* (right to host) contains both the word for "host" and the word for "rights" (*quan*) that is also found in the compound *renquan*, meaning "human rights." "Masters of their own house" (*dangjia zuo zhu*) is another phrase that uses the *zhu* character. *Zhu* and *quan* together form the compound *zhuquan* (sovereignty). And so, the vocabulary for "hosting" the Olympic Games directly linked up with the discourses of "sovereignty" as well as "human rights"; this made it an easy step for Chinese speakers to regard those who opposed China's hosting of the Games as opposing a fundamental right—the "national right" (*guoquan*) of the Chinese people. During Beijing's second Olympic bid, He Zhenliang responded to foreign journalists by arguing that "In fact, the entire populace of China hopes that Beijing's Olympic bid will succeed, and the desires and rights of over one billion people requesting to host the Olympic Games ought to be respected. If someone wants to ignore this unanimous desire, and deny their rights, what qualifications does he have to talk about human rights?"[40]

Clearly, this interpretation of a collective right held by a nation is a far cry from the individual civil and political rights advocated by Western NGOs and politicians. It is another indication of the vast gulf between the Western "rights talk" and the indigenous "rights talk" that mattered to the handful of Chinese people who thought about the issue at all. As much as the two Olympic bids had pushed China toward international norms, in 2008 Chinese people were simply not full participants in the Western human rights discourse. Needless to say, Western NGOs and governments, for their part, were almost completely ignorant of the Chinese worldview. This was not surprising, given the tiny trickle of communications that flowed between the Chinese public and the Western human rights interest groups.

Human Rights Discourse Between the IOC and BOCOG

However, there was another forum in which communication was more intensive, and that was in the close relationships between the IOC and its Chinese counterparts necessitated by the huge task of preparing a mega-event.

The IOC's approach was established early on by IOC president Samaranch during the evaluation of the bids in 2001. In early February 2001, Hein Verbruggen, chairman of the Evaluation Commission, telephoned Samaranch prior to the Executive Board meeting held before the commission's visits to the host cities. He told Samaranch that they had been under pressure from government representatives and the media concerning Beijing's candidature and the human rights situation in China. Verbruggen wanted clarification on the IOC's view on the Tibetan problem and asked whether the Evaluation Commission's report should refer to the human rights situation in the countries of the different candidate cities.[41]

The minutes of the meeting state that it was a unanimous decision among the director-general and seventeen IOC members (He Zhenliang was dismissed for the discussion) that the Evaluation Commission was a technical commission that should not engage in political issues. Judge Keba Mbaye from Senegal, who had been a leader in the anti-apartheid movement, observed that he had been closely involved with human rights issues since 1960 and could state with certainty that no country in the world fully respected human rights. The issue was a fundamentally political one, and judgments were based on the views held in the country concerned. Most of the world's countries had relations with China, as they did with other countries whose human rights policies they might not agree with. But this was not for the IOC's Evaluation Commission to deal with; rather, the commission should keep to purely technical concerns. As records of human rights questions dated from at least 1610, it was not for the IOC to start discussing these in a report on a city's technical capacity to stage the Games. Mbaye said that he personally was saddened to see China singled out for this kind of treatment.[42]

Samaranch wrote a letter to Verbruggen reiterating that the Evaluation Commission "is essentially technical in nature," and its report "shall not take into account any other political considerations; each IOC member is, of course, free to assess them according to his/her personal convictions." This policy was then stated in the report of the Evaluation Commission that was presented to IOC members before they voted on the candidate cities: "the Commission has a defined technical evaluation role but it is impossible to ignore the public debate on political issues such as human rights which, in the present context, is imposed on sport. The Commission will not deal with this issue other than to acknowledge the existence of the debate and its continuation."[43]

Samaranch had been a longtime supporter of China. In 2001 Samaranch's twenty-one-year term ended, and Jacques Rogge was elected at the IOC session three days after the selection of Beijing, meaning that the Beijing Olympics were Samaranch's legacy. Over the seven years of the preparatory work, the IOC consistently maintained the nonpolitical approach first established by Samaranch. Verbruggen was the chairman of both the Evaluation Commission and then the Coordination Commission. He explained to me that in the meetings with BOCOG, they avoided using the phrase "human rights" for many years, instead discussing whether there would be "disruptions" or "demonstrations." In January 2007 Verbruggen was struck—enough to make a written note of it—that his Chinese counterparts directly mentioned human rights in their meetings. He sensed that it became easier to talk about sensitive issues because they were bringing them up themselves. By this time, they had gradually built up personal relationships. By the end they could speak very openly about human rights issues.[44]

During those seven years, Verbruggen felt that his counterparts in BOCOG did not worry very much about public opinion in the West because they were so accustomed to criticism. He and his IOC colleagues had the impression that the BOCOG leadership was not well informed about what foreign press was saying; they never asked the Coordination Commission to react to attacks. Verbruggen asked them many times, "Why don't you have better communication with the outside world?" The reply was that they knew that the general opinion of the press was antagonistic, they were used to it, and they could only accept it.[45]

Conclusion: The Importance of Words

With respect to most of the issues that incited such heated sentiments in the West leading up to the 2008 Olympics—press freedom, Internet censorship, suppression of dissidents and rights advocates, Tibet, labor rights, housing evictions, and so on—the general assessment in the West has been that not much improvement was seen in the years before or after the Games. One exception is that the death penalty review system was improved, gaining a positive reaction from HRW.[46] It is easy to jump to the conclusion that hosting the Olympic Games either made no difference or worsened some human rights in China.

I would like to argue that the problem with this conclusion is that the question is too broad and vague. A rigorous academic analysis should track the people who were directly connected with the bids and the organization of the Olympic Games, the actions they took, and the consequences of their actions. As I have shown, the human rights discourse among Western politicians, advocacy groups, and in the media had very little direct connection with the people organizing the Games. The criticism outside China was largely unknown inside China: average people had little access to it, and the leaders of BOCOG were either indifferent or hostile to it. The main conduit for conveying this information was the IOC's Coordination Commission and the staff and consultants working on communications issues. The Coordination Commission had been instructed that political issues were not its concern, and given the attitudes of their Chinese counterparts, it is doubtful that even a concerted effort to promote dialogue on human rights would have been feasible had the IOC been inclined to attempt it.

Despite all of these obstacles, I argue that the Olympic bids and Games *did* have an impact in the realm of vocabulary, discourse, and the exchange of ideas. The two bids and the seven years of preparatory work facilitated the acceptance of Western concepts. In particular, the bid process pressured the Chinese leadership to make a conscientious effort—less conscientious in 1993 and more conscientious in 2001—to comprehend a few key notions of Western culture to which they were initially hostile. After the Beijing Olympics, He Zhenliang told me that an important lesson that China had learned through the Olympic Games was that in order to win over the audience to one's side, the message must be crafted in such a way as to connect with the audience's way of thinking. The Chinese assumption had been that it is enough to be principled and to be right. In retrospect, this erroneous assumption was the main reason that their arguments had fallen on insensitive ears from the 1950s through the 1980s. I asked him if he meant that in the late 1950s, when he was crafting all those vituperative letters to the IOC, no one had considered how to appeal to Western ways of thinking. He answered, "In any case, *I* did not."

In the process, Chinese decision makers discovered concepts that actually had some appeal, such as the Olympic notion of the harmonious development of human beings. They reinterpreted Western human rights concepts into Chinese idioms such as "people-orientation," "humanism" (*renwen*), and "master of one's own house." This made the concepts more palatable and eased the introduction of the actual words "human rights" into policies, documents, and speeches. The fact that key changes occurred in close association with key moments for Olympic bids indicates that Olympic sport and human rights discourse were closely bound together in China's efforts to reach out and establish greater connections with the outside world, particularly the developed West. Moreover, by framing the hosting of the Games within the Chinese understanding of the host/guest relationship and of national sovereignty, Chinese leaders and the public experienced the Games as, finally, a confirmation of China's rightful position in the world.

At the end of all this, readers will no doubt wonder about real human rights on the ground. Without trying to predict the future, I can only observe that the entry of the concepts that I have discussed into popular discourse has changed the nature of the conversation between the governed and those who govern and has provided society with new tools in its ongoing negotiations with the party state. How those negotiations will play out remains to be seen.

Notes

1. See Habermas's description of human rights as a "construction" rather than as "pre-given moral truths" as well as his analysis of the strategic response to this construction in emerging Asian nations. Jürgen Habermas, *The Postnational Constellation: Political Essays*, trans. Max Pensky (Cambridge, MA: MIT Press, 2001), 122–129.

2. Stephen C. Angle, *Human Rights and Chinese Thought: A Cross-Cultural Inquiry* (Cambridge: Cambridge University Press, 2002), 3–4.

3. Philip C. Huang, *Code, Custom, and Legal Practice in China: The Qing and the Republic Compared* (Palo Alto, CA: Stanford University Press, 2001), 26–27.

4. The clearest indication of this attitude is found in the petition (*shenfang*) system, in which local citizens personally make trips to Beijing to present petitions to central government bureaus, often by kneeling outside the gates holding up a written sign. The right to petition is supported by Chinese law and is considered an important recourse for righting wrongs by local government officials (in recent years the process has been increasingly moved to the Internet to avoid the publicly embarrassing convergence on Beijing). The petition system could be considered a kind of rights consciousness in that it is an accepted avenue for making claims against the state, but the logic is different from Western rights consciousness because it reinforces the imaginary of the benevolent central government. There is no power higher than the central government to which citizens could submit a petition to make a claim against the central government.

5. For a fuller account, see Susan Brownell, "'Sport and Politics Don't Mix': China's Relationship with the IOC During the Cold War," in *East Plays West: Essays on Sport and the Cold War*, ed. Stephen Wagg and David Andrews, 261–278 (New York: Routledge, 2007).

6. Dong Yunhu, "'Renquan' ru xian: Zhongguo renquan fazhande zhongyao lichengbei" ['Human Rights' Enter the Constitution: Important Milestones in the Development of China's Human Rights], Xinhuanet, March 14, 2004, www.people.com.cn/GB/paper2086/11949 /1075760.html.

7. Deng Xiaoping, "Gao zichanjieji ziyouhua jiushi zou zibenzhuyi daolu" [To Engage in Capitalist Liberalization Is to Follow the Capitalist Road], in *Deng Xiaoping wenji* [*Collected Writings of Deng Xiaoping*], Vol. 3 (Beijing: Renmin chubanshe), 125.

8. Dong, "'Renquan' ru xian."

9. Website of the People's Republic of China State Council Information Office, November 1991, www.china.org.cn/e-white/7/index.htm.

10. Dong, "'Renquan' ru xian."

11. Wu Zhongxi, *Shehuizhuyi yu Renquan* [*Socialism and Human Rights*] (Shanghai: Xuelin Chubanshe, 2007), 369.

12. "Human Rights in China," White Papers of the Chinese Government, Official website of the Chinese government, www.china.org.cn/e-white/7/index.htm.

13. Liang Lijuan, *He Zhenliang yu Aolinpike* [*He Zhenliang and Olympism*], (Beijing: Olympic Press, 2000), republished as *He Zhenliang yu wuhuan zhilu* [*He Zhenliang and the Road of the Olympic Rings*], (Beijing: World Knowledge, 2005); Liang Lijuan, *Qinli shen Ao* [*Personal Experiences of the Olympic Bid*] (Hangzhou: Zhejiang Renmin Chubanshe, 2008).

14. Liang Lijuan, *He Zhenliang and China's Olympic Dream*, translated by Susan Brownell (Beijing: Foreign Languages, 2007), library.la84.org/SportsLibrary/Books/HeZhenliang.pdf.

15. Ibid., 420. I use my original translation and not the "corrected" one that was published.

16. Dick Pound, telephone interview with the author, April 27, 2011.

17. Based on my experience in translating from Chinese into English the Shanghai Declaration, a document on urban sustainability that was issued at the conclusion of the Shanghai World Expo 2010. The university academics who drafted the document originally included the words for "human rights," but the higher-ups nixed it and eventually settled on "masters of their own house."

18. Jiang Zemin, "*Zai Zhongguo Gongchandang dishiliuci daibiao dahuishangde baogao*" [Report to the 16th Congress of the Chinese Communist Party], August 8, 2002, cpc.people .com.cn/GB/64162/64168/64569/65444/4429125.html.

19. Personal communication with Lu Yuanzhen, Beijing, January 21, 2008.

20. Wei Jizhong, "*Yi ren wei ben bu jinjin shi yi yundongyuan wei ben*" ["Taking People as the Root Is Not Just About Taking Athletes as the Root"], People's Net (renminwang), February 2, 2002, www.peopledaily.edu.cn/BIG5/paper53/5387/559547.html.

21. Ibid.

22. International Olympic Committee, *Olympic Charter: In Force as of 14 July 2001* (Lausanne, Switzerland, 2001), 8, www.olympic.org/Documents/Olympic%20Charter/Olympic_Charter _through_time/2001-Olympic_Charter.pdf.

23. *Yi ren wei ben*, Baidu.com, baike.baidu.com/view/93347.htm.

24. Liang, *Qinli shen Ao*, 158–159.

25. Ibid.

26. Yuan Weimin, *Titan Fengyun* [*Stormy Weather in the World of Sports*] (Nanjing: Jiangsu Renmin Chubanshe, 2009), 80.

27. International Olympic Committee, *Manual for Candidate Cities for the Games of the XXIX Olympiad 2008* (Lausanne, Switzerland: IOC, 2001), 23.

28. International Olympic Committee, *Report of the IOC Evaluation Commission for the Games of the XXIX Olympiad in 2008* (Lausanne, Switzerland: IOC, April 3, 2001), 60.

29. For a longer description, see Susan Brownell, *Beijing's Games: What the Olympics Mean to China* (Lanham, MD: Rowman and Littlefield, 2008), 143–144; Susan Brownell, "Human Rights and the Beijing Olympics: Imagined Global Community and the Transnational Public Sphere," *British Journal of Sociology* 63, no. 2 (2012): 313.

30. Yuan, *Titan Fengyun*, 82.

31. Ibid.

32. Ibid., 84.

33. "Mr. Liu Qi's Speech," official English translation originally on the BOCOG Official Website, Chinese text available at www.people.com.cn/GB/shizheng/252/5934/5935/20010713 /511372.html.

34. Confucius, *Analects (Lunyu)*, Book 13, passage 3 (my translation), modified from Roger T. Ames and Henry Rosemont Jr., *The Analects of Confucius: A Philosophical Translation* (New York: Ballatine Books, 1998), 161–162.

35. See Brownell, "Human Rights and the Beijing Olympics," 306–327; Susan Brownell, "'Brand China' in the Olympic Context: Communications Challenges of China's Soft Power Initiative," *Javnost—The Public, Journal of the European Institute for Communication and Culture* 20, no. 4 (2013): 65–82.

36. Author's telephone interview with Eduard Nazarski, director of Amnesty International the Netherlands, March 2, 2011.

37. Human Rights Watch, "Beijing 2008: China's Olympian Human Rights Challenges."

38. Brownell, "Human Rights and the Beijing Olympics," 308.

39. Interview with Susan Brownell, Beijing, 2008.

40. Liang, *He Zhenliang and China's Olympic Dream*, 158.

41. This account is based on the Minutes of the IOC Executive Board Meeting, Dakar, February 5, 6, and 7, 2001.

42. Ibid.

43. Ibid.

44. Interviews with Hein Verbruggen, Lausanne, Switzerland, January 15–16, 2009.

45. Ibid.

46. Kathleen Kingsbury, "An Olympic Reprieve for China's Convicts," *Time*, June 11, 2007, www.time.com/time/world/article/0,8599,1631399,00.html.

CHAPTER 9

Competing for Rights?

Human Rights and Recent Sport
Mega-Events in Brazil

João Roriz and Renata Nagamine

Human rights was a prominent theme at the 2014 men's soccer World Cup in Brazil and the 2016 Rio Summer Olympic Games. These events became a platform for two competing visions over which human rights were most central for sport mega-events. The Brazilian government, the Fédération Internationale de Football Association (FIFA), and the International Olympic Committee (IOC) tried to privilege issues of racism and discrimination. Activists and nongovernmental organizations (NGOs) used human rights language to resist the problems that they believed sport mega-events caused or exacerbated, such as police violence, violations of freedom of expression, and eviction. These important differences can be explained by seeing human rights as what linguistic anthropologists call a "strategically deployable shifter," a term that lacks content outside of specific contexts and can hide important political differences. Like corporate social responsibility, a concept that has been embraced by corporations more as a marketing tool than a genuinely new operational philosophy, human rights is a virtuous language that sport mega-event organizers can mobilize in part to conceal a lack of genuine change.[1]

The association between human rights and sport has grown in recent years. Both FIFA and the IOC have tried to align the events they stage with the values of the United Nations (UN), including peace and human rights. Thus, before every World Cup match, a joint message by Brazil, the UN, and FIFA was communicated at the stadiums: "Today we come together to strive not only for victory in the game but also for the victory of peace. Brazil, the United Nations and FIFA wish to share a message of peace, tolerance and respect for human rights," specifically by combating "all forms of discrimination" and working for "mutual respect."[2] The message reflected an official emphasis on antidiscrimination as the core value associated with sport mega-events, but organizers also included chronic problems in Brazil: the fight against sexual exploitation and human trafficking and for development and antipoverty measures, environmental issues, and LGBT rights.

Despite such efforts, human rights had gone virtually without mention in the bids for the World Cup and the Olympic Games. Although the Brazilian football federation Confederação Brasileira de Futebol (CBF), the sole candidate for the 2014 World Cup, did not publicize its dossier and gave no details about its budget, publicity focused on infrastructure problems that could be solved during the preparations to stage the event.[3] In the three volumes of the Rio Olympic bid, social, environmental, and infrastructure benefits were discussed, but in six hundred pages the term "human rights" appeared only once, in a section on the media.[4]

Rights talk was gradually incorporated into public policies once preparations got under way. The organizers of the World Cup emphasized three main issues: disability rights, sexual exploitation, and racism.[5] The first two issues were highlighted by the Secretariat of Human Rights of the Presidency (an agency with ministerial level), which was part of the working group responsible for the World Cup. The Brazilian federal administration had been trying to implement policies to increase public access for persons with disabilities. Brazil ratified the UN Convention on the Rights of Persons with Disabilities and its Additional Protocol in 2008, and at home the sport mega-events offered an opportunity to increase enforcement of preexisting legislation, in particular by requiring adaptation to buildings such as hotel, sports facilities, and public transport.

According to then head of the Secretariat of Human Rights, Ideli Salvatti, the "structure of protection" to fight sexual exploitation would be the World Cup's main legacy to Brazil.[6] New policies included the creation of a call center (Disque Direitos Humanos) to receive claims of violations; joint action by police officers, social workers, and "child care councils" (conselhos tutelares) before, during, and after World Cup matches; information campaigns for foreigners; a ban on visas for those convicted or suspected of pornography and child sexual abuse (as listed by Interpol); and federal legislation that turned the sexual exploitation of children and teenagers into a "heinous crime."[7] Yet, several reports indicate that there was an increase in sexual exploitation and child abuse complaints during the events. During the World Cup, there were 11,251 complaints against child abuse, 15.6 percent more than during the FIFA 2013 Confederations Cup, which had been held in Brazil as a prelude to the World Cup.[8]

The struggle against racism and other forms of discrimination played a major role in official documents, campaigns, and speeches of the organizers, though few concrete actions and public policies came along with the rhetoric. Racism is recognized as a major problem in Brazil, stemming from the legacy of slavery, the persistence of black poverty, and a culture of negative appreciation of racial diversity, although in public debate the existence of racial discrimination is often denied.[9]

Combating racism is enshrined in the Brazilian Constitution as one of the principles guiding Brazilian foreign policy. FIFA and the CBF, in turn, boosted their public fight against racism in the last decade as episodes of racial offenses during matches drew more attention in different corners of the world, including in Brazil. FIFA has placed racism at the core of its social message since 2006, when it launched the campaign "Say No to Racism" at the global level.[10] FIFA's charter prohibits any kind of discrimination, and in response to highly publicized incidents of racism at soccer matches, FIFA promised "zero tolerance" for racism during the World Cup.[11]

Antiracism also was often cited at the highest levels as one of the distinguishing features of the Brazilian World Cup. Former president Dilma Rousseff more than once proclaimed that this "will be the World Cup against racism and all forms of discrimination."[12] Lecturing to Brazilian diplomats, she stated that "We, as a country, have defined that the 'Cup of the Cups' that now awaits us next June has to be not only the Cup of peace but the Cup of the fight against racism."[13] However, FIFA failed to fulfill its promise to appoint staff to record discriminatory practices during the matches, which generated disappointed comments from the head of FIFA's antiracism task force.[14]

Human rights talk proved to be a resourceful vocabulary for different political agendas. The three largest Brazilian newspapers, O Globo, Folha de S. Paulo, and O Estado de S. Paulo, published hundreds of articles about human rights in connection with the 2014 World Cup and the 2016 Olympics.[15] Media coverage of the issues increased sharply as the events approached. In contrast to the 2018 and 2020 World Cups in Russia and Qatar, respectively, which have seen considerable discussion of human rights problems well before the events, human rights made a late appearance in relation to Brazil's World Cup. From 2007 to 2009 when Brazil and Rio were elected to host the World Cup and the Olympics, respectively, fewer than twenty articles on the subject were published in those three Brazilian newspapers. Almost all of them reported episodes involving police violence and speculated about what might happen during the events. None were more broadly concerned with human rights.[16]

Human rights came to be more directly associated with the mega-events only from 2009 onward. Two remarks are important here. First, in the years of the mega-events, the Brazilian newspapers published more articles about human rights violations that had occurred in the year before than in the year of publication (with the exception of *Estado* in 2015–2016). Second, the 2014 FIFA World Cup was more associated with human rights than the 2016 Olympics (except in *O Globo*). Taken together, these observations suggest that the unusually large number of articles on human rights and sport mega-events in 2014 was in part a product of the major social protests in some Brazilian cities that took place in 2013 and 2014.

The three Brazilian newspapers, *O Globo, Folha de S. Paulo*, and *O Estado de S. Paulo*, related human rights mainly to police violence, the right to protest/freedom of expression, and housing/evictions. The absence of discussion of the human rights issues most strongly advocated by FIFA, the IOC, and the Brazilian government is striking. In the mainstream media, human rights were associated with chronic political and sociopolitical problems. Discrimination on the basis of race, gender, and sexual orientation are chronic problems in Brazil. And so are police violence, violations of the right to protest, and housing evictions; nevertheless, unlike the others, these tend to draw the attention of the mainstream press more. One possible explanation is that media attached to the uses of human rights language by political activists, NGOs, and other groups. The UN and Amnesty International were the most prominent groups mentioned in the press, but local groups, such as Justiça Global, the Articulação Nacional dos Comitês Populares da Copa (National Coordination of Popular Committees Cup, ANCOP), and its local Rio Committee, also received substantial coverage. The UN and its special rapporteur on adequate housing, Raquel Rolnik, along with ANCOP and the Rio Committee, were the strongest advocates on housing issues. Local groups and Amnesty International primarily took up the issues of police violence, the right to protest, and freedom of expression.

"Não vai ter Copa!": Protests and Police Violence

The battle cry "Não vai ter Copa!"—"There won't be a Cup!"—echoed in the streets of Brazilian cities in the middle of 2013, right before and during FIFA's Confederations Cup. Chanted by the multitudes that took to Brazil's streets, the slogan alarmed FIFA officials, Brazilian World Cup coordinators, and politicians. The turmoil contrasted with the carnival-like celebration when the country had won the bid to host the event and images of the people celebrating in Copacabana had been broadcasted to the world.

The rights to host the world's two largest sporting events came in quick succession and might have been socially perceived as the coronation of the bourgeoning socioeconomic growth that the country had been experiencing since the beginning of the twenty-first century. But opinion polls indicate that support for hosting these events gradually declined. In 2008, only 10 percent of the population disapproved of hosting the FIFA World Cup. Opposition rose steadily: it was 26 percent in 2013 and 41 percent by 2014. After the World Cup, 54 percent of the Brazilians answered that the event was more disadvantageous than beneficial to the country. The pattern was the same with regard to the Olympics. In 2013, 25 percent opposed hosting the Games; one month before the opening ceremony, the majority of the population disapproved: 50 percent against and 40 percent in favor.[17]

The turning point for popular approval of the events appears to have been the year 2013. In 2013–2014 mass protests erupted in more than 350 Brazilian cities, making the scale of protest unprecedented since redemocratization in the 1980s. A comprehensive study of their causes is yet to be done, but the sporting events seem to have been a major contributor, offering targets to blame and opportunities for mobilization.[18] Criticism targeted a widespread culture of corruption involving familiar politicians and construction companies. Before the World Cup, CBF president Ricardo Teixeira fled to the United States allegedly to avoid being arrested on corruption charges. His daughter Joana Havelange, who is also former FIFA president João Havelange's granddaughter, remained part of the local committee, as did Ronaldo Nazário, owner of a marketing company with contracts with World Cup sponsors. Corruption scandals that resulted in the arrest of well-known politicians were still fresh news, and the ones involving the ruling parties, such as the Partido dos Trabalhadores and the Partido do Movimento Democrático Brasileiro, were widely broadcasted. Critics argued that the Brazilian model of representative democracy was in crisis.[19]

During the World Cup preparations, there were abundant media reports about FIFA's strict demands for the construction of the stadiums and other facilities. FIFA defended exigencies that seemed extreme to many Brazilians. According to its executives, a "FIFA standard of quality" had to be guaranteed for competitors, fans, and the media at the events. Huge financial investments were made to construct and refinish stadiums, including some in places such as Manaus in Amazonas, where soccer teams are scarce. A considerable part of the population contrasted the exorbitant expenditure on stadia to Brazil's social reality, noting that Brazil spent more than was spent for the 2006 FIFA World Cup in Germany and the 2010 Cup in South Africa combined.[20] Brazilians contrasted the so-called FIFA standard of quality with the traditionally poor quality of public services, particularly in education, health, and policing. Insensitivity by organizers—such as Ronaldo Nazário's comment that a "World Cup isn't made with hospitals, my friend. It's made with stadiums"— spurred further public indignation.[21] Later, economic recession and political crisis were added to a context in which the phrase "FIFA standard of quality" became widely used by hundreds of protesters in the streets to criticize the events, the state, and Brazilian democracy.

Brazilian officials, concerned with the potential impact on World Cup events, resorted to force to restore law and order, leading to police violence. In this context, rights institutions, activists, and the media began to use the strategy of naming and shaming to address police brutality.[22] Brazilian officials tried to justify the use of violence by citing the need to ensure that the 2013 FIFA Confederations Cup went ahead, including the right of ticket holders to get to the stadiums. In the midst of the protests, FIFA officials publicly affirmed respect for the right of the Brazilian people to exercise their civil liberties but also expressed concerns about prospects for the World Cup.

International NGOs, including Amnesty International and Human Rights Watch, together with local civil society organizations, such as Justiça Global and Conectas, became outspoken critics of police violence and associated violations during the protests. They produced reports, wrote opinion articles, offered legal assistance to activists who were arrested, and helped to place the topic in the mainstream media.

Amnesty International, for example, published a report titled "'They Use a Strategy of Fear': Protecting the Right to Protest in Brazil" and inaugurated a campaign called "No Foul Play, Brazil!" ("Brasil, chega de bola fora!") that targeted excessive force and advocated the use of nonlethal weapons by police as well as better police training.[23] Such documents used the language of human rights, highlighting rights to free speech, freedom of the press, and peaceful assembly.[24] In their annual reports, both Amnesty International and Human Rights Watch connected the sport mega-events to police violence. Amnesty International criticized the use of "excessive and unnecessary force by the security forces" in connection with the protests around the World Cup in 2013.[25] Human Rights Watch labeled police torture a "chronic problem" in the country and said that during the protests related to the World Cup the "police used excessive force, including beating people who had not resisted arrest and firing teargas canisters at protesters from short range."[26] Another report on police violence and protests was published by the British human rights organization Article 19, a group devoted to protecting freedom of expression and freedom of information. Its report argued that the government had reacted with "a campaign of intimidation, hasty legislation, and police tactics reminiscent of those used under the old authoritarian regime" and that the World Cup General Law bans protests that do not contribute to a "festive and friendly" event.[27] Article 19 urged the government to introduce a new law regulating the right to protest and freedom of expression.[28] Human Rights Watch issued press releases about activists arrested during protests and journalists injured or detained, and its reports echoed UN special rapporteur Rolnik's concerns about housing.[29]

NGOs also sought to bring problems to the attention of international governmental organizations. Justiça Global, Conectas, and eight local NGOs discussed the 2014 protests in a public hearing at the Inter-American Commission on Human Rights. They provided information on police violence, criminal proceedings against demonstrators (1,700 arrests during the protests), and judicial orders to prohibit protests during the Confederations Cup and the World Cup as well as fifteen draft legislative bills that could negatively impact activists and protests.[30] In the words of an NGO representative, the situation in Brazil was a "state of exception."[31]

The UN and some NGOs suggested that police violence was associated with the sport mega-events, but their official documents stopped short of establishing a causal relation between the two. An Amnesty International report titled "You Killed My Son: Homicides by Military Police in the City of Rio de Janeiro" stated that police operations in favelas intensified after the World Cup and before the Olympics.[32] Amnesty International reported that extrajudicial executions committed by the police in the favelas increased 39.4 percent between 2013 and 2014 and that there was an "environment of terror in the favelas" before the Olympics.[33] On the same day that the government tried to convince the UN Human Rights Council that the Olympic Games would have positive effects, Amnesty International and other NGOs stated that since the Pan-American Games in 2007, 1,300 people had been murdered in Rio during police operations. The government acknowledged that police violence was a problem but denied any relation with the sporting event.[34] In its official report, the UN Committee on the Rights of the Child questioned extrajudicial executions of children that increased during the preparations for the 2016 Olympics but did not affirm that the event was directly responsible for the deaths.[35] One commissioner, however, claimed that the committee received "concrete information" that the killings were "a way to clean [the city] to host international events."[36]

The newspaper *Estado de S. Paulo* reported that the UN sent confidential letters from different rapporteurs to the Brazilian government that raised questions about police brutality during the 2014 World Cup. According to the newspaper, the letters were not very diplomatic and mentioned specific violations. There was "an excessive use of force and arbitrary imprisonment of protesters" in São Paulo and Rio de Janeiro, the letters concluded in a tone common in fact-finding reports and judicial proceedings. Moreover, such letters noted the beating and detention of more than ten journalists as well as extrajudicial executions of more than thirty people in the Acari favela. The UN demanded a reply that never came, and when *Estado de S. Paulo* requested one from the government, it blamed police brutality on the states of Rio and São Paulo, which controlled the local police.[37]

The "Exclusion Games": Housing and Evictions

Problems related to housing in Brazilian cities are endemic. Social conflict around housing issues is a long-term problem that has worsened as access by the poor to the city and its communal life has been restricted. The modernization advocated by enthusiasts of the "rapid development" model from the mid-twentieth century imported industrialization but not the European social welfare state.[38] On the contrary, the fragile urban model that incorporated workers within the city contributed to their marginalization, and the law played a pivotal role in excluding the poor.[39] Alongside rural exclusion, urbanization laid the groundwork for a strong real estate market while shunting a large percentage of the population to the margins.[40]

The housing issue and its association with sport mega-events were vigorously taken up by local groups, notably the Comitês Populares da Copa

(Popular Committees of the Cup, CPCs) and ANCOP.[41] These groups have been described as "event-actors," for using the fluid space connecting several demands and actors, as well as "hybrid forums" because of their composition, which includes civil society, social movements, NGOs, representatives from the affected communities, politicians, researchers, and students, with a flexible organizational structure.[42] The CPCs and ANCOP functioned as a forum where different institutions gathered, discussed, and coordinated joint policies. Their actions included drafting dossiers, organizing protests and public debates, empowering local communities, and conducting campaigns to raise national awareness.

ANCOP and the CPCs were created in 2010, triggered by threats of forced displacement of poor people and drawing from the experience of the Comitê Social do Pan (Social Committee of the Pan), established in 2005. They had a specific repertoire for social action, adopting a broad vocabulary of human rights to frame their focus on housing issues. According to one of the founders, the committees aimed "to track spending and be a mobilizing agent of society to ensure that human rights are not violated . . . [at the] organization of these mega-events."[43] After some local mobilizations in places such as Porto Alegre, two workshops in São Paulo and Rio de Janeiro discussed local and national strategies.[44] The presence of Raquel Rolnik,[45] then UN special rapporteur on adequate housing, on both occasions probably contributed to framing the issue as a matter of human rights. In an article from October 2009 titled "Adequate Housing Is a Right for Everyone," Rolnik argued that it is the responsibility of the state to guarantee policies to implement the right to housing for the people who do not have access to it through the market.[46] Speaking as the UN special rapporteur, she raised concerns regarding the staging of sporting events in Brazil: "I am particularly concerned about the practice of forced evictions, criminalization of homeless persons and informal activities, and the dismantling of informal settlements in the context of mega-events."[47]

As shown above, concerns about the impact of the sporting events grew over time. Whereas other organizations used human rights language to address specific issues or react to certain incidents such as the violence during the protests, it was only ANCOP and the CPCs that presented a comprehensive critique of the events using rights talk. They used human rights as an umbrella concept to appraise the mega-events from different perspectives. Rights were the main vehicle for resisting a list of wrongdoings caused by such events—even when certain issues were not placed easily within a rights framework, such as corruption or budget matters.

The dossiers that were the key documents produced by ANCOP and the CPCs listed and publicized rights violations through a naming and shaming strategy. They attracted some attention and contributed to placing housing and evictions among the news published by the mainstream Brazilian media. International newspapers also wrote articles based on the dossiers.[48] ANCOP's first dossier, published in 2011 and titled "Mega-Events and Human Rights Violations in Brazil," was aimed at highlighting the "dark side" of the sporting events in Brazil.[49] After ANCOP's dossier appeared some regional committees published local versions, but the ones from the Rio de Janeiro Committee were the most comprehensive. With the same titles as ANCOP's, the four versions produced by the Rio de Janeiro Committee (2012, 2013, 2014, and 2015) were broader in scope and received much more attention.[50]

The information cataloging proved to be useful when cases against Brazil were brought to human rights organizations. At the twenty-second session of the UN Human Rights Council in March 2013 during the presentation of the special rapporteur on adequate housing, representatives of ANCOP, Conectas, and Rede Jubileu Sul and Wittnes presented a case against the Brazilian state and the institutions organizing the mega-events.[51] Again at the twenty-sixth regular session in June 2014, Conectas and the São Paulo Committee denounced "forced evictions, violations of the freedom of movement and the freedom to work, the creation of exclusion zones, and the criminalization of the right to protest" during the preparations for the event.[52]

The dossiers documented mounting discontent with the mega-events, and their contents grew through time, but not all the issues covered sat easily with human rights as a broader framework. The first two ANCOP dossiers included chapters on housing; labor; access to information, participation, and popular representation; the environment; access to services and public goods and mobility; and public safety. These issues were maintained in the following dossiers, and more were added: sport as well as budget and finances first, and in 2015 gender as well as children and adolescents.[53] Most chapters listed specific rights that were allegedly violated, but others seemed more concerned about broader public policy issues. The "elitization of football" and the high prices of tickets to World Cup games were stretched to be portrayed as human rights issues.[54] Chapters on public security centered on state-related violence and dealt mainly with public policy matters—from police abuse during early protests to increasing militarization, surveillance in slums, and money being wasted on private companies that would leave after the event—but human rights were not directly mentioned, nor were any legal documents referred to.[55]

The dossiers used international law, primarily human rights instruments, as their leading source. Uncommonly among reports by Brazilian NGOs, the dossiers cited international treaties alongside national legislation. When presenting the juridical-institutional framework of the right to housing, for example, not only Article 6 of the Brazilian Constitution and Article 2 of the city statute (Estatuto da Cidade, Lei n. 10.257/2001) were quoted but also Article 11 of the ICCPR, Article 25(1) of the Universal Declaration of Human Rights, 5(e)(iii) of the International Convention on the Elimination of All Forms of Racial Discrimination, and Article 16(1) of the Convention on the Rights of the Child.

In all editions, the dossiers drafted by the Rio de Janeiro Committee contain a section about human rights violations according to international law. After invoking several treaties to which Brazil is a signatory, stating their primacy within the domestic legal system, the section builds the case for the right to housing using legal arguments: "in terms of the international legislation recognized and signed by Brazilian law, evictions are a grave violation of human rights."[56] The main target is forced removals. And after quoting several documents, such as Resolution 1993/77 of the UN Commission on Human Rights, jurisprudence from the Inter-American Court of Human Rights, and general comments from UN organs and proposed guidelines from rapporteurs, the section affirms that "it is possible to conclude that the international legal order safely opted for the assurance of the right to adequate housing of communities by large impact developments."[57]

The strategy of placing all issues into a human rights framework has proved useful to local actors but also had limits. Rights language is far from straightforward, and broad interpretations might weaken its rhetoric. Not all legal texts are easily matched: Article 23(a) of the American Convention, about the right of public participation, was placed alongside Article 37 of the Brazilian Constitution, which states the general principle of publicity in public administration policies.[58] When Article 19 published its report on excessive police force against demonstrators, it recognized that "there is no explicit right to protest within international human rights standards" even though it argued that such a right is "protected implicitly" with the rights of expression, peaceful assembly, and association.[59]

Part of the attraction of human rights as a political language is its ability to assemble relative consensus around its moral appeal and its apparent capacity to provide self-evident facts. Its rhetoric still promises a realm separate from or above politics, one that can bridge right/left, local/international, and other substantial gaps. In this way, its normative strength gives it strategic leverage to generate sympathy and attention in domestic and international spheres.[60] Nonetheless, if "these days human rights only have friends," their vocabulary can be invoked by both sides of a political dispute.[61]

In this chapter we highlighted how different actors used human rights language to construct narratives about the recent sport mega-events in Brazil. Early public debates about hosting the World Cup and the Olympics were mostly about economic costs, legacy, and the country's ability to stage them. The organizers referred to rights in the context of a larger campaign to convince domestic audience about the value of the events, and while doing so rights were associated with the fight against racism, other forms of discrimination, and sexual exploitation and for disability rights. Such framing had limited impact on the mainstream media: analysis of the three most prominent Brazilian newspapers confirm that during the initial years, human rights were seldom mentioned in the news about the events.

From 2010 onward, the mainstream media progressively began to discuss human rights but did not adopt the organizers' rhetoric to gather support for the events. Instead of discussing racism and other forms of discrimination that are critical in Brazil, such as gender and sexual orientation, the events became increasingly associated with violations of political and socioeconomic human rights, including police violence, violations of freedom of expression, and housing evictions. Such matters triggered questions about the desirability of the events and their legacy. The predominant rhetoric in which those problems were framed as human rights violations was advanced by activists and local and international organizations. They found in human rights a useful vocabulary to draw attention to domestic issues, even though other framing processes were in competition, as shown above.

The two most prominent issues associated with rights and the events, namely the protests (i.e., police violence and freedom of expression) and housing evictions, have some unique characteristics. The first arose in connection with the unusual demonstrations in Brazilian cities in 2013 and 2014, and the police violence to suppress it led traditional organizations such as Amnesty International and some UN agencies to pressure the state. These institutions were already accustomed to a certain usage of the rights vocabulary, and they instrumentalized it to address the mega-events. Nonetheless, they did not use the rights framework to address the broader situation or criticize the sport mega-events in fundamental terms. Instead, they reacted to specific episodes engaging specific rights involving activists and journalists being detained and injured and police abuse related to protests. Other matters such as housing were mentioned marginally. Another approach was chosen by activists and organizations connected with ANCOP and the local committees. As shown, they emphasized the issue of housing evictions and produced comprehensive dossiers that listed some violations caused by the organizers. The events, which they called the "exclusion games," were criticized in their entirety, and human rights became the main vocabulary in this fight.

Notes

We would like to thank Aline Schwaderer and Ana Flávia da Costa for their research assistance cataloging newspaper articles.

1. See Stuart Kirsch, "Virtuous Language in Industry and the Academy," in *Corporate Social Responsibility? Human Rights in the New Global Economy*, ed. Charlotte Walker-Said, 92–112 (Chicago: University of Chicago Press, 2015).

2. FIFA, "FIFA World Cup in Brazil to Promote Peace and Fight All Forms of Discrimination," June 12, 2014, www.fifa.com/worldcup/news/y=2014/m=6/news=fifa-world-cuptm-in -brazil-to-promote-peace-and-fight-all-forms-of-dis-2-2368962.html.

3. See, e.g., "Brasil formaliza candidatura à Copa de 2014," *Reuters*, July 31, 2007, esporte .uol.com.br/ultimas/reuters/2007/07/31/ult28u51768.jhtm.

4. Brazil, *Dossiê de Candidatura do Rio de Janeiro a Sede dos Jogos Olímpicos e Paraolímpicos de 2016*, 3 vols. (Comitê Olímpico Brasileiro: Rio de Janeiro, 2009), 19.

5. The idea of sustainability has been at the core of documents from FIFA, the IOC, and the Brazilian government but was seldom associated directly with human rights. The concept was largely used by the organizers. The environmental meaning was replaced by a managerial one, which set a guide for the relationship with local stakeholders and set the parameters to "reduce the negative and increase the positive impact." Human rights were placed alongside other "principles" to guide the organizational governance, such as transparency, accountability, ethics, rule of law, and others. See "FIFA World Cup 2014 Sustainability Strategy: Concept," FIFA, May 2012, de.fifa.com/mm/document/fifaworldcup/generic/02/11/18/55/sustainabilitystrategyconcept _neutral.pdf.

6. "O legado da Copa para a infância," Folha de S. Paulo, May 27, 2014, www1.folha.uol.com .br/fsp/opiniao/167903-o-legado-da-copa-para-a-infancia.shtml.

7. "SDH/PR faz balanço da Agenda de Convergencia para proteção de crianças e adolescentes durante a Copa," Secretaria de Direitos Humanos, 2014, www.sdh.gov.br/noticias /2014/agosto/sdh-pr-faz-balanco-da-agenda-de-convergencia-para-protecao-de-criancas-e -adolescentes-durante-a-copa.

8. "Agosto," Secretaria de Direitos Humanos, 2014, www.sdh.gov.br/noticias/2014/agosto.

9. On racism in Brazil, see, e.g., Lilia Moritz Schwarcz, *Nem Preto Nem Branco, Muito Pelo Contrário: Cor e Raça na Sociabilidade Brasileira* (São Paulo: Claro Enigma, 2012).

10. Episodes of racist chanting by supporters are not uncommon in soccer. For example, it allegedly happened with the French team during the 2006 World Cup, when Spanish fans received French black players by making monkey chants ("Spanish Fans Accused of Racism,"

BBC, June 28, 2006, news.bbc.co.uk/sport2/hi/football/world_cup_2006/5127374.stm) and against an English soccer player who was racially abused during the 2010 World Cup qualifier against Croatia ("FA Calls for Inquiry into Racist Chants," *The Guardian*, September 11, 2011, www.theguardian.com/football/2008/sep/11/croatiafootballteam.englandfootballteam). During the 2014 World Cup, a report pointed at homophobic chanting by Brazilian and Mexican fans as well as discriminatory banners from supporters of Germany, Russia, and Croatia ("Fifa Fails to Punish a Dozen of Clear Racist and Homophobic Incidents at World Cup 2014, According to Fare Report," *The Telegraph*, July 10, 2014, www.telegraph.co.uk/sport/football /world-cup/10958490/Fifa-fails-to-punish-a-dozen-of-clear-racist-and-homophobic-incidents -at-World-Cup-2014-according-to-Fare-report.html).

11. According to an evaluation report after the event, because racism was "high on the public policy agenda in Brazil," FIFA decided to have a "pre-match ceremony by the captains, the teams and match officials," which was complemented "by a TV spot on inclusivity and a social media campaign launched by FIFA on June 5, 2014 calling on fans around the world to upload 'selfies' to social media platforms holding a mini-banner reading #SayNoToRacism." FIFA, *Sustainability Report* (Zurich: FIFA, 2014), 39–40. These were the only actions mentioned in the document, and there are no references to the antiracism task force.

12. "Fifa Destaca Copa de 2014 como 'Ocasião Perfeita' para Combater Racismo," Portal Brasil, March 21, 2014, www.brasil.gov.br/esporte/2014/03/fifa-destaca-copa-de-2014-como -ocasiao-perfeita-para-combater-racismo.

13. "Discurso da Presidenta da República, Dilma Rousseff, durante Cerimônia de Formatura da Turma 2012–2014 do Instituto Rio Branco e de Imposição de Insígnias da Ordem de Rio Branco," Ministério das Relações Exteriores, April 30, 2014, www2.planalto.gov.br/acompanhe -o-planalto/discursos/discursos-da-presidenta/discurso-da-presidenta-da-republica-dilma -rousseff-durante-cerimonia-de-formatura-da-turma-2012-2014-do-instituto-rio-branco-e-de -imposicao-de-insignias-da-ordem-de-rio-branco.

14. "FIFA Accused of Not Taking Racism Seriously Enough at World Cup," *The Guardian*, July 3, 2014, www.theguardian.com/football/2014/jul/03/fifa-racism-world-cup. FIFA recently disbanded the antiracism task force, stating that its mission has been "completely fulfilled." "FIFA Says It's Solved Racism in Football—But It's Nowhere Near," *The Guardian*, September 26, 2016, www.theguardian.com/commentisfree/2016/sep/26/fifa-anti-racism-football-taskforce -solved-nowhere-near.

15. According to the Brazilian Newspapers National Association, these three were the main broadsheet newspapers in Brazil in 2015. One tabloid, *Super Notícia*, exceeded them in the total number of copies per day, but its news coverage is quite limited. The association does not count website visits. See Associação Nacional De Jornais, www.anj.org.br/maiores-jornais-do-brasil/. We first counted articles from January 1, 2007, to October 31, 2016, in which the words "direitos humanos" ("human rights") appeared with "Copa" ([World] "Cup"), "jogos olímpicos" ("Olympic Games") and/or "olimpíadas" ("Olympics") on three newspapers' websites: O Globo (acervo .oglobo.globo.com), Folha de S. Paulo (acervo.folha.uol.com.br), and Estado de S. Paulo (acervo .estadao.com.br). Initially we found more than 3,000 articles. Then, the articles were analyzed to locate those that directly connected "human rights" with the events. The majority that were excluded matched the key words incidentally (there was no correlation) or were letters or were about sport events elsewhere (e.g., the 2008 Beijing Olympics). The final total was 386 articles. The remaining were categorized in three different ways: type ("news," "opinion article," "editorial," or "interview"), contents ("police violence," "housing," "LGBT rights," etc.); and the

institutions involved ("UN," "Amnesty International," "Human Rights Watch," etc.). It is important to state that for the second and third categories we did not intend to include all possible rights or all the institutions mentioned in the articles. In the third category we excluded the Brazilian state, FIFA, and the IOC as institutions. Of the 386 articles, there were 3 editorials, 22 interviews, 41 opinion articles, and 317 news articles.

16. For example, eight of nine articles published by *Estado* in 2009 mentioned an incident in which drug dealers shot down a police helicopter. The police clashes in the favelas following the episode left at least forty people dead, triggering a series of articles that included condemnation by Navi Pillay, then UN high commissioner for human rights. See "Marginalização de índios e negros prejudica Brasil, diz ONU," *Estado de S. Paulo*, November 13, 2009, politica.estadao.com .br/noticias/geral,marginalizacao-de-indios-e-negros-prejudica-brasil-diz-onu,466113. Pillay also wrote an article for *Folha* in which she highlighted opportunities and threats to rights but did not mention police violence specifically ("O Brasil e os direitos humanos," *Folha de S. Paulo*, November 8, 2009).

17. The opinion polls were conducted by the Instituto Datafolha from 2008 to 2014 and can be found at its website (datafolha.folha.uol.com.br). The most important ones quoted here are "Após fim da Copa do Mundo, aumenta taxa de insatisfação com torneio," Datafolha, July 18, 2017, datafolha.folha.uol.com.br/opiniaopublica/2014/07/1488044-apos-fim-da-copa-do -mundo-aumenta-taxa-de-insatisfacao-com-torneio.shtml; "Rejeição dobra e metade dos brasileiros é contra Olimpíada," Datafolha, July 19, 2016, datafolha.folha.uol.com.br/opiniaopublica /2016/07/1793176-rejeicao-dobra-e-metade-dos-brasileiros-e-contra-olimpiada.shtml.

18. See, e.g., André Singer, "Rebellion in Brazil: Social and Political Complexion of the June Events," *New Left Review* 85 (2014): 19–37.

19. Venício A. de Lima, "Mídia, rebeldia urbana e crise de representação," in *Cidades Rebeldes: Passe Livre e as Manifestações que tomaram as ruas no Brasil*, ed. Carlos Vainer et al., 88–94 (São Paulo: Boitempo, 2013).

20. "Copa levará o Brasil a ter os estádios de futebol mais caros do mundo," *Estado de S. Paulo*, December 13, 2016, esportes.estadao.com.br/noticias/futebol,copa-levara-o-brasil-a-ter -os-estadios-de-futebol-mais-caros-do-mundo,1108986.

21. "Brazil's Protests Raise Fears for World Cup as a Million Take to the Streets," *The Guardian*, June 21, 2013, www.theguardian.com/world/2013/jun/21/brazil-protests-football-world-cup.

22. These strategies can be understood as "advocacy designed to hold governments to account in relation to legal commitments they have accepted by ratifying international human rights treaties or other standards." Mary Robinson, "Advancing Economic, Social, and Cultural Rights: The Way Forward," *Human Rights Quarterly* 26, no. 4 (2004): 869.

23. Amnesty International, *"They Use a Strategy of Fear": Protecting the Right to Protest in Brazil* (London: Amnesty International, 2014).

24. The campaign gathered more than 140,000 signatures from people of 106 different countries in condemnation of police violence during the protests. See "Brasil, chega de bola fora!," Anistia International, anistia.org.br/entre-em-acao/peticao/brasil-chega-de-bola-fora/.

25. Amnesty International, *Report 2014/15: The State of the World's Human Rights* (London: Amnesty International, 2015), 82.

26. Human Rights Watch, *World Report, 2015: Events of 2014* (New York: Human Rights Watch, 2015), 115.

27. In June 2012 the president sanctioned the World Cup General Law that formalizes the hosting agreement with FIFA. The law regulates a number of issues, from alcoholic beverages

sold in stadiums (which was forbidden under Brazilian law) and trademark and copyright issues (FIFA considered Brazilian regulation too loose) to the prohibition of political manifestations during the games. On this matter, see Cícero Krupp da Luz, "A Ordem Transnacional da Lex Sportiva e os Megaeventos da FIFA," *Revista de Direito Constitucional e Internacional* 89 (2014): 277–300; Sarah Longhofer, "Contracting away Sovereignty: The Case of Brazil, FIFA, and the Agreement for the Right to Host the 2014 World Cup," *Transnational Law & Contemporary Problems* 23, no. 1 (2014): 147–171.

28. "Brazil: Police Must Be Regulated During Protests," May 30, 2014, Article 19, www .article19.org/resources/brazil-police-must-regulated-protests/.

29. Press release, "Brazil: Investigate World Cup Protest Arrests," Human Rights Watch, July 1, 2014, www.hrw.org/news/2014/07/01/brazil-investigate-world-cup-protest-arrests; "World Report 2013, Brazil: Events of 2012," Human Rights Watch, www.hrw.org/world-report/2013 /country-chapters/brazil; "World Report 2014: Brazil," Human Rights Watch, www.hrw.org /world-report/2015/country-chapters/brazil.

30. Press release, "Report on the 150th Session of the IACHR," Organization of American States, May 13, 2014, www.oas.org/en/iachr/media_center/preleases/2014/035a.asp.

31. "Brasil é acusado na OEA de violar direitos humanos," O Globo, March 29, 2014, oglobo .globo.com/brasil/brasil-acusado-na-oea-de-violar-direitos-humanos-em-protestos-12016170.

32. Amnesty International, *You Killed My Son: Homicides by Military Police in the City of Rio de Janeiro* (London: Amnesty International, 2015). During 2014, the year of the World Cup, the number of people murdered by the police in Rio increased 40 percent from 2013. In São Paulo it increased 100 percent. See Fórum Brasileiro de Segurança Pública, "Anuário Brasileiro de Segurança Pública 2014," www.forumseguranca.org.br/storage/8_anuario_2014 _20150309.pdf.

33. Amnesty International, '*A violência não faz parte desse jogo!': Risco de violações de direitos humanos nas Olimpíadas Rio 2016* (Rio de Janeiro: Anistia Internacional Brasil, 2016); "A 100 dias da Olimpíada, favelas vivem clima de terror, afirma Anistia," *Folha de S. Paulo*, April 27, 2016, www1.folha.uol.com.br/cotidiano/2016/04/1765131-a-100-dias-da-olimpiada-favelas -vivem-clima-de-terror-afirma-anistia.shtml.

34. "Anistia Internacional denuncia alta de homicídios no Rio," *Estado de S. Paulo*, June 26, 2016, esportes.estadao.com.br/noticias/jogos-olimpicos,na-onu-anistia-internacional -denuncia-alta-de-homicidios-as-vesperas-da-olimpiada,10000059580.

35. Committee for the Rights of the Child, "Consideration of Reports Submitted by States Parties Under Article 44 of the Convention: Combined Second to Fourth Periodic Reports of States Parties Due in 2007, Brazil," CRC/C/BRA/2–4, December 8, 2014.

36. "ONU denuncia mortes de crianças como forma de 'limpar' Rio," *Estado de S. Paulo*, October 8, 2015, brasil.estadao.com.br/noticias/rio-de-janeiro,onu-denuncia-execucoes-de-criancas -como-forma-de-limpar-rio-para-olimpiada-,1776826.

37. "Em cartas sigilosas, ONU criticou governo brasileiro por repressão policial na Copa," *Estado de S. Paulo*, February 25, 2015, brasil.estadao.com.br/noticias/geral,em-cartas-sigilosas -onu-criticou-governo-brasileiro-por-repressao-policial-na-copa,1639719.

38. Lúcio Kowarick, *A espoliação urbana* (Rio de Janeiro: Paz e Terra, 1980).

39. Rafael Gonçalves, *Favelas do Rio de Janeiro: História e Direito* (Rio de Janeiro: Pallas/ PUL-RIO, 2013).

40. Raquel Rolnik, *Guerra dos Lugares: A colonização da torra e da moradia na era das finanças* (São Paulo: Boitempo, 2015).

41. Monika Dowborl and José Szwako, "Respeitável público . . . Performance e organização dos movimentos antes dos protestos de 2013," *Novos estudos CEBRAP* 97 (November 2013): 43–55. The event was promoted by the following organizations: Fórum Brasil de Orçamento, Assembleia Popular, Jubileu Sul, Rede Brasil sobre Instituições Financeiras Multilaterais, Associação Brasileira de ONGs and Central dos Movimentos Populares.

42. Leticia de Luna Freire, "Mobilizações coletivas em contexto de megaeventos esportivos no Rio de Janeiro," *O Social em Questão* 29 (2013): 101–128.

43. Richardo Michado, "Comitês Populares da Copa, o nascimento de uma resistência," Revista do Instituto Humanitas Unisinos, June 10, 2013, www.ihuonline.unisinos.br/index.php ?option=com_content&view=article&id=5055&secao=422.

44. The event "Impactos Urbanos e Violações de Direitos Humanos nos Megaeventos Esportivos," held at the Faculty of Law, Univeristy of São Paulo, took place November 8–9, 2010, and was organized by the UN special rapporteur on adequate housing together with the Faculty of Architecture and Urbanism and the Juridical Department XI August (Departamento Jurídico XI de Agosto). The workshops included academics who studied the impacts of mega-events in South Africa and Greece and also facilitated links with activists from Belo Horizonte, Curitiba, Fortaleza, Manaus, Natal, Porto Alegre, Recife, Rio de Janeiro, Salvador, and São Paulo. The meeting in Rio de Janeiro took place later the same month. It was titled "O Desafio Popular aos Megaeventos Esportivos" and was organized by social movements. See "Impactos Urbanos e Violações de Direitos Humanos nos Megaeventos Esportivos," Carta Capital, November 8, 2011, www.cartacapital.com.br/sociedade/impactos-urbanos-e-violacoes-de-direitos-humanos -nos-megaeventos-esportivos.

45. Rolnik, an architect, urban planner, and professor at the University of São Paulo, was appointed as special rapporteur in 2008, serving in an unpaid capacity.

46. Raquel Rolnik, "Moradia adequada é direito de todos," *Estado de S. Paulo*, October 18, 2009, www.estadao.com.br/noticias/geral,moradia-adequada-e-direito-de-todos,452437.

47."Olympics and World Cup Soccer Must Take Up Cause of Rights to Housing—UN Expert," UN News Centre, March 9, 2010, www.un.org/apps/news/story.asp?NewsID=34028# .WKJ3qBAfWZZ.

48. See, e.g., "Rio Olympics Linked to Widespread Human Rights Violations, Report Reveals," *The Guardian*, December 8, 2015, www.theguardian.com/world/2015/dec/08/rio-olympics-2016 -human-rights-violations-report.

49. Articulação Nacional dos Comitês Populares da Copa, *Megaeventos e Violações de Direitos Humanos no Brasil* (Rio de Janeiro: ANCOP, 2011), 6.

50. The São Paulo Committee published two editions (2012 and 2015) of "[World] Cup for Whom?" ("Copa pra Quem?"); the committee in Pernambuco launched its publication "From Violations to Resistance: The Action of the Pernambuco Popular Committee of the Cup" ("Das Violações às Resistências: A atuação do Comitê Popular da Copa PE") in 2015 and also dedicated a report to the impact of the World Cup on women.

51."Red Card to the Human Rights Violations of the World Cup and Olympic Games," Conectas Human Rights, May 23 2014, www.conectas.org/en/actions/justice/news/red-card-to-the -human-rights-violations-of-the-world-cup-and-olympic-games.

52. "Conectas Addresses the World Cup, Immigration, Business and Foreign Policy at the Human Rights Council," Conectas Human Rights, November 6, 2014, www.conectas.org/en /news/26th-session.

53. Another significant difference from the early versions of the first documents is aesthetic: whereas ANCOP's 2011 and 2012 documents and the Rio de Janeiro Committee's 2012 one are mainly textual and have simple designs, the versions from 2013 onward are full of pictures, have sophisticated design, and contain posters with strong messages. There is a small note on the end of the 2014 dossier stating that it was funded by several organizations, among others the Heinrich Böll Foundation.

54. Comitê Popular da Copa e das Olimpíadas do Rio de Janeiro, *Megaeventos e Violações dos Direitos Humanos no Rio de Janeiro Dossiê do Comitê Popular da Copa e Olimpíadas do Rio de Janeiro* (Rio de Janeiro: CPC, 2012).

55. Ibid.; Articulação Nacional dos Comitês Populares da Copa, *Megaeventos e Violações de Direitos Humanos no Brasil* (Rio de Janeiro: ANCOP, 2011).

56. Comitê Popular da Copa, *Megaeventos*, 179.

57. Ibid., 182.

58. Articulação Nacional dos Comitês Populares da Copa, *Megaeventos e Violações de Direitos Humanos no Brasil* (Rio de Janeiro: ANCOP, 2011, 2014). The Inter-American Court of Human Rights understood Article 23 as the right of a person to be elected to public office and to serve in such position (cf. Case of Yatama v. Nicaragua, Preliminary Objections, Merits, Reparations and Costs, Judgment of June 23, 2005, Series C No. 127, para. 201, www.corteidh.or.cr /docs/casos/articulos/seriec_127_ing.pdf; Case of Luna López v. Honduras, Merits, Reparations and Costs, Judgment of October 10, 2013, Series C No. 269, para. 142, www.corteidh.or.cr/docs /casos/articulos/seriec_269_ing.pdf).

59. Article 19, *Brazil's Own Goal: Protests, Police and the World Cup* (São Paulo: Artigo 19, 2014), 12.

60. Makau W. Mutua, "The Ideology of Human Rights," *Virginia Journal of International Law* 36 (1996): 589–657.

61. Michel Villey, *Le droit et les droits de l'homme* (Paris: PUF, 1983), 17.

CONCLUSION

The Future of Idealism in Sport

Barbara J. Keys and Roland Burke

The biggest international sporting events are today caught in a vise. Thanks to their enormous popularity, the Olympic Games and the men's soccer World Cup draw in two competing forces. On the one hand, their vast scale compels their organizers and fans to endow them with lofty moral attributes, even though—as this volume has shown—such ascriptions float on an airy bed of unfounded assumptions and outright fantasies. It is not enough that the events entertain us. We crave a transcendent meaning for endeavors that require great effort. Sport is no different.

On the other hand, because these events are hugely popular they are also hugely profitable, and when vast sums flow with little accountability, corruption follows. The scandal that engulfed the Olympic Games in the wake of the Salt Lake City bribery revelations of the late 1990s, the large-scale Russian doping conspiracy of 2016, reports that thousands of exploited workers will die building stadiums for the Qatar 2022 Men's World Cup, and the U.S. indictments of Fédération Internationale de Football Association (FIFA) officials in 2015 for fraud, racketeering, and money laundering have corroded the moral claims that underpin the legitimacy of the Olympic Games and the men's World Cup. The same scale that makes us so eager to seek a moral purpose in these events ensures that there will also be pernicious forces at work.

Corruption scandals combined with the obscene costs of staging mega-events in an age of global terrorism have forced the International Olympic Committee (IOC) and FIFA into defensive positions. Weakened by other blows, they are less able to resist pressures around human rights and other issues from nongovernmental groups such as Human Rights Watch. They are also increasingly savvy about the benefits of coopting rather than resisting these forces. Their turn to human rights has been instrumental, more about pretense than practice. As João Roriz and Renata Nagamine note in this volume, sports organizations have come to use human rights much as businesses deploy corporate social responsibility: as a virtuous language that bridges deep political divides with rhetorical gestures rather than serious change. The contributions to this volume make clear that the claims do not match reality, with the IOC falling short at the 2014 Sochi Winter Games and FIFA skimping on even minimal efforts at antiracism at the 2014 World Cup in Brazil. These two organizations host the largest and most significant events, and their actions and rhetoric influence how other sport organizations feel compelled to behave. The IOC and FIFA, in other words, set the tone and create an example for sport in general.

Both organizations make similar claims about making the world a better place. Both tout their history of promoting antiracism and antidiscrimination. When IOC heavyweight Dick Pound wrote an "insider's account" of the Olympics in 2004, he held up the IOC's allegedly good record on antiracism as its key contribution to the promotion of human rights. Pound acknowledged—as Robert Skinner amply demonstrates in this volume—that the IOC had to be dragged into the fight against apartheid. But he still made the exclusion of South Africa the main exhibit in the list of the IOC's moral accomplishments. FIFA also emphasizes its record of antiracism, as Roriz and Nagamine show in their analysis of the 2014 men's World Cup. Both organizations make fantastical claims about fostering world peace. Peace and football "walk hand in hand," crowed one FIFA press release in 2003.[1]

IOC president Thomas Bach, despite a lackluster response to LGBT issues at the 2014 Games, has moved the organization toward significant reform since his election in 2013. Confronted first by a crescendo of negative publicity in preparation for the Sochi Games and then by a wave of Western cities dropping out of contention to host the Olympics because of cost concerns and low public support, Bach pushed through an Olympic 2020 reform agenda.[2] Among the agenda's aims is rebuilding the IOC's credibility by focusing on good governance, transparency, and ethics. Directly responding to the concerns raised at the 2014 Sochi Olympics, the Olympic Agenda 2020 reworded the sixth fundamental principle of Olympism to bring it in line with the United Nations (UN) Universal Declaration of Human Rights so as to include a prohibition on discrimination on the basis of sexual orientation.[3] Veteran Olympic scholar John MacAloon is skeptical of Olympic 2020's significance for issues such as antidoping and environmental protection but sees the IOC's cooperation with Human Rights Watch as pointing to a new paradigm for the Olympic leadership.[4]

As a measure of the new primacy of human rights as the rhetorical mold in which the moral claims of sport mega-events are now cast, the IOC has flagged the centrality of novel human rights provisions in host city contracts for future Games. The IOC also amended the Tokyo 2020 Games contract to meet the new standards.[5] Even so, the new wording is narrowly circumscribed, merely stating that "in their activities related to the organisation of the Games," the host city, the host National Olympic Committee, and the organizing committee of the Olympic Games shall prohibit discrimination and "protect and respect human rights" consistent with international law.[6] The government of the host country—the most relevant legislative and judicial authority—is not subject to these strictures, nor does the contract address human rights violations that might be only indirectly related to the Games.

Like the IOC, FIFA has moved toward greater rhetorical respect for human rights. In 2015 FIFA asked John Ruggie, the Berthold Beitz Professor in Human Rights and International Affairs at Harvard's Kennedy School of Government and the lead author of the UN's 2011 Guiding Principles on Business and Human Rights, to report on how FIFA could embed human rights in its operations.[7] In 2016 FIFA revised its statutes to include explicit recognition of human rights: "FIFA is committed to respecting all internationally recognised human rights and shall strive to promote the protection of these rights." In March 2017 FIFA established an independent Human Rights Advisory Board and created the position of human rights manager.[8] The advisory board consists of representatives from business (Adidas, the Coca-Cola Company), humanitarian bodies (the children's rights group Terre des Hommes, Transparency International Germany, the Office of the UN High Commissioner for Human Rights), and labor groups (FIFPro, the Building and Wood Workers' International), among others.[9] FIFA has promised to follow the IOC in including human rights provisions in future bidding documents (beginning in 2026). The Human Rights Advisory Board is also concerning itself with women's football, antidiscrimination efforts, Israeli-Palestinian relations, and the mistreatment of workers on building sites for the 2018 and 2022 World Cups, which has drawn loud, sustained criticism. FIFA published a new Human Rights Policy in May 2017, reiterating its commitment to respect and promote human rights.[10]

Capping these developments is the creation in June 2018 of a Centre for Sport and Human Rights: the premier symbol of a new symbiosis between sport mega-events interest groups and global human rights actors. Based in Geneva, the humanitarian capital of the world, and chaired by the high-profile former UN high commissioner for human rights, Mary Robinson, the new body promises to "share knowledge" and "strengthen accountability." The result of three years of discussion within the Platform on Mega-Sporting Events and Human Rights, a body created under the auspices of the United Kingdom-based Institute for Human Rights and Business, the Geneva center includes representatives of nearly every "stakeholder" in international sport: intergovernmental organizations, governments, sports bodies, athletes, local organizing committees, sponsors, broadcasters, nongovernmental organizations, trade unions, employers, and national human rights institutions. The creation of this center underscores the extent to which human rights movements and sport mega-events are now mutually constitutive endeavors, each hoping to gain legitimacy from the other.[11]

What is most surprising is not that the IOC and FIFA have embraced human rights goals but that it took them so long to jump on the bandwagon. The UN, governments, and nongovernmental organizations have been flocking to human rights as a moral lingua franca since at least the end of the Cold War. While some analysts argue that human rights movements have brought significant if limited improvements to individuals and communities, critics who charge that human rights has proved weak and ineffectual now have the upper hand.[12] The language has proved malleable, capable of being stretched to fit disparate causes while retaining sufficient legitimacy that its mere invocation can confer respectability. Such a language is perfectly suited to the aims and needs of global sport. The language is ostensibly universal, even while promulgated mostly by elites. Because its achievements are almost impossible to measure and its aspirations are varied and sometimes conflicting, it is possible to make a case that almost any endeavor has promoted some human rights for some beneficiaries.[13] As Roriz and Negamine show in their contribution to this volume, both FIFA and the IOC can claim to promote human rights while ignoring the injustices that human rights groups are combating: it is simply a matter of defining which human rights matter. Like political language as George Orwell defined it, human rights as a vocabulary can "give an appearance of solidity to pure wind."

Despite meager evidence that significant improvements will result from sport organizations' newfound embrace of human rights rhetoric, human rights organizations have declared victory. In early 2015, Amnesty International and Human Rights Watch joined a federation of like-minded groups, including Terre des Hommes and the International Trade Union Confederation, to form the Sports and Rights Alliance. Its mission is to ensure that sport mega-events are "always organized" in ways that "respect" human rights, labor rights, the environment, and anticorruption measures.[14] The alliance's recommendations for the IOC and FIFA provide a sensible framework for assessing how mega-events will affect the people whose lives are directly touched by events, especially residents of host cities and construction workers, using measures comparable to environmental impact assessments and mechanisms for imposing sanctions when strictures are violated.[15] But instead of acknowledging that sport mega-events will always impose some human rights costs, the alliance aims for purity and eradication of abuses. It is no coincidence that at a time when the issue of human rights is encountering its most serious challenge since the 1940s, its major actors would find in sport mega-events a unique opportunity for theatrical virtue-signaling on a global scale.

The relationship between the UN and major sports organizations continues to grow closer. Since 2011 the UN Human Rights Council has issued regular resolutions on "promoting human rights through sport and the Olympic ideal," extending the close relationship already developed on the "sport for development and peace" front.[16] In a world of terrorist attacks, forever wars, and devastating civil conflicts, the UN and the IOC have sought to buttress each other's faltering legitimacy with liturgical invocations of peace.

Although Joon Seok Hong shows in this volume that the democratizing effects of the 1988 Seoul Olympic Games have been exaggerated, the 2018 Pyeongchang Winter Olympic Games offered a stunning example of the apparent capacity of sport mega-events to foster peace. At the end of 2017, new nuclear testing by North Korea and U.S. president Donald Trump's bombastic reaction led experts to warn that the risk of war on the Korean Peninsula was at the highest level since the 1950s. But South Korean president Moon Jae-in, long a proponent of negotiations with North Korea, brokered a deal that allowed North Korea to share in the global spotlight. Hundreds of North Koreans, including athletes, cheerleaders, trainers, officials, a pop star, and the sister of North Korea dictator Kim Jong-un, the first member of the Kim dynasty to visit South Korea, descended on Pyeongchang. The countries marched together under the "unification flag" at the opening ceremony and fielded a joint women's ice hockey team.[17] Although U.S. vice president Mike Pence, attending the Games, seemed to spurn opportunities to engage in dialogue with representatives from North Korea, Moon scored a diplomatic breakthrough when a senior North Korean official attending the closing ceremony suggested a willingness to engage in talks with the United States. Not long after, in a stunning reversal, Trump agreed to meet with Kim Jong-un. The historic summit took place in June 2018.

Whatever the long-term outcome of the extraordinary détente initiated at the Olympic Games turns out to be, it is clear that the Olympic Games offered a unique opportunity to defuse tensions. Moralistic myth, even when deeply frayed, can be episodically useful. Amid the most florid bellicosity in a generation, the Olympic Games, as well as instrumental use of the pretenses of amity, fraternity, and peaceful competition, allowed a channel for progress. The substance of the Olympic ideal was to some extent superfluous—it was found useful by all parties for reframing an otherwise impassable rhetorical environment. The Games offered political cover for the kind of diplomacy that allowed North Korea to step onto the world stage in the guise of a normal power. The extraordinary popularity of the Games makes most nations covet a presence in them, and the mantle of apoliticism, fair play, a level playing field, and mutual understanding give the Olympics a veneer that makes them palatable to almost all types of government. As MacAloon noted years ago, "nowhere else do such favorable conditions exist for otherwise difficult meetings—on an invisible, informal, and agenda-less bases—among such a total range of global political elites, including from nations at war or having no diplomatic relations with one another."[18]

If the Pyeongchang Olympics offered an inspiring storyline, the continuing reverberations from Russia's systematic doping program, the staging of the men's 2018 FIFA World Cup in an ever more authoritarian Russia, and the questions swirling around the role of bribery in securing the 2022 men's FIFA World Cup for sweltering Qatar ensure that tensions over ethical questions will remain prominent on the agenda of sport mega-events.

The buzzwords "peace," "environmental protection," "antidiscrimination," "mutual understanding," and "legacy" remain crucial to global sport's positive "branding." We can expect that these mottoes will more and more be described in the terminology of human rights, which has a remarkable capacity to spread to new terrain and reshape concerns in its own image—even peace, which is the ultimate goal of human rights promotion.

As commercialism, doping, corruption, and gigantism spread an ever larger pall over sport mega-events, the need for a countervailing set of moral claims that can justify and excuse the excesses grows in tandem. The analyses in this volume have suggested that the moral claims are vastly inflated but also that the paucity of evidence—and the paucity of efforts even to find evidence—that the claims are grounded in fact have almost never acted as a brake on the impetus to make such claims.

What can we conclude? Our craving for meaning and moral value guarantees that we will continue to invest our most grandiose events with a capacity to do *good* that they have yet to earn. The moral veneer with which we cast global sport has often deflected attention from the wrongs that mega-events cause or exacerbate. But it has also, fitfully and sometimes unwittingly, helped reduce some of those wrongs.

Notes

1. "FIFA President Honoured in New York with Peace Prize," FIFA, February 19, 2003, www .fifa.com/about-fifa/news/y=2003/m=2/news=fifa-president-honoured-new-york-with-peace -prize-85542.html.

2. Oslo, Stockholm, Krakow, Munich, Davos, Boston, Barcelona, and Quebec City decided against bidding to host upcoming Games because public support proved lacking. In awarding the 2022 Winter Games, the IOC was left with two unpalatable choices: Almaty and Beijing. See Andy Bull, "Revealed: The Biggest Threat to the Future of the Olympic Games," *The Guardian*, July 27, 2016, www.theguardian.com/sport/2016/jul/27/biggest-threat-future-olympic-games -rio-2016-ioc-thomas-bach-hosts.

3. "Olympic Agenda 2020: 20+20 Recommendations," International Olympic Committee, stillmed.olympic.org/Documents/Olympic_Agenda_2020/Olympic_Agenda_2020-20-20 _Recommendations-ENG.pdf.

4. John J. MacAloon, "Agenda 2020 and the Olympic Movement," *Sport in Society* 19, no. 6 (July 2016): 769.

5. "Tokyo 2020 Hosting Contract Public After Meeting IOC Reforms," Around the Rings, May 9, 2017, aroundtherings.com/site/A__60068/Title__Tokyo-2020-Hosting-Contract-Public -After-Meeting-IOC-Reforms/292/Articles.

6. "Olympics: Host City Contract Requires Human Rights," Human Rights Watch, February 28, 2017, www.hrw.org/news/2017/02/28/olympics-host-city-contract-requires-human-rights.

7. See John G. Ruggie, "'For the Game. For the World': FIFA and Human Rights," Sports and Human Rights, 2016, www.sportandhumanrights.org/wordpress/wp-content/uploads/2015 /07/Ruggie_human-rights_FIFA_report_April_2016.pdf.

8. "Red Card: Exploitation of Construction Workers on World Cup Sites in Russia," Human Rights Watch, June 14, 2017, www.hrw.org/report/2017/06/14/red-card/exploitation -construction-workers-world-cup-sites-russia.

9. Press release, "Independent Advisory Board of Human Rights Experts to Meet on 13 March," FIFA, March 10, 2017, www.fifa.com/governance/news/y=2017/m=3/news=independent -advisory-board-of-human-rights-experts-to-meet-on-13-march-2875485.html.

10. See the Centre for Sport and Human Rights website, www.sporthumanrights.org.

11. "FIFA Activity Update on Human Rights," FIFA, May 2017, resources.fifa.com/mm
/document/affederation/footballgovernance/02/89/33/21/activityupdate_humanrights_may2017
_neutral.pdf.

12. Compare Samuel Moyn, *Not Enough: Human Rights in an Unequal World* (Cambridge,
MA: Harvard University Press, 2018), with Kathryn Sikkink, *Evidence for Hope: Making Human
Rights Work in the 21st Century* (Princeton, NJ: Princeton University Press, 2017).

13. For one effort at measuring, see Michael Ignatieff, "Human Rights, Global Ethics, and
the Ordinary Virtues," *Journal of International Law and International Relations* 13, no. 1 (Spring
2017): 1–9.

14. "Sports and Rights Alliance," Sports and Rights Alliance, www.sportandhumanrights
.org/wordpress/index.php/2015/07/06/sport-and-rights-alliance/.

15. "Requirements for Human Rights, Labour Rights, Anti-Corruption and Stakeholder
Involvement for Olympic Games," Sports and Rights Alliance, www.sportandhumanrights.org
/wordpress/wp-content/uploads/2016/12/SRA-IOC-requirements.pdf.

16. See the list at the Office on Sport for Development and Peace website: www.un.org/sport
/resources/documents/human-rights-council.

17. "Can South Korea's Leader Turn an Olympic Truce into a Lasting Peace?," *New York
Times*, February 25, 2018.

18. John J. MacAloon, "Politics and the Olympics: Some New Dimensions," Working Paper
no. 128, Institut de Ciències Polítiques i Socials, Barcelona 1997, 3, www.icps.cat/archivos
/WorkingPapers/WP_I_128.pdf?noga=1.

LIST OF CONTRIBUTORS

Jules Boykoff is a professor of political science at Pacific University. He is the author of three books on the Olympics: *Power Games: A Political History of the Olympics* (Verso, 2016), *Activism and the Olympics: Dissent at the Games in Vancouver and London* (Rutgers University Press, 2014), and *Celebration Capitalism and the Olympic Games* (Routledge, 2013). Boykoff also wrote two books on the suppression of political dissent: *Beyond Bullets: The Suppression of Dissent in the United States* (AK Press, 2007) and *The Suppression of Dissent: How the State and Mass Media Squelch US American Social Movements* (Routledge, 2006). He is an affiliate faculty member at the Institute for the Study of Sport, Society, and Social Change at San Jose State University.

Susan Brownell is a professor of anthropology at the University of Missouri–St. Louis. She is the author of *Training the Body for China: Sports in the Moral Order of the People's Republic* (University of Chicago Press, 1995), the first book on Chinese sports based on fieldwork in China by a Westerner. Brownell is also the author of *Beijing's Games: What the Olympics Mean to China* (Rowman and Littlefield, 2008), the coauthor of *The Anthropology of Sport: Bodies, Borders, Biopolitics* (University of California Press, 2017), and the author of articles on human rights and the Beijing Olympic Games.

Roland Burke is senior lecturer in history at La Trobe University. He is a leading expert on Third World engagement with international human rights since World War II. Burke is the author of *Human Rights in Eclipse: The Fate of the Universal Declaration of Human Rights, 1948–1998* (University of Pennsylvania Press, forthcoming), *Decolonization and the Evolution of International Human Rights* (University of Pennsylvania Press, 2010), and articles and book chapters on human rights.

Simon Creak is an assistant professor of history in the National Institute of Education at Nanyang Technological University, Singapore. He is a historian of Southeast Asia and modern sport. Creak is the author of *Embodied Nation: Sport, Masculinity, and the Making of Modern Laos* (University of Hawai'i Press, 2015) and numerous recent articles and chapters on the history and politics of Laos and of modern sport. He is currently writing a history of the South East Asia Peninsular/Southeast Asian Games in the context of decolonization and the Cold War.

Dmitry Dubrovskiy is an associate professor at the Higher School of Economics (Moscow) and associate research fellow at the Center for Independent Social Research (St. Petersburg). He is the former director of the Human Rights Program in the Department of Liberal Arts and Science (Smolny Institute) at St. Petersburg State University and a former lecturer at the Harriman Institute at Columbia University. He researches Russian human rights and sport. In addition to other articles and essays on Russian human rights advocacy, hate speech and hate crimes, and academic rights and freedoms, Dubrovskiy is the author of "Sport and Politics: Football as a National Idea in Contemporary Russia," in *Contemporary Interpretations of Russian Nationalism*, ed. M. Laruelle (Ibidem, 2007), and, with A. Tarasenko and A. Starodubtsev, *Create the Bridge: The Dialogue between Civil Society and the State* (St. Petersburg, 2011), both in Russian, titles translated here into English, as well as "Violence and the Defense of 'Traditional Values' in the Russian Federation," in *Religion and Violence in Russia*, ed. Olga Oliker (Center for Strategic and International Studies, 2018), published in English.

Joon Seok Hong is an honorary fellow at the School of Historical and Philosophical Studies at the University of Melbourne and a director of the International Sports Relations Foundation (iSR) in Seoul, South Korea. He is the former Koret Junior Fellow in Korean Studies at the Walter H. Shorenstein Asia-Pacific Research Center at Stanford University and a former lecturer with the Center for East Asian Studies at Stanford University. Hong is the coeditor of the volume *Sports Relations in East Asia: Theory and Practice* (iSR Forum Series, 2014) and the author of a chapter on democracy, law, and the institutionalization of social movements in *South Korean Social Movements: From Democracy to Civil Society*, edited by Gi-wook Shin and Paul Y. Chang (Routledge, 2011).

Barbara J. Keys is an associate professor of history at the University of Melbourne. She has published widely on the politics of international sport, the role of emotions in diplomacy, and the history of human rights movements. Keys is the author of *Globalizing Sport: National Rivalry and International Community in the 1930s* (Harvard University Press, 2006) and *Reclaiming American Virtue: The Human Rights Revolution of the 1970s* (Harvard University Press, 2014). She is finishing a book on antitorture campaigns since 1945 and is chief investigator of an Australian Research Council Discovery Project grant with Roland Burke and Xu Guoqi to study moral claims making around international sports events.

Renate Nagamine is a postdoctoral fellow in the Graduate Program in International Relations at the Federal University of Bahia, Brazil. She received her PhD in international law from the University of São Paulo Law School. Nagamine has worked as a researcher (collaborator) at the Brazilian Centre of Analysis and Planning and is a Kathleen Fitzpatrick Visiting Fellow with the Laureate Program in International Law at the University of Melbourne. Her areas of interest are public international law, international humanitarian law and human rights, political theory, and sexuality and gender studies.

João Roriz is an associate professor with the Faculty of Social Sciences, Federal University of Goiás. He has published on human rights and international relations. Roriz was a visiting research fellow at the Centre for International Studies, University of Oxford (2015–2016). He received his PhD (2013) in international law from the University of São Paulo and his LLM (2007) from the London School of Economics and Political Science.

Robert Skinner is a lecturer in modern history at the University of Bristol. He teaches the social and political history of South Africa, with a particular interest in the relations between South Africa and the rest of the world. Skinner is the author of *The Foundations of Anti-Apartheid* (Palgrave, 2010), which examines the emergence of anti-apartheid in the 1950s, and *South Africa in World History* (Bloomsbury, 2017). He is currently working on a series of projects exploring the local dimensions of global activism and the politics of everyday life.

INDEX

ACKNOWLEDGMENTS

The preparation of this volume and the contributions by Barbara Keys and Roland Burke were supported by Australian Research Council Discovery Project Grant DP170100291, "Moral Claims in International Sports Events and the Ethics of World Order." The preparation of the index was supported by a Publication Grant from the University of Melbourne Faculty of Arts. Jack Davies provided expert research assistance. Part of Chapter 5 appeared in Barbara Keys, "Harnessing Human Rights to the Olympic Games: Human Rights Watch and the 1993 'Stop-Beijing' Campaign," *Journal of Contemporary History* 52, no. 2 (2018): 415–438, reprinted by permission of Sage Publications. The valuable suggestions of two anonymous reviewers were very much appreciated. Thanks are also due to editor Peter Agree and the team at Penn Press and BookComp, who brought to the publication process an extraordinary level of care and professionalism.